MAKING THE CASE
FOR LEADERSHIP

MAKING THE CASE FOR LEADERSHIP

Profiles of Chief Advancement Officers in Higher Education

Jon Derek Croteau and Zachary A. Smith

ROWMAN & LITTLEFIELD PUBLISHERS, INC.

Lanham • Boulder • New York • Toronto • Plymouth, UK

Published by Rowman & Littlefield Publishers, Inc.
A wholly owned subsidiary of The Rowman & Littlefield Publishing Group, Inc.
4501 Forbes Boulevard, Suite 200, Lanham, Maryland 20706
http://www.rowmanlittlefield.com

Estover Road, Plymouth PL6 7PY, United Kingdom

British Library Cataloguing in Publication Information Available

Library of Congress Cataloging-in-Publication Data

Croteau, Jon Derek, 1975–
  Making the case for leadership : profiles of chief advancement officers in higher
education / Jon Derek Croteau and Zachary A. Smith.
      p. cm.
  Summary: "Strong higher education advancement leadership is more important
today than ever. The success of advancement and development offices rests largely on
the shoulders of chief advancement officers. Through groundbreaking research, this
book identifies details and themes of leadership along with theoretical and practical
implications important to a broad academic audience"— Provided by publisher.
  ISBN 978-1-4422-0633-5 (hardback) — ISBN 978-1-4422-0635-9 (ebook)
  1. Educational fund raising—United States. 2. Educational leadership—United States.
I. Smith, Zachary A., 1974– II. Title.
  LB2336.C75 2012
  371.2'06—dc23

                                                                    2011032957

♾™ The paper used in this publication meets the minimum requirements of American
National Standard for Information Sciences—Permanence of Paper for Printed Library
Materials, ANSI/NISO Z39.48-1992.

Printed in the United States of America

Contents

Foreword by Peter Hayashida

"SOMETIMES YOU DON'T take up enough space in a room," said my boss during a quiet moment of reflection. It was a curiously ironic observation as I'm quite a slender guy, but I understood that the feedback was clearly figurative. The mysterious yet wise words still echo in my head almost a decade later, and I think I'm finally getting it.

The boss was Michael Eicher, the subject of one of this book's case studies and the former University of California, Los Angeles, vice chancellor who has helped to shape me into the leader I strive to become. His point was elegant in its simplicity: my natural inclination to yield to others was preventing my colleagues from understanding what I had to offer. Mike's urging was to spread my wings, test the boundaries of my comfort, and demonstrate through words and actions the vision and creativity I could bring to bear on organizational problems.

This skill would prove even more essential when the world as we knew it seemed to crumble in the fall of 2008. Seemingly unprecedented economic turmoil would chip away at the foundations of our vaunted institutions of higher education and create uncertainty and anxiety among our universities' most generous supporters. Managing change through such adversity would require a different kind of leadership than had sown the early seeds of our profession—leadership that was focused on change management, talent development, and organizational improvement.

While there was no corner of society untouched by the fiscal crisis, chief advancement officers were faced with a unique blend of leadership challenges. High among them was disinvestment by increasingly stretched federal, state, and local agencies; increased competition for philanthropic dollars; media clutter caused by a rapid succession of both man-made and natural disasters around the world; a supply-and-demand problem in the labor pool with too many vacancies and too few qualified candidates; and disruptively high turn-over among the front-line relationship-builders in advancement.

We can take comfort in the historic cyclicality of the economy; that is, what goes up must come down and vice versa. On the other hand, this dip—or perhaps *plummet* is a more apt description—will have lasting consequences for states like California, Florida, New York, Texas, Washington, and others facing multi-billion-dollar deficit budgets. The long-term implications for higher education advancement are only beginning to reveal themselves in this "new normal" of slow economic growth, static corporate profits, increased regulation, and reduced consumer spending (Gross 2009). One thing is clear: this dynamic, volatile, and unpredictable world will require an army of differ-ent advancement leaders who are strategic, adaptable, focused, and insightful.

Like many in the field, I am an accidental advancement officer. I graduated from UCLA with a communication studies degree and no career plan. Para-doxically, I found my options were simultaneously constrained and bound-less. A relatively brief stint in private sector finance and marketing convinced me that I needed to be in a mission-driven environment. That is probably the most important professional revelation I've made in my career, and it led to untold satisfaction.

I returned to my alma mater as a student affairs officer, determined to apply my passion by counseling students seeking to realize their hopes, dreams, and aspirations. At the time, this truly felt like my calling. I was young and en-ergetic, and I still remembered the undergraduate experience well enough to be useful. My joy was short-lived when, after a few years, the recession of the early 1990s led to a dire threat to my job security. As a fairly junior employee, I knew that to stay would be folly, so I quickly changed course and landed in what was then the only job for which I seemed nominally qualified.

I began my career in advancement as a program manager for alumni scholarships. Our alumni association's executive director, John Kobara, was active in both the Council for Advancement and Support of Education (CASE) and the Council of Alumni Association Executives (CAAE), so he was a helpful mentor, role model, and advocate. He was also the first senior administrator I met who was Asian-American, and he quickly disabused me of any notion that my cultural background prevented me from being strong, assertive, and direct.

When John was succeeded by Keith Brant, currently vice president for development at St. Mary's College in Moraga, California, I negotiated the creation of a new role as chief financial and operating officer for the separately incorporated alumni association. I relied heavily on resources at CASE as well as the American Society of Association Executives to get my feet under me in this new position for which I had great apparent potential but very little in the way of directly relevant experience. Keith was certainly an important mentor, but he also took on the duties of sponsor, helping me grow into new responsibilities. He trusted me to figure out how to do this brand-new job that hadn't previously existed. I was determined to validate his confidence.

In the late 1990s, I decided that there was something missing from my professional portfolio of experience. While I had mastered the business mechanics of alumni relations, there were many operational phenomena that I did not truly grasp conceptually. I needed a pedagogical framework—a lens through which to view my work, define problems, assess solutions, and implement change. I embarked on a part-time MBA at California State University, Northridge—another influential experience that would transform how I viewed not just my job, but my entire institution.

As I started my MBA, I initiated a relationship with my then–vice chancellor, Mike Eicher, who would eventually rank alongside my own father as one of my most influential role models. Mike is a brilliant strategist, savvy manager, inspiring coach, and disciplined analyst. But above all else, he has a deep commitment to organizational development, culture building, and talent management. Much of what I know about building, motivating, measuring, and rewarding teams derives from the work Mike and I did together beginning in 2000 when he appointed me as his assistant vice chancellor. In fact, it was his mentoring of me when I was at the alumni association that prepared me to compete in a national pool for the promotion that landed me on his immediate team for five and a half years.

It is not possible to overstate the impact Mike had on my subsequent development—as a leader, as a manager, as an advancement officer, and as a person. His unwavering integrity, compassion, and humility represented dimensions of leadership I had never observed in such perfect balance. Most of us who worked for Mike would have walked across hot coals for him, but his only desire was to make his team and his campus successful. That, in my humble opinion, is the measure of a true leader. There were eight of us on Mike's senior leadership team during his last year at UCLA—three are now sitting vice chancellors or vice presidents. We stand as living testament to the investment Mike made in developing people and supporting their growth.

If Mike was my coach on strategy and leadership, his successor Rhea Turtletaub was my tutor in humanity and humor. An accomplished and respected national leader in development, Rhea's personality is balanced with distinct cleverness, whimsy, and passion that distinguishes her from many in the field. She is serious without taking herself too seriously, and competitive without forgetting to have fun. Rhea's influence in helping to balance my personality was profound, as my detractors would argue that I've always been a bit too serious and not as much fun as I could be. I don't dispute this, but I also realize I am fundamentally who I am. Still, I often hear Rhea's voice in my head when chaos reigns around me, and then I try to stop for a good laugh before pushing on to the next challenge.

My current appointment as vice chancellor for university advancement at the University of California, Riverside, represents the largest and most daunting jump in my career so far. During my transition into this role, I felt extremely exposed. I couldn't have imagined the pressure involved in running my own program, yet I also couldn't imagine not experiencing the exhilaration when the wheels all start turning in the same direction. People who know me well know I don't start things I don't plan to finish. My focused intensity, drive, and competitive spirit eliminate failure as an option.

Fortunately, it was at UC Riverside where I found my most recent mentor in Chancellor Timothy White. An immigrant from Latin America who was the first in his family to attend college, Tim is the walking embodiment of inspiration. Like me, he is the product of public education; in fact, he is living proof that California's 1960 Master Plan for Higher Education transforms lives. In addition to a doctorate from the University of California, Berkeley, Tim earned degrees from California State University and a California community college.

But Tim's impact on my life derives from the truly exceptional manner in which his leadership manifests itself and how he treats others around him. During a time of great turbulence and controversy, Tim remains beloved by students, faculty, staff, alumni, and community members alike. He is a brilliant strategist with a heart of pure gold. He has carefully nurtured me as a leader, guiding me around landmines while being an advocate, sponsor, and supporter. He has pulled no punches in helping me improve, yet I have never received feedback from him that made me feel anything but a renewed commitment to do better. Tim's self-deprecating style and accessible manner belie his remarkable talent as a leader, persuader, and change manager. To the extent that I have experienced success in my current role, I can trace it directly to the support I've enjoyed from above and the ideal ecosystem Tim creates for individuals who are motivated to succeed.

As I reflect on eighteen years in advancement, it's hard to escape several conclusions. First, changes in society—demographic, economic, social, political, and cultural—will demand evolution in the way we do the work of promoting our institutions and bringing external support to bear on their missions. The United States Census Bureau predicts that by 2019 a majority of

Americans under the age of eighteen will be non-white (Tavernise 2011). The gap between the richest and poorest citizens of our nation will have grown into a gaping chasm, larger than at any time in recorded history (*CBS News* 2011). Globalization dominates the rest of the world while the United States continues to be an insular outlier among industrialized countries, with only 30 percent of U.S. citizens holding valid passports versus 60 percent of Canadians and 75 percent of residents of the United Kingdom (Avon 2011). What will this mean for higher education and, specifically, for the professionals who work to advance their institutions?

Second, the segment of the U.S. population primarily in the workforce—those aged 20–64—will grow by only 21 percent by 2050 while the cohort of Americans aged 65 and older will grow by 115 percent, creating a likely wave of retirements and a succession crisis for many professions, including advancement (United States Census Bureau 2011). The dreaded "retirement of the baby boomers" may have been postponed by the financial crisis of 2008, but this population cannot continue to work forever and eventually must prepare the next generation of professionals to assume the mantle of leadership. How well we do that will influence the future success of not just our profession, but our institutions.

Finally, as a relationship-based profession, we are only as strong as our weakest link. This means the investments we make, both financial and non-financial, are the most influential drivers of our success or sources of our failure. Sending employees to conferences and giving them books is no longer enough; the annual performance evaluation is being replaced by the continual performance dialogue; and companies that aren't thoughtful about career paths proceed at their own peril. Mentoring, job-sculpting, telecommuting, and organizational re-engineering are not fads; they have become part of the permanent lexicon for savvy employers who want to attract and retain the very best talent.

The sum of these observations forms the backbone of the case for this book. When I became a vice chancellor, no one handed me a "chief advancement officer's manual." Indeed, even if such a volume existed, there are as many ways of approaching this task as there are practitioners. However, there are striking similarities among the most successful vice presidents and vice chancellors across higher education. As you will learn in the pages that follow, the strongest leaders in our profession are unbridled optimists committed to lifelong learning. They possess uncommon emotional intelligence and maintain a keen focus on others. Finally, they never forget the context within which their work must be performed. We are not the main show, but rather we act in a supporting role and, if we act well, do so with little fanfare and seamless professionalism.

What has been lacking for aspiring chief advancement officers is a handbook of sorts—not a tome of recipes to be followed with mechanical precision, but a compendium of testimonials from which those with the greatest potential can learn the fundamental lessons of leadership and shape their journeys using the lessons of those who have walked the path before them. For sure, leadership is not for everyone. Some who read these pages will conclude that the costs outweigh the benefits of sitting in the corner office. Yet others will believe they have the requisite competencies but possess neither the temperament nor the judgment to succeed in such an endeavor. Readers will derive benefit commensurate with their self-awareness, openness to growth, innate potential, and ability to adapt to a dynamic and rapidly changing professional landscape.

There are few practitioners and scholars in this community better qualified to prepare the next generation of advancement leaders than Dr. Jon Derek Croteau and Dr. Zachary A. Smith. Jon and Zach have decades of both practical and theoretical experience in the advancement profession, and they devoted their academic careers to the study of organizational development, leadership, and talent management.

As a former assistant vice president for campaign planning and operations, founder of a nonprofit organization, and leadership solutions consultant, Jon has had ample opportunity to engage with advancement officers across a full spectrum of expertise and personalities. His work in talent management over the years has defined an entire field of inquiry and raised the bar on how advancement teams are built, managed, and grown. Under the leadership of Robbee Kosak at Carnegie Mellon University, he created a renowned talent management program in their advancement division. His contributions to the field include *The People First Approach: A Guide for Recruiting, Developing, and Retaining the Right People*, as well as regular speaking and consulting engagements across academe. He is also on the editorial board of the only refereed journal devoted to higher education advancement, the *International Journal of Educational Advancement.*

Zach is a seasoned development officer with experience ranging from health sciences to intercollegiate athletics. He has provided key staffing for university presidents and has a keen understanding of the politics of large, multi-campus public universities. Along with leaders in the field at the University of Michigan, UCLA, and Carnegie Mellon University, Zach was a pioneer in developing in-house talent-management expertise at the University of California, Irvine, and has built a national reputation helping organizations develop high performing teams through consulting projects, speaking engagements, and scholarship. His work has been so impressive that we were fortunate to have him join UC Riverside as assistant vice chancellor for development, responsible for managing a full complement of central services including annual giving, gift planning, corporate and foundation relations, and stewardship, as well as the recruitment and retention of development staff. Zach continues to be a leading voice in advancement in support of talent management strategy and practice and is widely published on the topic in publications including the *Journal of Leadership and Organizational Studies* and the *International Journal of Educational Advancement.*

While this book is groundbreaking in both its content and the application of qualitative methodology to the study of leadership in the advancement profession, it represents only the beginning of a larger conversation that will be critical to the future of our institutions of higher learning. Rarely has the future held so much promise and potential in the face of staggering uncertainty and volatility. The strongest advancement shops will flourish during this period. As the eulogy was being delivered in the trade media for so-called mega gifts, several institutions within a one-hour drive of me closed nine-figure donations.

But what of the rest? How do medium-sized and small organizations compete with the likes of Stanford, Harvard, Johns Hopkins, Columbia, Penn, Yale, and New York University? I suspect the only realistic answer is that they don't. Leadership is no accident, and it can happen anywhere within the capabilities of the institution and the individuals involved. No one will dispute that sustained, double-digit growth in annual fundraising production is impressive and laudable, but if such a program is raising less than $100 million per year, it won't likely garner much national attention.

That doesn't mean that a college or university won't continue on its rapid ascent; in fact, it begs the question of how such growth is even possible in this day and age. I would argue that the answer can be found in the nuggets of wisdom that my colleagues share throughout this book, and that Jon and Zach frame in ways that are practical, actionable, and sustainable. Chinese philosopher Lao Tzu once said, "A leader is best when people barely know he exists. When his work is done, his aim fulfilled, they will say: We did it ourselves." Instilling in others the belief that they can do things they thought impossible is the essence of great leadership. You will see that theme repeated in these pages.

You will also find reasons to hope as you consider the work of these great leaders, for many of them are already quietly engaged in training future generations of chief advancement officers. Like major gift fundraising itself, this work requires patience, commitment, and compassion. And like the advancement officers they manage, these leaders have created complex ecosystems of learning, organizations that go beyond workbooks and training modules to think holistically about what leadership means and how to achieve it. These are places where continuous education is the norm and great ideas come from all levels of the organization chart. It's not an absence of order, but rather the presence of a *new* order—one that strategically develops talent, fosters smooth integration across an enterprise, and creates opportunities for professional and personal growth.

The poet Robert Browning said, "A man's reach should exceed his grasp, or what's a heaven for?" It is surely the case that good enough is rarely good enough in the world of advancement, but when it comes to the current and future leadership of our organizations, we must be at the cutting edge if we are to remain vibrant and valuable to our institutions. In doing so, we will set the stage for new and creative approaches to training not for the sake of training, but with an eye toward a future characterized by stability, consistency, and innovation. Glimpse the private thoughts of these public people and consider how their lessons might form the basis for your future as a great advancement leader.

Acknowledgments

THIS BOOK IS THE END PRODUCT of an incredible partnership that began many years ago as a grassroots venture between two academically curious professionals. It eventually grew into a dynamic, collegial, and highly productive relationship built largely on mutual respect and a common vision for the future. We have thoroughly enjoyed collaborating on this book and look forward to partnering on future projects. We share a unifying passion for making a positive impact on the leadership success, effectiveness, and performance of our nation's higher education institution leaders, while helping them to develop human capital and reach maximum organizational potential.

There are several people we would like to thank for their support and contributions to this book. Our doctoral dissertation advisors, Dr. Alan K. Gaynor and Dr. Mimi Wolverton, have provided us with sage counsel and advice over the years and have prepared us with the necessary skills and competence to take on a research and writing project of this nature. Peter A. Hayashida has been an invaluable resource and an ongoing champion of our work. He has a deep understanding of leadership and its importance, serving as an advocate and a credible voice on the topic throughout the advancement industry. We would especially like to thank Peter for writing such a clear, concise, and relevant foreword to this book. Thank you to our colleagues at the University of California, Riverside, including Joel Munson, and our colleagues at the University of California, Irvine, who have supported this project each step of the way. Thanks to the leadership solutions firm Witt/Kieffer, especially the education and not-for-profit practice leaders past and present—Dennis M. Barden, Lucy A. Leske, and John K. Thornburgh—for their support. Thanks to Dr. Patrick J. Ferrillo Jr. for serving as a mentor, role model, and leader and for always making himself available for practical advice and wise counsel when needed. Jenni Oliver and Joan B. Croteau reviewed our manuscript and provided much needed feedback and editing—we appreciate their help and assistance. Also, thanks to Patti Belcher, our editor at Rowman & Littlefield, for believing in our ability to produce a quality manuscript.

Thank you to the participants across the country, and in some cases overseas, who responded to our surveys and questionnaires. And a very special thanks to our case-study participants for their time, expertise, honesty, patience, and knowledge. Without them, this book would not have been possible. Their contributions will be felt and measured well into the future, and will surely have a positive, longstanding impact on the advancement industry. Thank you to Lisa Calvert, Mike Eicher, Susan Feagin, Trish Jackson, Connie Kravas, Jerry May, Sarah Pearson, Carrie Pelzel, Martin Shell, and Curt Simic.

Lastly, we are forever grateful to our families, who continue to make tremendous sacrifices that enable us to pursue our research, writing, and many other professional endeavors. We would like to extend a special, heartfelt thank you to Justin Croteau and Jennifer, Carter, and Campbell Smith (the newest addition to Zach and Jennifer's family) for all of their love and support. This book is dedicated to you!

Introduction

A S BOTH PRACTITIONERS AND RESEARCHERS in the field, we observed years ago that truly great higher education advancement leaders are rare. This is not a criticism of current chief advancement officers, but rather an acknowledgement that the industry has fallen short in leadership preparation, development, and training. It is not uncommon for today's fundraising professionals to be promoted into management and leadership positions for which they are not ready and to draw upon skills and abilities that have neither been developed nor refined, or that simply don't exist. In addition, succession planning has been largely ignored, leaving many advancement units structurally exposed and at risk. And finally, there are simply not enough advancement professionals in the pipeline to meet current and future staffing demands, especially at senior-level positions. In an industry with such high stakes, these issues are alarming. So we pose the following questions: How did we get here? What does it mean for the future? What should be done to address the problem?

We think about these questions often and have a basic sense of what caused the current void of leadership. During the second half of the twentieth century, advancement programs grew exponentially and demand for fundraisers increased tremendously. As growth exploded, new positions were created, and there were simply not enough competent fundraising professionals to meet rising demand. As a result, ill-prepared and inexperienced fundraisers were hired into positions for which they were not ready. Fast forward three to five years, and these same ill-prepared and inexperienced fundraisers began assuming higher-level management and leadership positions. They moved up fast, taking jobs with increasing levels of responsibility, scope, and salary. In addition, there has never been a clear entry point into the profession. Academic programs didn't exist until recently (and there are only a few that exist today), so no formal pipeline of advancement professionals was established. Contributing to the problem, no comprehensive or substantial management and leadership training programs exist for senior-level executives, forcing them to learn important skills on the job. On-the-job training is an inadequate model for a leadership position that has such tremendous responsibility.

Today, a significant number of advancement leaders self-describe their entry into the profession as unplanned. They advanced through their careers without any formal training or professional development to be leaders of people and programs. Their resumes are stellar, as they usually have fifteen to twenty years of experience. But some lack the necessary competence to be effective leaders. Of course many advancement leaders are highly successful and have what it takes to occupy the corner office and lead high-performing organizations. But a large cohort do not, putting the organizations and institutions they serve at risk.

What does it all mean for the future? For one, missed fundraising opportunities and less-effective advancement divisions will result without strong leadership. It's hard to quantify, but less-effective organizations most certainly result in fewer funds raised for endowments, scholarships, research, and capital improvements. Perhaps equally important, the industry is setting future leaders up for failure. Chief advancement officers serve in high-profile and highly political positions. They must be able to navigate ambiguous, dynamic environments. They must be able to sit across the table from accomplished faculty and wealthy donors. They must be able to communicate effectively with college presidents and politicians. And they must be able to do so with savvy, diplomacy, and tact, while always focusing on strategic outcomes and objectives.

These are challenging positions, requiring senior, high-level executives. Which brings us to the last question: How can we address the problem? How can we better prepare current and future chief advancement officers for current and future demands of the position? We certainly don't have all the answers, but our hope is to get at the core of these and other related questions. Before we can better prepare advancement leaders, we must first understand what it takes to be successful in the position. Once we know this, we can begin to create leadership development and training programs that are relevant and meaningful to the profession.

In this book, we've identified a set of leadership competencies necessary for the individual who wishes to be successful and effective as a chief advancement officer in higher education. We've broadened our understanding of this important leadership position and identified the knowledge, skills, abilities, attributes, and behaviors necessary for high performance. After an introduction and historical overview of the profession, a review of leadership literature, and a discussion of methodology, ten case studies of successful chief advancement officers, as nominated by their peers, are presented. We interviewed industry leaders, reviewed resumes and professional documents, and surveyed colleagues of these chief advancement officers in an effort to learn more about their career paths, leadership philosophies, and thoughts on professional development and leadership training. In short, we teased out the secrets to their success and present them in this book.

Through our research, we offer a thorough and comprehensive advancement leadership competency model that we hope will lead to relevant leadership and management training programs for the profession. Analyzing and identifying competencies of successful chief advancement officers, as we've done in this book, provides a blueprint for preparing future advancement leaders for the rigors of the job. Imagine for a moment a higher education advancement program that is highly functional, highly collegial and collaborative, and more effective and productive. This type of organizational environment is possible, but only if its leaders have the competence, experience, and training necessary for success. Now imagine the potential outcomes of this type of organization. Strong advancement leadership would help institutions raise more funds for faculty teaching and research through endowed chairs and professorships; they would have more funds for student aid through scholarships and fellowships; and they would have more funds for facilities and capital improvements. It's difficult to monetize competent leadership, but we believe the stakes are high and that the profession can no longer ignore this issue.

1

A Brief History of
Higher Education Advancement

IN TODAY'S COMPETITIVE WORKFORCE ENVIRONMENT, demand for higher education has reached unprecedented levels. The bachelor's degree has become
an essential credential for a middle-class lifestyle. More students than ever
are attending colleges and universities worldwide in an effort to compete
in a global economy. As a result, postsecondary educational resources have
become strained. For most public institutions, a perfect storm of declining
state support and increasing enrollments has pushed campus funding models
beyond capacity. There are simply not enough funds to support the demand.
And as institutions face ongoing pressure to become more self-sustaining,
rudimentary fundraising tactics employed during the founding years of
our country have evolved into sophisticated and strategic development and
advancement operations today. Although fundraising alone will not solve
campus budget problems, it can complement existing revenue sources and
increase academic quality, access, and affordability.

As Martin Shell, Stanford's vice president of development and alumni
relations, suggests, higher education fundraising has become a full-contact
sport. Once a passive activity managed by a few faculty members and the
institution's president, the art and science of academic fundraising is now a
multi-billion-dollar industry managed by highly skilled executives. High net
worth individuals are aggressively solicited for transformational gifts; foundations are peppered with million-dollar grant requests; and corporations are
asked to gift equipment and supplies as well as to engage in creative financial
and strategic partnerships with institutions of higher learning. Today's advancement professionals require a breadth and depth of knowledge spanning

a functional spectrum that includes finance, budgeting, human capital and talent management, constituent relations, fund development, marketing, advertising, communications, writing, public relations, and event management. Because of the complexity of the chief advancement officer position, it is perhaps one of the most difficult and demanding jobs to carry out in all of higher education.

The following pages outline a brief history of the growth of higher education and the corresponding development of the higher education fundraising and advancement profession. We begin with the founding of the first colonial institution, Harvard College, and journey through the proliferation of the thousands of institutions that exist today. Much of the information was drawn from Arthur Cohen's detailed history of the United States system of higher education in his book *The Shaping of American Higher Education: Emergence and Growth of the Contemporary System* (1998). This chapter presents a solid historical description of the foundation of the higher education advancement industry and the evolution of the chief advancement officer position.

The Colonial Period

As one might expect, Harvard College, founded as New College in 1636, was the first institution of higher education to receive a philanthropic donation, as well as the first college to launch an organized development program. In 1638, a young minister by the name of John Harvard donated a collection of approximately four hundred books and cash from his estate to New College. At the time this was enough private support to rename the school in his honor. His donation marked the first naming gift in the history of American higher education philanthropy, spawning what would eventually become the world's largest endowment.

The colonial period was a time of society building with "varying degrees of oversight" from the British (Cohen 1998, 9). Although the population grew considerably from the late 1600s to the late 1700s, with the city of Boston leading the way, most wealth was still concentrated in England. Shortly after John Harvard made his gift, a man by the name of William Hibbens, along with his two partners Hugh Peter and Thomas Weld, traveled to London on behalf of the newly renamed Harvard College to raise much-needed funds from the British (Worth 2002). It was the first documented fundraising strategy employed by an American institution of higher education, paving the way for future advances in the field. Hibbens created and developed the first fundraising brochure, or what today is often referred to as a "case statement," and presented it to donor prospects. Hibbens returned to Boston with five hundred pounds for the institution, and his journey was considered a tremendous success (Worth 2002). Combined with John Harvard's donation, these funds helped stabilize the start-up institution's financial position.

After the founding of Harvard, the first 150 years of higher education fundraising were mostly defined by church-sponsored events consisting of rudimentary and amateur processes including passing the plate, church dinners, bazaars, and an occasional "ask" by presidents and paid consultants (Worth 1993). The concept lacked any sort of strategic planning. Fundraising results were inconsistent and unpredictable. However, these early attempts were important insofar as they yielded systems and processes that are prevalent today. Although highly unsophisticated, prospect management, donor research, alumni engagement, pipeline development, and other tactics arose during this period.

The growth of the colonial era was marked by an intense effort on the part of the colonists to differentiate themselves and become independent from the European way of life. Explorers settled the vast landscape of North America (Cohen 1998). Religious reformation was prevalent as various sects and denominations fractured, reorganized, and proliferated. During the 1700s, the population grew from 250,000 to nearly 4 million; the number of postsecondary institutions grew from two to nine; and student enrollments grew nearly sevenfold from 150 to 1,000. Cohen summarizes higher education's development during this period:

> The nine colleges that were organized in the colonies were modeled on educational forms that had been developed in Europe over the prior five hundred years. This development has been traced well by Rashdall (1936) and, more recently, by Lucas (1994). One incipient university form was organized by groups of students who established their own organizations and assemblies, employing the faculty, deciding on how they would spend their funds, and setting rules governing the courses of study, examinations, and awarding of degrees (15).

From the beginning, there was a quasi-public relationship between private institutions and early state governments regarding control and funding (Whitehead and Herbst 1986). It wasn't until the Dartmouth College case of 1819, whereby the Supreme Court protected private institutions from state encroachment, that a distinction between public and private institutions emerged (Whitehead and Herbst 1986).

A vast array of methods was implemented to generate resources for start-up institutions during the colonial era, with government programs typically providing the majority of funding. Cohen describes how the original nine colonial institutions—Harvard College (1636); the College of William and Mary (1693; the nation's first public institution); Yale University (1701); the

University of Pennsylvania (1740); Princeton University (1746); Columbia University (1754); Brown University (1765); Rutgers (1766); and Dartmouth College (1769)—relied on taxes, military exemptions, lotteries, student fees, tuition, and, of course, private donations for funding. Although no formal fundraising programs existed, philanthropy was an important capital resource. For example, Elihu Yale donated assets valued at approximately five hundred pounds, which helped establish an endowment to pay the faculty on an annual basis. The University of Pennsylvania used a pledge system for start-up capital, securing four hundred pounds annually from twenty-five donors, including Benjamin Franklin, over a five-year period. Donations of land, assets, and cash were targeted and institutions were persistent in their fundraising efforts. However, endowments were small and a long way off from providing a steady and reliable revenue stream.

A Nation Develops

With the nation growing quickly in size and economic force, the number of higher education institutions and enrolled students exploded. The nineteenth century was a period of expansion, emergence, and industrialization. From 1790 to 1869, the United States grew in population from just under four million to over thirty-eight million, influenced by key events including the Louisiana Purchase, the acquisition of territories in the South and West, an emphasis on manufacturing and agriculture, and a developing infrastructure. Likewise, the number of higher education institutions grew from 11 to 240, and enrollments grew from 1,050 to 61,000. Cohen (1998) suggests the increase was staggering and swift:

> The distances between settlements were great. The splintering of religious denominations continued, and each sect had to have its own college. In each newly formed community, town boosters felt they needed a college to legitimate their settlement. The field was open for philanthropic groups, churches, and community developers. But the overriding reason has to be the general feeling of expansiveness that swept across the United States in the first few generations after independence (57).

Financing methods during this period grew out of the methods employed during the colonial era, which leaned heavily on private donations and state support. It was a difficult period as funds were scarce and students continued to pay little tuition (Cohen 1998). Most institutions operated year to year on shoestring budgets, as funding models continued to evolve. Many schools failed. However, as the nation's population grew in size, wealth, and prosperity, philanthropic pledges and donations became more frequent. Around 1800, Williams College reportedly raised $14,000 in small gifts and contributions, and a short time thereafter, Amherst raised $50,000 (Cohen 1998). Other institutions, such as Princeton, Columbia, and Union College, also found success. However, to put it in context, Cohen states that "little cash was available; as late as 1870, the colleges of the nation were receiving a total of approximately $8 to $9 million per year through private donations" (1998, 88).

Also during the 1800s, the first formal alumni associations were created with a primary mission to "perpetuate memories and intellectual interests" among graduates (Worth 1993, 19). Alumni funds provided a way for associations to give back to a school and its students, often in the form of scholarships. In addition, as a result of the Morrill Acts of 1862 and 1890, land grant public institutions proliferated and fundraising strategies migrated from private institutions into public institutions. The East Coast was dominated by private institutions, so most public institution fundraising began in the Midwest (Worth 1993). As institutions continued to open across the country, more-sophisticated methods of fundraising emerged. But there were still no formal development programs. Most fundraising responsibilities continued to fall on the shoulders of faculty, university presidents, and paid consultants. However, methods including the development of prospect rating systems and donor contact lists, and advanced methods for soliciting gifts, took hold as more people on campus participated in philanthropic endeavors to raise highly sought-after funds for various projects and programs.

Growth and Prosperity

The late 1800s through the mid-1900s was a transformational period, to put it mildly. The United States experienced another generation of incredible population growth. Higher education institutions grew in number and size, increasing access for more and more students. The purchase of Alaska completed territorial expansion, and the nation began a period of industrialization that would help shape and transform universities (Cohen 1998). The population grew from nearly 40 million in 1870 to approximately 140 million by 1945 (Snyder 1993), representing a staggering growth rate of 250 percent in a seventy-five-year period. Snyder further estimates that the number of higher education institutions grew from 250 to 1,768, a sevenfold increase, with enrollments climbing from 63,000 students to over 1.6 million.

Two pieces of legislation helped open the doors to more students: the College Land Grant (Morrill) Act, passed during the Civil War; and the Serviceman's Readjustment Act, or GI Bill. These bills thawed access to higher education and began what Cohen refers to as the "Mass Higher Education Era." The Morrill Act of 1862, which gave each state thirty thousand acres of federal land per number of congressmen, was used to open institutions such as the University of Illinois in 1867 and the University of California in 1868 (Cohen 1998). Many prestigious private institutions were also founded during this period, including Stanford in 1891 and the University of Chicago in 1892. As more and more schools opened, governing bodies, professional associations, and advocacy groups began to arise, like the Association of American Universities, founded in 1900.

In addition to an increase in government funding, private funds began flowing from wealthy investors and businessmen who struck it rich during and after the Civil War period (Cohen 1998). For instance, Johns Hopkins was founded in 1876 with private support, and Cornell opened in part due to a $500,000 gift from Ezra Cornell. As the nation continued to prosper, philanthropic gifts grew in number and size and provided start-up capital for institutions nationwide, typically in the form of endowments that generated annual financial payouts in perpetuity. As Cohen (1998) describes it,

> Private donations, always an important source of revenue, accelerated rapidly, so that by the 1890s some single institutions were receiving $1 million or more. After the turn of the twentieth century, even before tax laws changed, many of the large private donors organized philanthropic foundations as conduits for their funds. As income and inheritance taxes grew, foundations became even more prominent (159–160).

Transformational gifts were becoming more frequent during this time, allowing institutions to establish themselves with a stable balance sheet and engage in high-quality teaching and research from the outset. Cornelius Vanderbilt donated $1 million; Andrew Carnegie gave $1 million; Johns Hopkins donated $3.5 million; the Stanford estate provided $20 million; and John D. Rockefeller gifted $30 million to the University of Chicago. While these major donations were transformative and influential, and received widespread press and public attention, most institutions relied on much smaller gifts that were largely restricted to specific programs and purposes such as student scholarships and other student-focused activities (Cohen 1998). As a percentage of giving, unrestricted gifts began to shrink and restricted gifts rose. With more restricted gifts donated toward specific programs, an increase in financial management and oversight of funds was necessary. Schools fortunate enough to receive large capital infusions, such as Harvard, Johns Hopkins, and Stanford, continued to build their endowments, which provided the majority of their operating income. But most public institutions were not so fortunate and relied on government support to stay afloat.

As private institutions became wealthier, they attracted the most talented faculty and brightest students, which helped to establish the finest programs and ultimately graduate the country's most successful professionals and affluent alumni. Accordingly, fundraising and alumni relations programs grew more robust in the early 1900s, with more-prosperous institutions building their endowments by soliciting alumni on a regular basis. "As the number of alumni grew larger, the funds they contributed grew as well. These organized campaigns rapidly replaced the occasional individual appeals, but institutional presidents continued to cultivate and steward large donors who provided funding" (Cohen 1998). Wealthy private institutions became exponentially wealthier, growing in size and stature compared to most public institutions. As the country prospered, total giving grew from $65 million in 1920 to approximately $148 million by 1930 (Cohen 1998). In 1909, Harvard's endowment stood at $20 million, which provided enough income to fund all annual expenditures (Cohen 1998).

As one might expect, the Great Depression had a tremendous impact on the overall financial health of higher education institutions. With a decrease in revenue from all sources, including endowment payouts, individual gifts, alumni giving, foundation grants, and other forms of donations, schools had to make draconian cuts to their enterprises. Capital spending fell to nearly zero, faculty salaries declined by about 15 percent, and instructional costs per full-time-equivalent faculty member declined by over 10 percent at public institutions (Cohen 1998). However, within the greater context of the nation's broken economy, higher education institutions suffered far less during the Great Depression than most social organizations and institutions. Furthermore, in 1936 legislation was passed exempting gifts from taxation, which began a new phase of growth in fundraising and philanthropy (Elliot 2006).

Fundraising and Advancement Programs Professionalize

Toward the end of the nineteenth and beginning of the twentieth century, faculty governance, and in some cases student governance, surrendered to a more formal administrative structure tasked with managing the operations of higher education institutions. Chief student affairs officers, chief financial officers, athletics directors, provosts, and other senior administrators began emerging. Faculty no longer had the time, and students were much too young and ill-prepared, to handle the growing administrative tasks of running colleges and universities. Likewise, presidents were forced to spend less time in the classroom and laboratory and more time tending to various campus operations. While many executive-level responsibilities and positions surfaced during this time, the chief advancement officer position came much later.

Not surprisingly, Harvard is credited with the establishment of the first formal fundraising office (in the 1920s), and Northwestern University is credited with first using the term *development* in its current sense (Oliver 2007). But an organization outside the higher education industry had a much greater influence on the formalization of the fundraising and advancement profession in the early 1900s. In 1902, Lyman L. Pierce, an executive with the YMCA, undertook a campaign to raise $300,000 to build a new facility in Washington, DC (Cutlip 1990). Pierce joined with another notable YMCA executive from Chicago, Charles Sumner Ward, and together they organized, planned, and guided to successful completion one of the first formal fundraising campaigns. Ward essentially became known as the founding father of today's modern campaign fundraising techniques, developing the first campaign thermometer to publicly display an organization's success over time, creating strategic prospect lists, establishing campaign time limits, identifying volunteers and leadership gifts, and publicizing successes (Cutlip 1990).

Ward eventually made his mark on higher education philanthropy when he was hired to help raise $3 million for the University of Pittsburgh's campaign in 1914 (Worth 2002), the largest campaign of its time. He and a handful of other notable fundraisers, including Arnaud Marts, who later cofounded the well-known firm Marts and Lundy, introduced effective campaign methods and strategies to universities and other organizations nationwide. Their approaches to fundraising eventually became standard practices that remain influential today.

Throughout the first half of the 1900s, most higher education fundraising campaigns were led by paid consultants such as Ward. Campaign strategies and tactics were managed by the consultant and the actual fundraising was carried out by volunteers, faculty, and campus leaders (Worth 2002). Charles Ward never personally solicited gifts himself, yet he helped raise millions for the institutions and organizations he represented. Rather than savvy interpersonal skills, his application of strategy was the key to his success. To some, it was a very controversial approach, but highly effective.

Around the middle of the twentieth century, Ward and other notable consultants continued to develop the art and science of fundraising into a legitimate and credible profession. Higher education organizations began adding full-time development and advancement staff to their operations. Charles Ward laid the foundation for a new breed of professionals, including major gift officers, development directors, planned giving experts, communication and marketing executives, and alumni relations managers who were employed directly by the institution. According to Pray (1981), the first director of development was appointed in the 1940s. By 1949, the American College Public Relations Association found only two members with the title

Director of Development. But by 1952 it found thirteen (Pray 1981). Since then the profession has grown by leaps and bounds. Every major college and university employs a comprehensive development or advancement staff, and the demand for competent fundraisers is high. Institutions recognize that an investment in resource development through private support pays off in spades. As Worth (2002) acknowledges,

> Development has emerged within the past fifty years as an identifiable field within higher education administration, with its own specialized body of knowledge, standards, training programs, and career patterns. Concomitantly, the development officer or institutional advancement officer has risen to the most senior ranks of college and university administration, with a significant role in the overall management of the institution. In the past decade, development has become a common route to the college or university presidency (29).

In 1958, the advancement structure began to professionalize further when the American Alumni Council (AAC) and the American College Public Relations Association (ACPRA) convened for a meeting at the Greenbrier Hotel in West Virginia. Historically, a culture of collaboration had not existed between these two groups, and in fact they were often in competition with each other (Worth 2002). However, the meeting in 1958 resulted in a landmark publication, the "Greenbrier Report," which led to the formalization and professionalization of advancement as we know it today. In 1974, the AAC and the ACPRA merged to become the Council for Advancement and Support of Education (CASE; Worth 2002). As a result of these key events, the chief advancement officer has emerged as a senior executive with a seat in the president's cabinet and as a critical player in the successful operation of colleges and universities.

Advancement Modernizes

As Cohen (1998) outlines, from 1945 through 1975 the U.S. population continued to expand, growing from 140 million to over 215 million. In addition, the number of higher education institutions grew from 1,768 to 2,747, and the number of students enrolled rose from just over 1.6 million to over 11 million. Growth was steady and consistent, and led to a stable and booming economy. By 1995, student enrollment grew to over 14 million at over 3,700 institutions. Today, the U.S. population has surpassed 300 million; there are over 4,400 postsecondary institutions; and in 2010, the number of students enrolled in these postsecondary institutions was expected to set a record of over 19 million (National Center for Education Statistics).

Philanthropic donations have risen steadily alongside the booming economy and population. From 1949–50 to 1975–76, voluntary private support increased tenfold (Cohen 1998). In 1957, Harvard launched an $82 million campaign, with Stanford announcing an even larger goal of $100 million shortly thereafter (Cohen 1998). Transformational gifts were growing larger. The University of Richmond received a $50 million gift from E. Claiborne Robbins in 1969, the largest gift of its time. In 1979, the first $100 million gift was a donation by Robert Woodruff, former CEO of Coca-Cola, and his brother to establish the Emory Scholars program at Emory University. Today, $100 million gifts are more common as notable philanthropists such as Bill Gates, Warren Buffet, George Lucas, T. Boone Pickens, William and Flora Hewlett, and Phil Night make $100 million or larger donations to colleges and universities nationwide.

With large, transformative gifts having such a profound impact on academic programs, a campaign arms race began to develop toward the end of the twentieth century as private institutions sought to out-raise each other. Worth (1993) documents that in 1984, Johns Hopkins launched a $450 million fundraising campaign, which was the largest campaign of its time. However, just three years later, Stanford University announced the first billion-dollar campaign:

> The explosion of fund-raising goals in the 1980s reflected the strong U.S. economy as well as the increasing needs of colleges and universities being called upon to serve a lengthening national agenda. Our colleges and universities are looked upon as vehicles for achieving social justice, enhancing national economic competitiveness, and advancing technological and medical knowledge, among other goals. The costs of needed facilities and equipment has continued to rise, as have faculty salaries, medical insurance costs, and all the other elements of the college or university (27).

Toward the end of the century, advancement units were increasingly called upon to meet the needs and priorities of institutions through private philanthropy. Private institutions had a long history of engaging in fundraising activities; however, public institutions began adding programs and ramping up staff as well. Colleges and universities realized a coordinated effort was most effective at generating and increasing private support, and as a result, the functions of alumni relations, development, marketing and communications, government and community relations, and public affairs departments began to merge into one *advancement* unit.

Today, the chief advancement officer is the senior executive responsible for managing advancement and external relations functions. Because fundraising is the primary focus, many executives at this level have a deep background in development. As pressures mount on institutions to develop new and creative revenue sources, chief advancement officers have become valuable professionals to the chief executives they serve. Campaigns have proliferated across the country to the extent that most institutions are always in campaign mode. Either in the planning stages, a silent phase, or preparing for public launch, institutions continuously campaign. Stanford may have launched the first billion-dollar campaign in the 1980s, but by 1990 Columbia reached new heights with a $2 billion campaign. Columbia went a step further and outdid itself by launching a $4 billion campaign in 2006, which was eclipsed when Stanford announced a $4.3 billion goal later that same year. However, campaign goals continued to push even higher. Columbia increased its original $4 billion goal to $5 billion in December 2010, and the University of Southern California announced a $6 billion campaign in August 2011, the largest ever. It is only a matter of time before new audacious goals are set and fundraising records are broken. Charles Ward, the founding father of fundraising, is surely rolling in his grave at such astronomical numbers.

To no one's surprise, the significant increase of and focus on private donations as an important source of revenue can be traced to declining government support. Private institutions, usually founded through transformational gifts to begin with, have always relied on private support. But public institutions never had to do so until recently. While fundraising in and of itself will likely never fill the shortfall of state support, it can certainly impact academic quality, launch innovative research projects, and provide access to students through scholarships.

With hundreds of millions and even billions of dollars at stake, colleges and universities have ramped up their staffs significantly, especially over the past twenty to thirty years. As Cohen (1998) notes,

> In public and private institutions alike, the drive to increase funding from the private sector led to sizable investments in staff. It was not unusual for a major university to have three hundred people working in the development office. The institution's president had to be involved, along with numerous people skilled in fundraising. The development officers proceeded with deliberate plans, targeting wealthy donors and establishing personal relationships with them where possible; they emphasized the prestige of their institutions, the scope of its programs, and the way it was serving the public. They were careful to tailor their requests to purposes identified as being favored by particular donors. Fundraising in both the public and private sector had become so important that the issue dominated presidential selection; individuals with unattractive lifestyles or mannerisms might well be rejected regardless of their academic credentials. Presidents who could relate well personally with private donors and with corporation and foundation officials were much more desirable (409).

As might be expected, the expansion of the advancement industry from the last half of the twentieth century through today has not evolved without its challenges. As new positions were created, a game of professional musical chairs began to unfold. Schools late to deploy fundraisers realized they needed to create development programs and add staff so as not to miss out on resource opportunities. Market forces have caused inexperienced professionals with short tenures to move from institution to institution, taking advantage of larger salaries and more-prestigious titles each step of the way. The growth has been good for development and advancement professionals individually. But higher education institutions have experienced peaks and valleys in their staffing levels, leading to instability and often chaotic organizational environments. It is widely known that development professionals with longer tenures have more fundraising success. However, demand for fundraisers and escalating salaries have led to a supply problem that has not been adequately addressed. In addition, the strategic priorities of the main campus, academic units (i.e., deans and faculty members), and advancement office are often at odds with each other, placing advancement and fundraising professionals in precarious situations. This results in job dissatisfaction, frustration, and burnout, causing development and advancement professionals to seek employment elsewhere.

The Chief Advancement Officer of the Twenty-First Century

The roles, responsibilities, and expectations of higher education advancement units and the chief advancement officer position have changed dramatically since the first development offices were established in the last century. Job descriptions have changed and become more complex, and senior administrative titles and portfolios have evolved to reflect the evolution of the profession. Common titles include Vice President of Development, Vice President of Philanthropy, Vice President of External Relations, and Vice President of Advancement. Some titles include the alumni relations function, such as that of Vice President for Development and Alumni Relations at Boston University and Vice President for Development and Alumni Relations at the University of Florida. Moreover, as the higher education industry continues to place a greater emphasis on marketing, branding, communications, and public affairs, the portfolios of chief advancement officers are broadening. For instance, Robbee Baker Kosak, vice president for university advancement at Carnegie Mellon University, and Carrie Pelzel, senior vice president for advancement at Dartmouth College, both carry these responsibilities. Some universities have created even loftier titles to emphasize the importance of the advancement function, such as Executive Vice President or Senior Vice President. Regardless of title, senior higher education advancement leaders are now considered the "chief" development officer or "chief" advancement officer of their institution. Some individuals even carry this title, such as James D. Thompson, who is the senior vice president and chief advancement officer at the University of Rochester.

As the case studies of the successful higher education chief advancement officers presented in this book illustrate, it is important to have a clear understanding and operational definition of the terms *advancement* and *chief advancement officer*. Today, one widely accepted operational definition includes the majority of institutional external relations functions, the most important of which is development. *Advancement* has a connotation that invokes meanings such as "bettering," "positioning," "advancing," "furthering," "deepening," and "broadening" an institution's brand and its reach and impact on its community, the nation, and the world. Therefore, colleges and universities want people both inside and outside the higher education industry to think of advancement as all-encompassing. For example, Education.com (2011) defines institutional advancement as "interpretation and promotion of an institution to its various constituencies—[including] fund raising, internal and external communications, government relations, and public relations."

For the purpose of this book, *advancement* is defined very similarly. It's widely accepted that advancement encompasses most of the external relations components discussed above. However, it must first and foremost include development. All advancement functions lead to or relate to fundraising in some way, shape, or form. Therefore, the executives profiled in this book include those with primary development responsibilities as part of their portfolio, like Jerry May at the University of Michigan. Executives with both development and alumni relations responsibilities are also profiled, like Sarah Pearson, formerly at Northwestern University. Finally, executives with the full range of advancement duties are profiled, like Carrie Pelzel at Dartmouth College. In this way, the essence of what advancement truly represents has been captured from multiple perspectives. Regardless of title and portfolio, all chief development and chief advancement officers work in unison with marketing, communications, alumni relations, and other external agents and officers to help raise private funds for their institution.

In the future, advancement units will continue to be faced with even greater pressure to raise money and increase revenue from private sources. Despite the recent "Great Recession," Americans have accumulated more wealth than ever. As the baby boom generation prepares to leave its legacy behind, the greatest transfer of wealth in the history of our nation is upon us. Higher education institutions have a unique opportunity to take advantage of billions of dollars

of wealth transfer through principal and legacy giving. In addition, venture philanthropy—that is, using concepts, strategies, and techniques from for-profit
venture capitalists and applying them to the nonprofit sector—is becoming
increasingly popular. The future of the advancement profession remains bright.
However, chief advancement officers must continue to evolve and develop their
skills as strategic planners and skilled leaders. They must ultimately become better prepared to meet the increasing expectations and professional demands of
twenty-first-century higher education institutions.

2

Leadership in Higher Education and Advancement

A LTHOUGH IT IS A CRITICALLY IMPORTANT DIVISION, the most astute and experi-enced higher education professionals will likely agree that advancement is an organizational unit that, on the surface, appears to operate under an ambiguous directive that is often confusing and misunderstood. In addition, many campus constituents view advancement as a bank. If an academic unit needs money, it calls advancement. If researchers need funding, they call advancement. For public institutions, if state funding is cut, advancement is often expected to help fill the void. The list of campus needs is infinite, and advancement is often looked upon to solve these various financial problems.

From a leadership perspective, high expectations are placed on chief ad-vancement officers, yet these professionals have little institutional power to move things forward independently. The success of chief advancement of-ficers is often less contingent on asking people for money and more on being able to coalesce the various forces on campus (i.e., deans, faculty, staff, ad-ministrators, and perhaps most importantly, volunteers) in an effort to lever-age their interest in and ability to raise money. Every good chief advancement officer knows that his or her success rests largely on the backs of multiple constituent groups. While this organizational paradox likely exists within other higher education units and senior-level administrative positions, there is arguably no individual who must balance the interests of more stakeholders than the chief advancement officer.

The purpose of this book is to identify, define, and articulate the variables, or underlying themes, of chief advancement officer leadership that are im-portant and necessary for effective advancement outcomes and organizational success. The leaders in any industry must possess a certain level and scope of competence to be successful. However, in higher education, shared governance and faculty tenure are the underpinnings of a distinctive culture that drives its operational processes. Few industries have these unique horizontal organizational characteristics. Therefore, it is important to have a greater understanding of the competencies that are important for chief advancement officers who want to lead effectively within their own units and their campuses as a whole.

The following pages provide a summary of previous research, propositions, and existing theories on higher education and advancement leadership. This chapter will aid in developing a general understanding of our approach to studying leadership and the chief advancement officer position, beginning first with a review of general leadership theory, followed by some of the more-popular and well-respected studies on higher education and advancement leadership.

What Is Leadership?

Most would agree that leadership is a fluid process that is not only difficult to characterize theoretically, but seemingly more difficult to replicate in practice. James MacGregor Burns, a distinguished leadership researcher, believed that leadership is among the "least understood phenomena on earth" (1978, 2). Many propositions and theories have been introduced on the topic spanning a wide spectrum of academic and practical perspectives. But the past one hundred years of research has resulted in multiple theories, spanning domains from psychology to sociology and education to business (Green 1988; Moilanen 2002).

One of the earliest theories of leadership dates to the late 1800s and early 1900s. The trait approach, as it was called, found that certain individual characteristics were important for effective leadership, and it was these characteristics, or traits, that differentiated leaders from their followers (Bass 1990; Northouse 2004; Stogdill 1974). Commonly known as the Great Man theory, it followed the premise that power is given to a select few individuals whose "inheritance and destiny" move them into leadership positions (Bennis and Nanus 1997, 5). Essentially, great man, or trait, theory said that leaders are born and not made and that leadership is largely the result of certain traits that only certain people possess. Although only a select few are born with these traits and characteristics, these traits and characteristics are nonetheless important and essential for leadership success.

While popular during its time, trait theory came with obvious limitations. Stogdill (1974) found inconclusive evidence related to the impact of a leader's qualities and characteristics on an organization. He believed that a person does not rise to a leadership position because of traits alone, but rather the personal characteristics of the leader must match the characteristics and goals of the leader's followers in any given situation—which is constantly changing. Leadership, Stogdill argued, is a "working relationship among members of a group in which the leader acquires status through active participation and demonstration of his capacity for carrying cooperative tasks through to completion" (1974, 65). In short, situational context, or environment, was found to be a significant variable left out of the original trait theory.

Evidence accumulated that required a modification of how one differentiated between leaders and followers (Stogdill 1974; Bass 1990). Environment was thought to have a significant influence over who assumed leadership positions. This belief led to a shift from the trait approach to situational leadership. The situational approach, as it became known, held that great leaders emerge as a result of the environment (Bass 1990). "The situationalists advanced the view that the emergence of a great leader is a result of time, place, and circumstance" (38). Contrary to supporters of the trait approach, situational theorists believed leaders are not born, but rather are the product of a situation that requires a certain type of leader at a certain time (Bass 1990).

Hersey and Blanchard (1969) agreed with situational theorists, but believed that a leader must either be task-oriented or relations-oriented, depending on the skill level and maturity of the subordinate. For instance, new, inexperienced employees might require a more task-oriented leader and might need to be told specifically what to do. Hersey and Blanchard argued that as "their 'life-cycle' on the job continues and their experience increases, they [the employees] have to be sold to continue performance" (Bass 1990, 489). Or simply, as subordinates fully mature and have a better understanding of what needs to be done, a leader's responsibility shifts to relationship management and delegation.

Fiedler (1967) suggested that a leader's influence over group performance is contingent on matching the leader's style with the "degree of favorableness" of the group (151). Known as contingency theory, this argument asserts that if a leader's style is tailored to the environment, organizational performance should improve. However, Fiedler believed that rather than changing a leader's behavior, it is more important to *match* a leader's style with an appropriate organizational context. In short, he believed that "effective leadership is *contingent* on matching a leader's style to the right setting" (Northouse 2004, 109).

Fiedler's research had a far-reaching impact, as it led to future studies that looked more closely at leader-subordinate dynamics—that is, exchanges or interactions between a leader and a follower. Leadership characteristics, context, and environment had been widely researched; however, little was understood of the processes and relationships between leaders and followers.

In 1976, Graen proposed that informally developed roles were negotiated between each individual group member and the leader. This is commonly referred to as leader-member exchange theory (LMX). "Co-workers may get involved in the role definition, but the leader, in particular, has a vested interest in the member's role. The definition of a member's role defines what the member and the leader will expect the member to do" (Bass 1990, 333). Early research focused on the dynamics between in-group and out-group relationships and how leaders interact with subordinates in both types of groups. Mutual trust, respect, liking, and reciprocal influence defined leader/in-group relationships, while formal communication based on job descriptions defined leader/out-group relationships. According to Graen (1976), a division between inner-circle and outer-circle relationships occurs because a leader does not have time to give equal attention to all subordinates. Later studies shifted focus from in-group and out-group relationships to how leader-member exchanges contribute to effective organizational outcomes (Northouse 2004). High-quality leader-member exchanges increase employee morale, which leads to an increase in organizational productivity and job satisfaction (Northouse 2004).

Consistent with Graen's (1976) theory on the process of leadership, transformational leadership emerged to describe the dynamic relationship between leaders, followers, and organizational outcomes. J. M. Burns's book *Leadership* (1978) first proposed the idea of the "transforming" leader, which was later extended by Bass (1985, 1998). Since then, thousands of articles have been published on transformational leadership. Transformational leadership continues to drive a large body of research today and helps to frame discussions around the leader and his or her impact on an organization from a much broader, visionary perspective.

In transformational leadership, Burns believed leadership to be a process, or a series of transactions, between leaders and followers whereby leaders influence followers to move an organization above and beyond what is typically expected to achieve a greater purpose (Bass 1990). More specifically, transformational leaders are responsible for motivating followers to put their self-interests aside for the good of the organization (Bass 1990). Bass (1985) asserted that "increased awareness and the arousal of higher-level needs which transcend self-interests can produce extraordinary effort" (15). By raising the consciousness of followers to focus on higher-level needs rather than self-interest, the transformational leader can achieve significant organizational results (Bass 1985). Four factors of influence define transformational leadership: charisma, inspirational motivation, intellectual stimulation, and individualized consideration. Burns's (1978) theory of the transforming leader was based to some extent on Maslow's hierarchy of needs. A transformational leader is responsible for motivating, persuading, and coercing individuals to "upgrade" their self-interest needs to the needs and interests of a group or organization (Bass 1985).

Burns's contributions to the body of knowledge on leadership are significant and have led to further study of the transformational leader. In 1994, Ronald Heifetz introduced a quasi-variation of transformational theory. Heifetz centered his premise on the mobilization of subordinates through adaptive work. He built on interaction and exchange theories that suggest effective leadership is more about process rather than authority or a personal set of characteristics. For Heifetz, leadership is an activity involving the mobilization of people to face difficult problems. Leadership helps people make progress against challenges through adaptive work. Adaptive work consists of the "learning required to address conflicts in the values people hold, or to diminish the gap between the values people stand for and the reality they face" (1994, 22). More specifically, adaptive work involves *changing* one's values, beliefs, or behavior for the good of an organization, and it is the leader's responsibility to assist followers with change. Heifetz's conclusions offer an alternative approach to the process of leadership and relationships that are necessary between leaders and followers to foster positive organizational outcomes.

In his book *Good to Great* (2001), Jim Collins uses the term *Level 5 leadership* to describe executives who are interested in "the larger goal of building a great company" (21). His empirical, longitudinal study compared good companies to great companies. Collins found that all great companies had Level 5 leaders, whereas the comparison companies employed leaders who fell into the bottom four levels. Collins believed Level 5 leaders embody a "paradoxical mix of personal humility and professional will" (2001, 39). They are ambitious, modest, self-effacing, and understated, and they plan for succession for the greater good of the company (39). Collins's work is consistent with the idea of a transformational leader; however, he points to specific *leadership competencies* within the context of what he believes to be important for taking good companies and making them great. Based on his research, he outlines specific knowledge, skills, abilities, attributes, and behaviors—emphasizing professional will and personal humility—that are important to achieve Level 5 leadership status. While not everyone has the potential to become a Level 5 leader, Collins hypothesizes that there are

many people with the potential to reach Level 5 status under the right circumstances and with the right professional development.

A large body of more recent leadership research focuses on work groups,
teams, and team dynamics. Northouse defines teams as "organized groups
composed of members who are interdependent, who share common goals,
and who must coordinate their activities to accomplish these goals" (2004,
203). Multiple models and theories exist; however, the main impetus of team
leadership research looks at the core function of a leader and his or her role
in facilitating high-performing and effective teams (Northouse 2004). It is
the leader's responsibility to ensure ongoing analysis and management of the
team by selecting an appropriate course of action and implementing contex-
tual behaviors conducive to team productivity. In short, "effective leaders
have the ability to determine what leadership interventions are needed (if
any) to solve team problems" (207).

Higher Education Leadership

While the previous section outlined leadership theory in general, this section
reviews leadership within the context of higher education. It is important to
consider leadership success and effectiveness within context, especially when
thinking about higher education institutions and their unique organizational
structure. Universities are multi-unit, highly bureaucratic organizations that
have been referred to in the past as "organized anarchies" (Cohen and March
1986). They often move at a glacial pace, with multiple layers of policies and
procedures. Some scholars have even suggested that the traditional values,
historic perspectives, shared governance, and faculty independence of higher
education institutions have resulted in inefficient systems, outdated policies,
and ill-prepared administrators (Raines and Alberg 2003). While little attention has traditionally been devoted to studying leadership in higher education, education leadership studies have been gaining ground in recent years.
Funders, including government agencies, state legislators, and institutional
trustees, expect higher education leaders to not only be savvy and competent
academic professionals, but also to have a keen business sense.

A large portion of existing higher education leadership literature consists
of anecdotal, qualitative information with unclear propositions that are
difficult to replicate (Bensimon, Neumann, and Birnbaum 1989). As one
might expect, most higher education leadership research has focused on the
presidency and the extent to which presidential leadership actually makes a
difference (Cohen and March 1986; Fisher, Tack, and Wheeler 1988; Fisher
and Koch 1996, 2004; Peck 1983). However, Bensimon, Neumann, and

Birnbaum (1989) contended that higher education leadership theories were too narrow, discounting the emergence of leadership from sources other than the president (79). In order to advance the higher education leadership research agenda, Bensimon, Neumann, and Birnbaum believed scholars should "use theories that give attention to multiple sources of leadership" (79). This observation strengthens the case for studying leadership across the academy from multiple perspectives and contexts, including that of the chief advancement officer.

Some of the earliest observations of the president's position focused more on obligations and responsibilities rather than leadership (Day 1946). Interestingly, as far back as sixty years ago it was noted that presidents were responsible for managing public relations, increasing resources, mediating competing interests, maintaining moral, encouraging innovation, and promoting the general philosophy of the institution (Day 1946); this is consistent with many of a current president's responsibilities. However, Peck (1983) wrote of university presidents as more visionary and "entrepreneurial." This was an important shift, as Peck seemed to focus more on the president as a leader rather than as a manager. He believed that college presidents should be "future focused" and should possess entrepreneurial characteristics that enable them to appropriately navigate the complex system of higher education. Interestingly, Peck's findings contradicted other research suggesting that presidents have little impact or influence on the institutions they lead (Cohen and March 1986). In their research, Cohen and March found that the ambiguous nature of higher education institutions allows individuals and units to make decisions independently, without the blessing of a CEO. They suggested that the institution makes the leader and that the leader does not have great power to change the institution.

One of the most frequently cited empirical studies on the college presidency was conducted by Fisher, Tack, and Wheeler (1988). The authors identified effective presidents and compared them to representative presidents to expose and analyze differences between them. Specifically, they found effective presidents were more likely to be

- less collegial and more distant;
- less likely to be spontaneous in speech and actions;
- less restricted by organizational structure or by the consensus of those to be led;
- less likely to appear to make decisions easily;
- more confident;
- more inclined to rely on gaining respect than on being liked;
- more inclined to work long hours;

- more supportive of the controversial concept of merit pay;
- more interested in encouraging people to think differently and creatively; and
- more likely to be concerned with higher education in general than with one institution (111).

However, during the late 1980s and early 1990s, when team leadership theories became popular, researchers began looking at more horizontal and shared governance models of leadership (Bensimon and Neumann 1993; Birnbaum 1992; Green 1988) and their relevance to higher education. Considering the tremendous power academic senates have over the tenure and decision-making process of college and university presidents, this was a logical model to follow.

Green (1988) wanted to expand leadership theory beyond leadership roles to a more inclusive, shared model of leadership. She believed that the decentralized nature of colleges and universities combined with faculty independence creates an environment in which a CEO's leadership power is dependent on his or her legitimacy within the organization (15). Legitimate power requires the acceptance of followers as well as shared values and goals. This acceptance comes from a leader's credentials and in most cases academic experience more than anything else. As a result, Green offered a new model of higher education leadership emphasizing the importance of coalition and team building in which leaders serve as "knowledge executives" and "future agents" (50). To be a knowledge executive and future agent, the leader must possess extensive knowledge of postsecondary institutions, understanding their operation from wide-ranging perspectives. Green's analysis is consistent with the "future focused" leader of Peck (1983); however, Green's assertion refers to the behavior of a team of leaders rather than simply a president, as did Peck.

Consistent with Green (1988), Birnbaum (1992) also approached the topic from a team, or shared governance, context. Birnbaum conducted a rare, holistic, longitudinal academic leadership study known as the Institutional Leadership Project (ILP). Spanning five years, the ILP looked at multiple institutional types and leadership roles and used various data sources. In general, Birnbaum concluded that presidents can make a difference, but he cautioned against a "one size fits all" scenario. Extending Birnbaum's research, Bensimon and Neumann's book *Redesigning Collegiate Leadership: Teams and Teamwork in Higher Education* (1993) explored "models of teamwork in higher education, taking into account the leadership orientations of presidents and their executive officers" (xi). The authors looked at the horizontal nature of how leaders of multiple divisions work together and solve problems.

They argued that most models of higher education leadership assume the process of leadership is the result of an individual, discounting for the most part group dynamics altogether (16). Bensimon and Neumann's thesis is based primarily on the concept that team leadership accepts differences among individuals, embraces these differences, and brings them to the forefront for lively dialogue and open discussion, resulting in the exploration of multiple viewpoints that may not have otherwise been discovered. The authors concluded that a shared responsibility for thinking is as important as a shared responsibility for doing by enhancing team learning and team engagement with the campus as a whole (145).

A recent book by Adrianna J. Kezar and Jaime Lester, *Enhancing Campus Capacity for Leadership* (2011), builds on the argument for a team, collaborative, and shared leadership approach. The authors suggest that there are multiple sources of higher education leadership outside traditional administrative hierarchies. Through case study analyses, they posit that formal authoritative positions are not the sole source of leadership within higher education. Leadership emerges from faculty and staff interested in enacting change from the ground up, and it's manifested through informal networks, social interactions, and support systems.

Higher education leadership research has resulted in multiple propositions and theories. The debate appears to center on whether or not presidential leadership actually has an impact on the institution, and more recently, how leadership transcends the president's office. The latter discussion is of particular relevance to the focus of this book and opens the door for expanding the breadth and depth of leadership research within various domains of higher education. Presidential leadership is certainly important and should continue to be explored in greater detail. However, little is known about leadership below the presidency, especially as it relates to the chief advancement officer. We hope to further our understanding of this important administrative position.

Advancement Leadership

Due in large part to the chief advancement position's relatively slow evolution, few people have looked at variables of leadership related to the success of chief advancement officers. As noted in chapter 1, the advancement industry did not begin to fully professionalize until the mid 1950s and has only recently gained credibility as an invaluable addition to the president's cabinet. However, it is important to outline existing research, scholarship, and landmark events that have made modest contributions to our understanding of higher education advancement from a leadership perspective.

John Pollard was perhaps one of the first authors to provide a comprehensive summary of the applications and considerations of fundraising in the higher education setting. His book *Fund-Raising for Higher Education*, published in 1958, noted that a successful development program rests largely on the institution's ability to obtain a full-time staff member to be in charge of the program (242). However, an obvious omission of the book is a discussion on the topic of leadership.

Around the same time Pollard's book was published, a key event took place that had a profound impact on the profession. As discussed in chapter 1, the three-day meeting held at the Greenbrier Hotel in White Sulphur Springs, West Virginia, by the American Alumni Council and the American College Public Relations Association resulted in the "Greenbrier Report," which suggested that all external related functions, including public relations, fundraising, and alumni relations, should be subsumed under one unit managed by a senior-level executive at the vice-president level (Reck 1976). Since then, the chief advancement officer position has evolved, most notably in the past thirty to forty years, into a legitimate leadership position within higher education institutions, and it is now clearly an essential piece of the fundraising puzzle.

In her book *The Kindness of Strangers: Philanthropy and Higher Education* (2006), Deni Elliott offers a more recent review of the landscape of higher education fundraising and the important elements to consider in operating a successful advancement program. While her book is framed heavily within the context of ethics and fundraising, she provides a good overview of the development profession and its evolution. She points to the importance of identifying with donors, matching donor interests with university needs, researching prospects, accounting, and considering multiple constituent groups (including women) when raising funds for an institution. But similar to John Pollard's book nearly fifty years earlier, Elliot's book does not provide a meaningful discussion of leadership.

While there has yet to be a comprehensive attempt to understand chief advancement officers from the perspective of leadership and the important competencies necessary for success, a few authors have addressed the topic as part of much broader research. For instance, Nehls (2008) identified the characteristics of patience, perseverance, work drive, flexibility, belief in teamwork, confidence, altruism, resiliency, and focus as important qualities that chief higher education fundraisers should possess during presidential transitions. Nehls also found emerging themes of enthusiasm, optimism, extraversion, passion for work, and overall job satisfaction to be important. While her research outlined personality characteristics identified as important during a specific point in time—that is, during presidential transitions—one can argue that these characteristics are important regardless of the situation and environmental context.

From a somewhat different perspective, but relative to the current research, Smith and Wolverton's (2010) statistical analysis discovered the core leadership competency category of *external relations* to be one of five domains important for effective higher education leadership in general. While their research validated anecdotal observations on what most people had already thought to be important for higher education leaders, additional research is necessary to identify sub-competencies that more fully describe effective leadership within the external relations and advancement domain.

Another problem is the lack of existing academic programs focused on the advancement profession. In general, most educational leadership and higher education administration programs are relatively new and thus have not been in existence long enough to produce academically trained practitioners to move through the advancement pipeline. Magnifying the problem, most degree programs offer few, if any, courses specific to educational fundraising and advancement. Peabody College at Vanderbilt University offers a master's degree in institutional advancement in higher education, and Indiana University's Center on Philanthropy has been producing educational fundraisers since 1987 (Elliot 2006). However, most academic programs are more broadly based on nonprofit management and philanthropy in general, and they often reside in business schools and public administration programs. This is in stark contrast to the for-profit sector, where MBAs have existed as core programs at colleges and universities for decades, providing a steady flow of qualified practitioners to assume leadership positions in business and industry.

Without a workforce of faculty developing curriculums, teaching students, and conducting research on the topic of educational advancement, there is likewise a lack of scholars interested in and focused on studying the important discipline of advancement leadership. The current research broaches this topic from an exploratory perspective so that future scholars and practitioners can expand upon it and develop more-robust theories of leadership related to the chief advancement officer position. Higher education advancement organizations are becoming increasingly sophisticated to the point that this important topic should be given the attention it deserves.

3

Issues of Methodology

C HAPTER 1 REVIEWED THE HISTORY of advancement in higher education and the evolution of the roles and responsibilities of the chief advancement officer. Chapter 2 outlined existing leadership theory broadly and then narrowed its focus to leadership as it relates to higher education and advancement. These first two chapters lay the groundwork for thinking about chief advancement officers as leaders and offer an important framework for profiling the cases in this book. However, before the cases are presented, it would be useful to understand the process used to discover emerging competencies and themes of leadership necessary for success and high performance in higher education advancement. The intent here is to provide a lens through which leadership competence is revealed and to offer insight into the steps taken to do so.

The following chapters will then offer intimate details and insight into the background, education, experience, career path, and thought processes of highly successful chief advancement officers. These leaders were asked what they believe to be important factors of success necessary to lead high-performing advancement teams and also how they came to assume their positions of leadership. Questions related to defining moments in their careers, significant professional influences, and advice for aspiring advancement professionals interested in assuming the chief advancement officer position were posed. Furthermore, we sought insight into the leadership and management philosophies of these leaders and how they go about applying them in their quest for successful organizational outcomes. The goal was to collect enough data to discern variables of leadership important for success in the chief advancement officer position.

Leadership and Competence

Competence is an all-encompassing term that when applied to leadership provides a relevant context for understanding the knowledge, skills, abilities, attributes, and behaviors necessary to effectively lead people and organizations. While most leadership theory aims to understand the social phenomena underlying leaders and their interactions with subordinates and organizations, analyzing leadership through the lens of competence provides a more specific roadmap for guiding practitioners. Furthermore, identifying leadership competencies specific to an industry like higher education advancement helps shape our understanding and knowledge of the type of people who might be ripe for current and future leadership positions. It also helps in considering strategies for developing future generations of advancement leaders.

David McClelland (1973) pioneered the study of competence when he suggested that aptitude and intelligence alone were not sufficient predictors of high performance, effectiveness, and successful outcomes. He said, "For some purposes it may be desirable to assess competencies that are more generally useful in clusters of life outcomes, including not only occupational outcomes but social ones as well, such as leadership, interpersonal skills, etc." (9). McClelland's thesis discredited the validity of intelligence testing in general. He asserted that scores on intelligence and aptitude tests are not valid indicators for determining future job success or job status, dismissing highly correlated research that claimed otherwise. Stated another way, he believed that performance on tests of ability does not relate to job performance. According to McClelland, the high correlation between intelligence tests and job status found in multiple studies may be the result of socioeconomic factors and credentials rather than anything else. Individuals with more resources, power, and networking opportunities have more career opportunities in general, and, therefore, end up in better paying, high-profile jobs.

At the time, McClelland's conclusions were provocative and controversial. His work produced a paradigm shift regarding the relationship between exceptional school performance and successful life outcomes. Since then, studies have surfaced to support McClelland's claims. For example, Thomas Stanley (2000) published research consistent with McClelland's hypothesis, using economic outcomes as the primary indicator of success. He explored the ideas, beliefs, and behaviors of over seven hundred millionaires and found that clusters of social skills, orientation toward critics, integrity, and creativity outranked intelligence as factors leading to economic success (35). Stanley concluded, "The results of my research on millionaires are highly congruent with Professor McClelland's. Grades received in college do not explain a statistically significant portion of the variation in wealth or income, nor do SAT results" (69).

Furthermore, Daniel Goleman (1998) analyzed competency models from over 180 companies, suggesting that "emotional intelligence" components of self-awareness, self-regulation, motivation, empathy, and social skill play an increasingly important role at the highest levels of a company—more so than intelligence and technical skill. In fact, Goleman found that "nearly 90 percent of the difference in leaders' profiles was attributable to emotional intelligence factors rather than cognitive abilities" (94). This is important insofar as we expand our thinking beyond experience and technical skill and consider other factors that are perhaps more relevant in determining the leadership success of chief advancement officers.

To frame the context further, a brief review and specific definition of competence is in order. Multiple definitions exist; however, for a simple definition, Merriam-Webster's *Collegiate Dictionary* (2004) defines *competence* as "a sufficiency of means for the necessities and conveniences of life." From an organizational context, Athey and Orth (1999) define competencies as "a set of observable performance dimensions, including individual knowledge, skills, attitudes, and behaviors, as well as collective team, process, and organizational capabilities, that are linked to high performance, and provide the organization with sustainable competitive advantage" (216). Marrelli, Tondora, and Hoge (2005) define a competency as "a measurable human capability that is required for effective performance" (534). They further state, "A competency may be comprised of a knowledge, a single skill or ability, a personal characteristic, or a cluster of two or more of these attributes" (534). For the purpose of this book, and to synthesize existing definitions into a manageable form, competence is defined as an observable performance dimension of knowledge, skill, ability, attribute, or behavior that results in high performance and effective outcomes.

Leadership and Competence in Higher Education

Within the context of higher education, competence has been discussed as an important element, tenet, or dimension necessary for effective leadership. Birnbaum (1992) talked about competence related to the presidential role of articulating vision when he said, "The real purposes of articulating a vision are to give constituents confidence in the leader's competence" (25). Having confidence in a leader's competence is necessary for followers to buy in to and move toward shared goals and outcomes (Birnbaum 1992), which is certainly critical within the horizontal decision-making structure of higher education institutions. Furthermore, some have argued that competence is one of the most important qualities for deans to possess (Krahenbuhl 2004), suggesting that in addition to intelligence, there are many competencies essential for academic leadership effectiveness (Hoppe 2003).

Further empirical evidence of the importance of competent academic leaders is detailed in Wolverton and Gmelch's book *College Deans: Leading From Within* (2002). The authors identified competence as one of three keys to a dean's leadership success. They argued that "competence refers to a dean's ability to add value to an organization because of the technical knowledge base that he or she possesses" (91). Furthermore, Montez (2002) cited competence as one of five dimensions of higher education leadership. Competence "defines the work ethic of leaders" (49) and includes expertise, working hard and energetically, and balancing work with life. Finally, Kouzes and Posner (2003) found in their research that the majority of higher education constituents believe competence is an important leadership characteristic for leaders to posses (11).

There was no documented research identifying specific competencies necessary for effective higher education leadership until Elizabeth McDaniel (2002) developed a core leadership competency model. In her research, a group of thirty former American Council on Education (ACE) fellows convened in an effort to identify characteristics and behaviors of leadership in higher education. After developing a set of comprehensive leadership competencies, the ACE fellows distributed them for review to senior leaders and subject-matter experts in higher education. This process resulted in a final list of core higher education leadership competencies that was validated further by the American Council on Education Leadership Commission, which reviewed the leadership competencies and provided feedback. What emerged was a four-category model: leadership context competencies; leadership content competencies; leadership process competencies; and leadership communication competencies, with further sub-competencies listed within each category.

Smith and Wolverton (2010) extended McDaniel's qualitative findings and offered a more-quantitative analysis. They developed a refined model of higher education leadership competencies, resulting in five major leadership categories, or themes: analytical leadership; communication leadership; student affairs leadership; behavioral leadership; and external relations leadership. In part, this book seeks to expand on Smith and Wolverton's findings by further examining leadership competencies specific to the category of external relations leadership and the chief advancement officer position.

The Approach

Leadership competence in external relations and, more specifically, advancement is an important topic of inquiry. However, previous studies have determined that this domain is ill defined and in need of further study and clarity (Smith and Wolverton 2010). Thus, profiling highly competent chief advancement officers as identified by their peers and culling out themes of leadership competence through case-study methods leads to a greater understanding of the position among current and future advancement practitioners and offers a template for developing future leadership development and training programs.

Identifying the Cases

In March 2010, an electronic survey was e-mailed to a random selection of over three hundred university chief executive officers, chief advancement officers, associate vice presidents or chancellors of development and advancement, and subject-matter experts, including executives in the higher education search-firm industry, higher education professors, and advancement human resources professionals. The survey asked participants to identify up to six chief advancement officers they knew who they believed were highly competent leaders in the field of higher education advancement.

As a result, 127 chief advancement officers were nominated as highly competent leaders. Our next task was to review the nominations and sort them by number of nominations received. Anyone receiving more than one nomination was invited to participate in the study. Seventeen people were nominated more than once and invited to participate in the study with the assumption that not all of them would be willing and available. The final cohort of participants included the ten chief advancement officers selected and profiled in this book. Of these, six are female and four male. Seven are from private institutions and three from public institutions. It is noted that the majority of chief advancement officers profiled in this book are from large research institutions. While this may be perceived as a limitation, the emerging themes of leadership presented throughout the remainder of the book are relevant and applicable to chief advancement officers from institutions of all types and sizes. In other words, leadership is scalable.

The Interviews and Data Collection

Interviews included both face-to-face and telephone format. A digital recorder was used to capture as much information as possible. As a convenience, four chief advancement officers were interviewed at the CASE Leadership Summit in New York in July 2010. One participant was interviewed in person in California, and five were interviewed by phone. Prior to our conducting the interviews, conference calls were held with the participants to brief them on the overall research project, the process for data collection, the logistics of the interview, and the general themes of the interview questions.

Interview questions consisted of three primary lines of inquiry. The first focused on the chief advancement officer's professional background, career path, and the reason or reasons the chief advancement officer advanced his or her career into the chief advancement officer position. The second line of questioning focused specifically on leadership and the competencies each officer believed to be important for success in his or her position. Here, questions were also asked related to the challenges of the position as well as the benefits. The third and final line of questioning focused on leadership development and training; existing programs that the officer found beneficial for his or her own leadership development; the future of advancement leadership; and issues pertaining to the preparation of the next generation of advancement leaders.

In addition to interviews with the ten chief advancement officers themselves, up to three of their current or former subordinates were surveyed and asked to identify important competencies related to their boss's success as a leader. Furthermore, professional documents, including resumes, vitas, summary bios, and any other pertinent information related to the careers of the chief advancement officers, were also reviewed and analyzed.

Prior to our interviewing the participants, a pilot interview was conducted with one chief advancement officer who was not part of the study. The purpose of the pilot interview was to test the process, gain feedback regarding the interview questions and themes, ensure the reliability of the recording equipment, and make other adjustments, if necessary. The pilot interview was held approximately two weeks prior to data collection with the actual case-study participants. Feedback was gathered from the pilot-case participant and incorporated into the final data collection and analysis procedures.

Analyzing and Presenting the Cases

Rather than using statistical analyses and computer software to help analyze the data, the authors served as the main analysts (Yin 2009). For consistency in the following chapters, a summary and overview of each chief advancement officer is presented in an effort to tell a narrative story about his or her background, entry into the profession, career path, and variables that shaped his or her approach to and philosophy of leadership and thoughts on leadership development. The final chapters consolidate our findings based on the interviews, present a preliminary advancement leadership competency model relevant to the higher education advancement profession, and draw conclusions based on lessons learned throughout the research process.

4

Lisa D. Calvert: The Analytical Fundraiser

A N OFTEN-HELD BELIEF among many current and previous chief advancement officers is that the typical nontraditional career path in development and advancement is no longer sufficient for appropriate entry into the profession and sustainable success. As the argument goes, nontraditional candidates come with great risk and require significant training. Many believe that in today's fast-paced advancement organizations, few resources exist to adequately prepare nontraditional candidates for the rigors of the job. Presidents, deans, faculty, and other senior administrators have outsized fundraising expectations; therefore, nontraditional candidates do not have the skills to navigate the highly political environments in which they are often placed. This is an increasing perception of today's chief advancement officers even though, as detailed in this book, many current advancement leaders rose to their positions from nontraditional backgrounds themselves. The debate will likely live on for years, but as Lisa D. Calvert exemplifies, entering the advancement industry as a nontraditional professional was not only seamless for her but led to a highly successful career culminating in senior leadership positions at two highly regarded institutions: Creighton University, a private institution, and Purdue University, a public institution.

Calvert's advancement career began as a result of timing, a poor economy, and perhaps an innate recognition of person-job fit. She had big plans for herself on matriculating at Oklahoma State University, participating in internships, and visualizing a career path that would involve lobbying in Washington, DC. However, Calvert's plans were shaken in the early 1980s when the economy suffered through a significant recession. Inflation took off, unemployment was high, and interest rates rose to record levels. In short, it was a tough time to be a new graduate and young professional.

From 1983 to 1986, Calvert worked for Farm Credit Banks, gaining meaningful experience as a business development and management operations specialist. She created advertising and promotional materials for local and district banks, giving her meaningful, real-world experience fresh out of college. But sadly, she eventually got laid off and then accepted the reality that the banking industry would take years to recover:

> My work in the district bank and offices throughout a four-state area gave me the type of training to eventually become a lobbyist in Washington, DC, like I had planned. It was the mid-1980s and the farm economy, along with the rest of the economy, went south. We went through a series of layoffs at Farm Credit, resulting in a 50 percent reduction in staff for the district bank. I was one of the lucky ones, surviving multiple rounds of layoffs. But eventually, about five or six layoffs later, I was eliminated. I was one of the youngest in the division. The president, vice president, and his assistant were among the few left.

At Farm Credit, Calvert gained a strong background in finance, market research, and business development. But she had an opportunity to go to work for two U.S. Senators in Washington, DC, which had always been her dream. Her experience at the bank had taught her how to educate large constituencies through market research and data analysis, which is an important skill for a lobbyist. Unfortunately, due to personal reasons, she was not in a position to accept the Senate opportunity, and she began looking elsewhere for work.

Inspired by one of Kent Dove's first books on higher education fundraising, Calvert consulted with a few people in the advancement field and ultimately decided the advancement and development profession was a good match with her background, skills, and interests. So in 1986, she accepted an entry-level development position at Butler County Community College. She closed what was then the largest gift in school history and steadily climbed the advancement ladder. Throughout the early years of her career, Calvert gained a broad range of skills and experiences through multiple development positions at institutions including Wichita State University, Kansas State University, and the Institute of Logopedics (now Heartspring). At Logopedics, where she served as vice president of development, Calvert raised funds to help provide access to education and medical services for special needs children. As she recalled,

> The Institute of Logopedics had a very compelling mission. The organization was at a defining moment and the mission was becoming less and less relevant. Since the 1930s, professionals and staff created and provided educational and medical services to special needs children spanning the globe. Due to their great work, it eventually lead to federal laws providing all special needs children ac-

cess to public education. The organization's leadership was tasked to expand the mission, which focused on North America.

It was during her tenure at the Institute of Logopedics that Calvert found joy in working for an institution with a compelling mission and vision. For Calvert, the mission was inspiring and allowed her to speak genuinely and passionately about the cause, which in turn led to successful fundraising outcomes. "We had an amazing opportunity for about four years to redefine the institution," she recalls. "We built a new thirty-seven-acre campus and involved President Clinton, the who's who of Hollywood, and corporate CEOs. It was a truly phenomenal experience."

Calvert's career was not only shaped by her passion for mission, but also by geography. Education had always been her passion, but personal circumstances allowed her to explore new opportunities elsewhere at various stages in her career.

> I rose to leadership positions by default, in some ways, based on personal and family situations. In the formative stages of my career, I was married to a gentleman who was in retail management and we moved about every three to four years. I decided to use it as a professional opportunity for growth and development. As we moved, I tried different things. I love public higher education, so I decided to take a few career risks. I felt that if I liked it so much, and it seemed to come easy for me, then I should try different types of fundraising. I have always picked jobs that I am passionate about. I had opportunities to work at some very prestigious institutions, but followed my passions instead. For instance, I loved my position at Kansas State because I worked for the 4-H program. I am a third-generation 4-H'r. I drove 130 miles each day for about four and a half years, and I loved every minute of it.

In 1998, Calvert was on the move again. This time she accepted a position as regional vice president and senior consultant for Cargill Associates and tried her hand at consulting. There she counseled higher education and health care advancement programs on campaign operations, pre-campaign studies, and internal development assessments. Supporting more than 150 clients annually, she opened new markets and created one of the most comprehensive development assessment programs in the consulting industry. One of the firm's former clients, William Jewel College, liked the firm's work so much they offered her a senior position within their institution. The timing in her career was right, so in 2000 Calvert accepted the offer and assumed the position of vice president of institutional advancement.

Calvert's work at William Jewel was a defining moment in her career. Her consulting work, which included development audits, proved to be an invaluable asset due to accounting control issues within the advancement unit. Shortly after her arrival at William Jewel, Calvert discovered falsified grant documents from two prominent foundations. As she described it, "It was a real discovery moment in my career related to ethics, integrity, honesty, and how to approach a controversial situation. Uncovering this information took courage, and it was a very interesting and educational experience." At William Jewel, Calvert was forced to take on the role of change agent. "My experience at William Jewel was amazing," she recalls. "We helped an institution navigate through the complexities of very challenging issues that had to be resolved with transparency." There were massive financial challenges that required significant structural changes. Calvert understood that the decisions she made might have significant implications for her career, but there were few options. So after Calvert's nearly three years at William Jewel of taking on tough administrative challenges, her family was considering a move again. At the same time, Creighton University was seeking a chief advancement officer and recruited Calvert to their campus.

For Calvert, assuming the position of vice president for university relations at Creighton University was a natural fit and seamless transition. From her work at Farm Credit Banks to her position at William Jewel College, she had acquired a wide spectrum of skills and experiences as well as a diverse frame of reference. She gained savvy political skills that allowed her to navigate successfully through complex organizational matrixes. And she developed the strong interpersonal skills essential for working with volunteers, trustees, and campus leadership. In short, her body of work laid the foundation for her leadership position at Creighton University and subsequent seven-year tenure there.

Calvert's achievements at Creighton were significant. Her unit was presented with the 2007 and 2008 CASE awards for overall fundraising performance for superior programming over a three-year period. Under her leadership, university relations raised over $500 million, surpassing the institution's campaign goal a year ahead of schedule. She analyzed philanthropic capacity and developed an innovative affinity model based on 167 factors that was viewed as one of the most sophisticated and comprehensive fundraising analyses in the higher education advancement industry. After Calvert's seven years of success at Creighton and significant national attention, in 2010 she was lured away by Purdue University, where she assumed the position of vice president for development.

Calvert points to many influential factors during her career that have impacted her leadership philosophy, but none more so than the opportunity she has had to work with amazing volunteers:

> First and foremost, I would say the volunteer leadership at the Institute of Logopedics was profoundly influential. The organization . . . had incredible volunteer leadership, including cofounders of well-known companies like Pizza Hut and Shaklee Products as well as Fortune 500 board chairmen. At Creighton

University, there were multiple Fortune 500 chairmen of the boards, CEOs, and successful billionaires involved with the campus. To have access to those kinds of leaders is profound and amazing. These are individuals who are committed to the institution and the institution's success and, in turn, committed to the senior leadership of the institution. To have individuals in those capacities who are actively supporting you on a day-to-day basis is very influential. At Creighton University, there was a core group of six current and former board members who were also campaign steering committee members and chairmen of boards or top senior executives of ConAgra Foods, Peter Kiewit and Sons, Gannett Company, Commercial Federal, and Berkshire Hathaway. This group in particular was like my own think tank. I met with them frequently and relied on their counsel and advisement. They had a huge influence on shaping my leadership style and philosophy. They pushed us to think differently; they pushed us outside our boundaries; and perhaps most importantly, they pushed us to validate our industry because there is not a great deal of data to support what we do. These are individuals running Fortune 500 companies, some of whom helped Warren Buffet get started. They pushed us so far outside the box, but in a supportive manner, that we created a new methodology in the business that had never been developed before.

Calvert's development of both philanthropic capacity and affinity models are perhaps her most notable achievements. At Creighton, she worked with volunteers, consultants, and senior leadership to identify and measure philanthropic capacity through analytic methods. As a result, her team identified over two hundred people with $4 billion in potential lifetime capacity, significantly increasing the pipeline of principal gift donors. As noted, her team also developed an affinity model based on 167 factors in an effort to validate the propensity of newly identified prospects. Combined with existing research reports from Harvard, the entire process was an analytic approach to fundraising driven and supported in large part by the volunteer leadership at Creighton. While market research and analyses are common in the private sector, advancement organizations have been slow to adopt rigorous analytical methods for fundraising, relying more often on relationship-building than on anything else. Calvert developed at Creighton a highly successful method and approach to principal gift fundraising, which she implemented at Purdue as well.

In addition, Calvert's career has been influenced and shaped by a strategic willingness to take risks. She thinks outside the box and considers new ideas and alternative approaches for generating revenue for institutions. She credits her success in large part to being flexible and open to new ways of thinking. She believes it is important to keep learning while focusing first and foremost on institutional needs. As she describes it,

It's important to be open and receptive to learn from all of our experiences, while listening and being flexible. Early on I learned that I may not always think the president or volunteer is right, and that they might have really crazy ideas, but it's important to listen anyway. They are the president or volunteer leader for a reason. Even though I may not agree with their idea, I want to be open to it and not be rigid in my thinking. A dear friend and colleague once said to me, "You have to have a stomach of a goat and the backside of a seal," because it is truly not about us but rather it is about the institution. Sometimes you just have to be flexible and roll with both the good and the bad in our profession.

Perspectives on Leadership

Calvert defines leadership as a visionary process. It is about being strategic within the realm of the big picture while also considering what leadership looks like for each individual person. She thinks competent leaders communicate effectively, build strong relationships with multiple constituents, and are open to new ideas. She further states, "It is about learning how to manage up in a highly entrepreneurial way while respecting the culture of a specific institution." Without institutional respect, barriers often form, making it difficult to move anything forward. Calvert thinks leadership is about influencing departments, divisions, and programs that fall outside one's realm of control. Building successful working relationships with various stakeholders and academic units is important, she says. But it's also important to remain true to oneself and not take oneself too seriously.

Leadership versus Management

For Calvert, leadership and management are two very distinct concepts. She believes management is about empowering teams and providing resources for staff to be successful. It is about understanding employees' strengths and weaknesses and managing them toward excellence. She says management is more about people, resources, and programs, whereas leadership is focused more on vision and strategic planning. "I try to hire competent and talented people, build a mutual trust, and then work with them to identify opportunities for success. It is my job as a leader to help facilitate and manage their success."

Leadership Competencies Necessary for Success

Calvert points to self-awareness as the most important leadership competency necessary for success as a chief advancement officer. Prior to assuming the top position, she thinks advancement professionals should be comfortable with who they are, both personally and professionally. "I have learned this over time," she says. "I had a volunteer say to me once, 'You've really come into your own, and it's clear you are comfortable with who you are and where you are in your career.'" It imparts confidence, which is also important. Leaders must understand what they know and what they don't know. Being able to say "I don't know" is important and necessary for the ultimate success of an organization, Calvert says. Finally, Calvert thinks leaders must be courageous and have a forward-thinking frame of mind, as it often takes a combination of courage and vision to make difficult decisions.

Leadership Competencies Most Difficult to Carry Out

For Calvert, flexibility is perhaps the most difficult leadership competency for chief advancement officers to maintain. As she describes it, educational institutions are highly complex environments with multiple stakeholders guiding decisions. Chief advancement officers have significant responsibility with little authority. The lines of authority are often blurred, making flexibility a critical trait. "It is very different in higher education versus the private sector," she contends. "It's like herding cats, chickens, and rabbits. The government, faculty, and other stakeholders are involved in the decision-making process, so chief advancement officers must be flexible."

Who, other than the Chief Advancement Officer, Is Responsible for Leading Advancement Organizations?

Calvert is somewhat nontraditional in her thoughts about who, outside of the chief advancement officer, is responsible for leading the advancement function on campus. In her opinion, the advancement services unit plays a critical leadership role:

> The reason I believe advancement services plays such an important role is be-cause the infrastructure in advancement is first and foremost so critical. I think there is a great under-appreciation and lack of understanding for that function. In many ways, we have set ourselves up for expectations that are not manage-able in the industry. Because we focus so much on front-line fundraisers and alumni relations, we often forget about the data and the infrastructure—from HR, to budgeting, to database management—you need to be able to function successfully. The advancement services team is important for philanthropic analysis and forecasting. It needs to be a partner with finance and other parts of the organization to keep the operation moving forward. Working with the data is such an important component for us to be successful. I would say my number two is definitely my development person, but the success of the division runs off the back of the operations or advancement services person.

What Competencies Make You an Effective Leader?

Calvert's strengths are grounded in a philosophical outlook committed to life-long learning. There are many different ways of doing things, which inspires her to continue learning every day. She says she's nimble, flexible, and a good listener. She takes pride in considering multiple options and viewpoints in the decision-making process and being open to new ideas. Specifically, she says she is open to suggestions from campus leadership and her volunteer board, and she engages them in big-picture discussions. "Whether it is the CFO, president, or volunteer board, you must have measurable outcomes, and you must be able to communicate and translate them in a way people understand." Communication skills are also very important to Calvert. Over the years, she has learned that strategic, audience-based communication is important to her success.

Calvert thinks her staff would say she is much different today than in the past. During her early years at Creighton, she would have been described as a massive change agent. "My role was to come in, make quick assessments, and move rapidly." However, she resisted initial recommendations to dismiss staff and focused more on providing resources necessary to change the culture. By all measures, it was a challenging environment, but Calvert was supported by strong leadership across campus. "My staff had no goals or measurable objectives of success, but the stakes were incredibly high for the university." She continues, "It was a defining moment in the life of the institution, which required a transformation of how we conducted business on a daily basis." Ultimately, Calvert was forced to make very difficult decisions, causing many people within the organization to view her as a "hatchet man" and "change agent" who would never survive. Organizational resistance was pervasive. But it was her willingness to make tough decisions that, in her eyes, made her successful. She was resilient and resolute in her actions:

> I did a sixty-day assessment and discovered the organization was significantly behind industry best practices. I knew I could not say this publicly, so I brought in outside counsel to help. We initiated some programs to bring everybody up to a minimum standard, and many people were not willing to join us. Unfortunately, we had to let some of these people go.

Toward the end of Calvert's tenure at Creighton, internal promotions increased and turnover decreased significantly. She began focusing more on managing talent and working closely with human resources to help get the right people on her team. She made herself more visible by walking the halls and talking more to her staff. She states,

> We started investing in our team. We did an employee survey, which we knew would come back very low initially, but we needed a baseline to understand

where we were and where we needed to go. We started investing more in talent management. The new university HR associate vice president came from ConAgra Foods, so he understood massive change. We listened to our staff and committed to sharing feedback with them in very open groups. We tried to focus on two or three things we would change each year, and we started focusing more on reward and recognition programs. I learned a lot through the process, and made a lot of mistakes, but it was a positive experience.

One of Calvert's former directors reports describes her as "motivated to succeed, functionally competent and knowledgeable, and a leader who knows when to reach out for help." Furthermore, this same person said Calvert works very hard and ultimately wants the institution to be successful. Another person who worked for Calvert had this to say:

Lisa stays current regarding trends in the advancement field. She's very good at using think tanks to craft practical and realistic strategies and goals. She also has strong interpersonal skills with a contagious optimism. I would describe her leadership style as one of inclusion and consensus building. She took a parochial development organization and expanded it to be more broadly focused, more aggressive in goal setting and preached a philosophy of transformation. She put her sights on significantly larger gifts than was the case historically and did it quite successfully. She knows the profession very well and that results in an up-to-date philosophy of philanthropy that can be translated into action. She is also very graceful and generally puts people at ease.

Leadership Development and the Future of Advancement Leaders

Calvert presents herself well professionally and is likeable and generally enthusiastic about her work. She clearly enjoys her role as a chief advancement officer and is honored to have served innovative institutions with visionary leaders and volunteers. But like most of our chief advancement officers, Calvert is unimpressed with existing leadership development and training programs in advancement. "I think there is a real void in leadership training in the advancement industry, a huge void," she laments. "My greatest frustration, and one shared by my Jesuit colleagues, is that I have a strong desire to be a greater, more effective leader, but I cannot find a quality, affordable program." She would like to see programs that build stronger ties between presidents, deans, and advancement professionals, programs that help both advancement staff and academic leaders work together more effectively toward shared institutional goals and outcomes.

Calvert believes the advancement leader needed today is a different type than in years past. She says advancement professionals with fresh, progressive, and big ideas are highly sought after. "Many new leaders are much younger and assuming leadership positions earlier in their careers than they are probably ready. But it is a new world," she says. "The pace and complexity of institutions and advancement organizations have changed dramatically, requiring a different type of chief advancement officer. We need to be sure we develop programs that prepare these young leaders with the skills they need to be successful."

Existing Professional Development Programs for Chief Advancement Officers

For her own professional and career development, the void of existing leadership programs in the advancement industry forced Calvert to go outside the profession for training. She attended the University of Chicago's Strategic Business Leadership Program, which she describes as Chicago's capstone class associated with its MBA program. She also attended Harvard's program Leadership for Senior Executives. For Calvert, Chicago's course was a wonderful experience, but she thinks many programs miss the mark:

> How do you package these programs so that the complexity of higher education is reflected? That's the issue. There is also the issue of easing tension between the business world and the not-for-profit world. Corporations think higher education is wasteful and inefficient. However, they do not fully understand the complexities of operating higher education institutions.

At the Chicago program, many participants were interested in Calvert's perspective on the higher education business environment. "There were about thirty-five people from around the world in the class, but only two people, including myself, from higher education," she observes. "The rest were from the corporate sector, and they just could not get their heads around our operational environment. We had people waiting in line to talk to us about it."

But Calvert believes the best professional development for advancement professionals is to simply go out and assess quality programs at peer institutions. "I learn more by talking to my peers than I do from most conferences," she says. "I sent my new principal gifts person, who came from alumni relations, to meet with colleagues at Harvard, Boston College, and Stanford, and it was very effective." Because there is a lack of quality leadership training and professional development programs, Calvert thinks evaluating successful programs is a great way for someone in a relatively new role to sharpen skills and learn new ways of doing business.

The Future of Leadership Development and Training

Most advancement leaders understand the importance of using diplomacy and influence to get things done. But the difference between a good influencer and a great one can have a profound impact on one's career. As fundraising goals and expectations continue to increase, Calvert believes advancement leaders of the future must sharpen their skills in this area so they are more effective. She thinks chief advancement officers must pay closer attention to internal audiences, including faculty and staff, because advancement needs their support and cooperation to be successful:

> Faculty and staff can wreak havoc if they are not on board with the greater mission and goals of the advancement unit. The University of Chicago program was exceptional in teaching participants how to have influence over areas of the organization where you have no control. In the past, I have always used gut instinct to understand who has influence and power, who the decision makers are on campus, and how to navigate through various constituents to get work done. But the Chicago program put us through a series of exercises and used research to back up the strategies and tactics they taught us. It was very interesting. I know I can sell my programs to a volunteer or nonprofit board. But do faculty or department chairs care? They often do not. They are more concerned about their research or what is in it for them. So having strong influence skills will continue to be important for advancement leaders in the future.

Challenges Facing Chief Advancement Officers

According to Calvert, today's chief advancement officers must be deeply knowledgeable about the campuses they serve. They must have a cultural context and understand organizational nuances. They must be able to communicate effectively to external constituencies and be savvy story tellers in a way that translates "advancement speak" into compelling cases for support. Donors and prospects need to feel good about the mission of the institution. However, as Calvert laments, the challenge for advancement professionals is to connect donors with programs they feel passionate about. "We must tell our story differently because for many donors today, terms like *annual fund* and *endowment* are confusing and do not mean anything," she says. "In tough budgetary times with steep cuts to higher education, donors want to know where their money is being directed and how it can have the greatest impact."

Looking to the future, Calvert points to the leadership void as the greatest threat to the advancement industry. As previously mentioned, she thinks we need to better prepare and develop current advancement professionals to assume chief advancement officer positions that have grown in complexity and scope. In her mind, traditional career paths are no longer sufficient.

> One of the things we will have to be more comfortable with is the tactical approach to fundraising. For example, forecasting philanthropic potential and developing strategies, timelines, and measurable outcomes around goals and objectives will become increasingly important. I think that is something we have to figure out because the reality is we are a revenue-generating business unit. In the traditional higher education environment and culture, this way of thinking often creates tension. But we have to feel okay with this tension and learn how to manage innovative thinking more effectively.

In addition, Calvert believes we need to embrace accountability because future advancement professionals will be held to a different standard of performance than in decades past. "We have a responsibility as leaders in advancement to help our stakeholders understand our key responsibilities," she contends. "It sounds lofty and inspirational, but I think we have a tremendous responsibility because we have the ability to effect meaningful change." In this scenario, individuals who are uncomfortable with measures of accountability and increased performance metrics will either self-select out of the industry or be asked to step down, leaving an even greater leadership void in the future.

Positive Aspects of Serving as a Chief Advancement Officer

Calvert projects a sense of passion for her work. She enjoys speaking with and meeting fascinating people, but most of all, she gets tremendous fulfillment out of linking donor interests with institutional programs. She's entirely mission driven. For her, it's less about securing a specific dollar amount and more about feeling the emotions of the process.

> My mother still does not know what I do. But I picked up the phone and called her the other day to tell her how hard we have been working to fund a faculty member's research that might one day cure leukemia. And I think she began to understand. So for me, it is such a joy to talk about these important projects, and it makes me very happy to be able to contribute in some small way to solving major societal problems.

Preparation for Newcomers and Future Leaders in Advancement

For newcomers, Calvert has four primary pieces of advice: follow your heart; know your passions; be willing to try new things; and embrace lifelong learning. To succeed, advancement professionals must have a passion for the mission of the institution. They must constantly study the organization. And they must embrace learning as part of the job. There are many wonderful opportunities to develop a career in the advancement industry, but Calvert believes first and foremost one must be mission driven to realize success.

But helping newcomers find a mission-driven entry point into the advancement profession is only the first step. Developing these new professionals is where Calvert thinks the advancement industry falls short. Furthermore, she believes leadership and development training must happen concurrently within overall talent management programming:

> We, as current advancement leaders, must pay closer attention to career paths. Traditionally, I think most advancement career paths have been much less deliberate and more accidental. As leaders, we need to talk with our staff and help them along a path that makes sense for them and for the organization. There is so much going on in our industry that we keep focusing on the tactics of our work. We are being pushed so far into the tactical realm that most organizations and their leaders do not have the time or resources right now to focus on staff development.

Calvert says the solution needs to be calculated and planned. She thinks an informal group of thought-leaders and subject-matter experts in higher education and the advancement industry should get together and begin developing a strategic roadmap for addressing the leadership void. She feels strongly that if a high-caliber group created a model for leadership development and training, the model could have tremendous implications for the future of the profession. It is the responsibility of current advancement leaders to create new methodologies and new ways of addressing current challenges, she says, and then disseminating the information to the rest of the industry.

5

Michael C. Eicher: A Father's Influence

THE YMCA HAS PROFOUNDLY INFLUENCED the evolution of fundraising in America. Today's chief advancement officers rely on many strategies, techniques, systems, and processes established in the early 1900s by Lyman L. Pierce and Charles Sumner Ward, often referred to as the founding fathers of fundraising. While Pierce and Ward, early executives of the YMCA, have been credited with developing sophisticated campaign methods, Michael C. Eicher points to the YMCA for molding him in a way that impacted his career path and eventual rise to a leadership position in higher education. For Eicher, the YMCA taught him how to think critically, methodically, and strategically within the context of his own career, and provided the foundation he needed for future professional success.

From 1979 through 1986, Eicher worked at the YMCA, taking on progressively more responsible positions from program director to eventually interim executive director for a large branch. The YMCA influenced him well beyond his capacity as an employee as his father was a YMCA executive for over thirty years. As Eicher describes it, "I grew up in the YMCA. My dad was an executive there, and we moved around the country as he progressed in his career." It was his father's work that shaped Eicher's approach toward management and leadership. It wasn't just fate that led him to work for the YMCA, but rather his father's career, which molded him into a young professional who fit seamlessly within the YMCA's culture and values.

> When I graduated from college, I got recruited to work for one of the most innovative YMCAs in the country and had the opportunity to go work with some

amazing people doing really interesting work. I had always planned to go back to graduate school, but it turned out that the seven years I was at the YMCA was my graduate school. I learned a lot of important skills. Before I join the Y as a professional, when I was in college, I had the chance to run one of the largest YMCA summer camping programs in the country. I learned how to interview for and recruit talented people, how to manage a team, how to supervise, and how to fire. And I learned a lot about social dynamics. I learned how to plan and run meetings, when and how to lead, and I learned things that were really useful that I applied at the YMCA and beyond.

Early on, Eicher assumed he would have a long and prosperous career at the YMCA much like his father. His father was passionate about the YMCA, and his success inspired and motivated Eicher. It seemed like a logical path that would be both rewarding and meaningful. However, it was a demanding career that required late nights and long weekends, often with few breaks in between. After seven years, Eicher grew exhausted by the long hours, constant pressure, and demanding schedule. It was a period in his life when personal responsibilities forced him to reevaluate and reflect upon his future. His job seemed untenable with a growing family, so he made the difficult decision to leave. "All my colleagues thought I was committing professional suicide," he says. But Eicher had an epiphany that helped make his decision to change directions more palatable. A few of his close colleagues had left "the movement" and became highly successful fundraisers elsewhere. Their advice, counsel, and successful transitions into other prosperous nonprofit and advancement fields, including higher education, provided the incentive he needed to make a change.

So there he was, on the fast track to a senior management position at the YMCA, preparing to leave it all behind for new pursuits in hopes of a better quality of life. The road was not easy, but he quickly found his stride in the higher education advancement industry. After a few failed applications at several health-related foundations, museums, and other large nonprofit agencies, Eicher answered an ad for a job at the University of California, Los Angeles (UCLA). It was the summer of 1986 and UCLA was searching for a major gift officer in the humanities. There was mutual interest, and he was invited to campus for several rounds of interviews. At the very end of the process was a meeting with the dean. "From the beginning of this meeting, it was obvious we were not a good fit." It simply didn't work, Eicher says, adding, "The dean wanted somebody I wasn't." Rather than letting it demoralize him, Eicher remained persistent and realized UCLA was a place he could imagine himself working. UCLA also recognized that his skills and experiences were transferable and applicable, so they continued to engage him with other fundraising opportunities. He came back, met with another dean, and once again the fit did not seem right. "So literally I was typing a note back to the UCLA folks thanking them for their hospitality when the phone rang. They thought they had a job for me that would be a perfect fit and encouraged me to go back one last time to look at a couple of jobs in the health sciences: one in dentistry and one in medicine." Shortly thereafter, he was offered either job, and he chose medicine, where he found his calling.

Like most young development professionals, Eicher found his first months in the position completely disorienting. He went from running a large professional staff team and literally thousands of volunteers at the YMCA to supervising a part-time assistant in a mid-sized campus office. He began questioning his decision to leave the YMCA and felt trepidation about his new career path. After a little less than a year in his new role, he started to feel more comfortable with the academic culture, expanded his knowledge of higher education fundraising, and hit his stride. Roughly one year into his new role, he was asked to become the deputy director of health sciences development and director of development for the school of medicine. The opportunity in the school of medicine launched what would become a prosperous, and perhaps most importantly, meaningful twenty-year career at UCLA.

For the first nine years at UCLA, Eicher ascended through multiple promotions, eventually landing in a senior leadership role as vice provost of medical sciences development. It was a fulfilling career; one that ultimately provided management responsibilities over a full spectrum of fundraising programs for UCLA's health sciences, including the UCLA Medical Center, the Harbor UCLA Medical Center, and the schools of medicine, dentistry, public health, and nursing. But in the early 1990s, Eicher felt it was time for a change. Over the span of nine years, he had observed the external relations function from multiple levels and perspectives and felt he had learned all he could. Although his rise to management had been swift, as many in middle-management positions, Eicher questioned his future at UCLA and wondered if he had reached his full potential.

I needed a change. I went home to my wife and said, "I don't know where my next step will be, but it's not going to be at UCLA because nobody above me is going anywhere." Then about three weeks later, I was asked to assume the assistant vice chancellor position and to organize and run the university's next campaign, which began the second half of my tenure at UCLA. I remained in that role for a year, and then the chief campus fundraiser, the associate vice chancellor, stepped down, and the chancellor asked me to assume that position. It was a point in my career where I was very much in the right place at the right time. I became the chief fundraiser for the entire campus, including medicine, and I did that for about three years. Eventually I was made the vice chancellor for external affairs, which included alumni relations, development, government relations, communications, and the UCLA Foundation.

Over a twenty-year career at UCLA, Eicher found success in every role he assumed. During this time, he developed important operational skills, adopted a strategic approach to management and leadership, and learned how to be a successful principal gift fundraiser. His last position at UCLA was vice chancellor of external affairs, to which he was appointed in 1998. As vice chancellor of external affairs, he managed a staff of over 550, successfully completed a $3.1 billion fundraising campaign, and implemented dramatic organizational changes, improving customer service, teamwork, and efficiencies within the external affairs unit. He had seen and done just about everything a person could see or do in the higher education advancement industry. His accomplishments were many, but as a motivated and curious professional, Eicher was again ready for a new chapter in his career. This time it would take him thousands of miles away.

Surviving and thriving as a senior-level administrator is highly dependent on the chief executive officer and his or her support. Eicher was well-liked and highly respected, both at UCLA and nationally, but in 2006 UCLA's chancellor Albert Carnesale announced his resignation. With two kids in college and little interest in "training" another chancellor, Eicher responded to overtures from Bill Brody, the president of Johns Hopkins University. President Brody was searching for a new vice president of development and alumni relations, and Eicher fit Brody's profile for the position. While Eicher was not interested initially, a persuasive dinner-meeting with Brody eventually convinced him. As Eicher expounds, "I had great respect for Hopkins and Bill Brody. It felt right. It seemed crazy to think about moving three thousand miles away, but our kids were out of the house and the opportunity seemed like the right fit at the right time. It also was a chance to see if I could be successful at a private, East Coast institution." Eicher was born in Illinois and had lived in Massachusetts, but this would be the first time in his adult life he had worked outside California.

As he thinks about his career, Eicher credits the YMCA with providing a solid professional foundation and teaching him to be aware of the strategic context of any issue. His upbringing in a YMCA family influenced his values as a young man, and later, his work style as an executive. His approach to work is grounded in strategy and reflection. He reflects on organizational challenges through the lens of multiple views and stakeholders, and adopts a strategy to fit the overarching goals and objectives. He doesn't mince words, and he pushes his staff to think in much the same way. But one thing is certain: Eicher's leadership philosophy was profoundly influenced by his father.

> My dad taught me the importance of thinking strategically. One day, I came to him with a silly little camp problem—I had to figure out how to quickly and efficiently train eighty camp counselors. I showed him these really cool training

techniques I was excited about and outlined a whole day of great activities for the team. He took my papers and put them aside and asked, "What are you trying to accomplish?" I remember responding by pointing to the materials. He said, "No, that is what you want to do. Tell me what you want to accomplish. What is the end goal here?" I remember how frustrated I was at first because I just wanted to get something done, but he was right. In the end, we developed a much better training experience based on well-defined outcomes and strategic objectives. He always approached problems with the end goal in mind. It was a very strategic approach to problem solving.

Outside of his father, Eicher also points to a former chief of the Los Angeles Metro YMCA, Larry Rosen, as influencing his leadership philosophy. Rosen preached the notion of considering short-term problems within the context of long-term objectives. Eicher began thinking multidimensionally in a way that considered organizational challenges as not just about getting from point A to point B, but rather as the first step in a much larger context.

There is a book by Robert Fulghum titled *All I really Need to Know I Learned in Kindergarten*. Well, for Eicher it is "Everything I needed to learn, I learned in summer camp." From a staff training and professional development perspective, serving as a camp counselor during his high-school years gave him important team-building and group-dynamic skills he has applied throughout his career. As a camp counselor, he would take groups of eight to ten boys and build cohesive, team-focused units. He not only learned the positive aspects of that experience, but the negative ones as well. He explains that building cohesive teams can be achieved by getting the group to believe "everyone who is not in our circle is the enemy, and they are all bad and out to get you." This creates a very tight-knit group very quickly, but this approach is also self-defeating. "I've seen managers do just that with their own teams. It quickly creates a negative environment and discourages teamwork. In a cabin, you learn how to foster cohesiveness using positive team-building strategies."

In the workplace, running and facilitating a meeting is no different. Eicher contends, "Whether you are running it with a group of camp counselors or with a group of Wall Street executives, the essence of a good meeting is preparing everybody in advance, setting an agenda, having a structure, establishing clear roles and responsibilities, and having a good understanding of what you are trying to accomplish."

Perspectives on Leadership

Within the context of advancement, leadership is about motivating a team of professionals to pursue and actively support the vision of the institution and its goals and objectives. But Eicher believes leadership must be considered within the greater context of comparing leadership with management. He says that the boundaries between leadership and management are blurry, and that it's difficult to discuss one without understanding the other. "If you gave me a list of management and leadership words, I could probably put them in one category or another, but it doesn't tell you much."

Leadership versus Management

Differentiating between leadership and management is an interesting intellectual exercise, but Eicher does not spend much time worrying about it as a practitioner. Like many senior leaders, he reads a lot of books on the subject, but for him it's more about implementing appropriate strategies within the context of the current environment. Both leadership and management are important concepts, and applying definitions to them is a worthy task. But Eicher focuses more on strategic thinking and his overall leadership effectiveness, regardless of the context. In his mind, *leadership* and *management* are terms that are often confused and interchanged. "If we are working together on a project, we might be in a management mode. But as the chief advancement officer, I often switch into a leadership role in an effort to help bring whatever it is we're working on to fruition." For example, he believes the performance review process is generally a management task. However, a subordinate might need coaching, encouraging, and help being creative, which for Eicher is more about leadership. He thinks leaders often bounce back and forth between the two without consciously thinking about it. He also believes management is more about the short term and tactical, while leadership is about the long term, creativity, and strategy. Another view is that managers have subordinates and leaders have followers. When Eicher leads, he uses strategies of persuasion, consensus building, and logic. He tries to set a direction and vision people can see, as he says, by "calibrating everyone's compass to find true North." Leadership for him is often working in the realm of "softer" and less-tangible things that make people feel good about the work they're doing, whereas managing is more often about checking things off a list and getting actual day-to-day work completed.

Leadership Competencies Necessary for Success

Eicher cautions against the exercise of measuring leaders against a list of competencies since, as he believes, this doesn't take context and culture into consideration. But throughout Eicher's interview, strategic thinking emerged as his most valued competency necessary for success. He also values flexibility over the textbook. "There are a lot of things that fundraising textbooks say you should do, but they are all without context. The context at Johns Hopkins is much different than the context at UCLA or Cornell or Stanford," says Eicher. But in all organizations, he believes flexibility and thoughtfulness about context is important.

Creativity is also important and often difficult to find in leaders. "It is not about creativity for creativity's sake. It is about taking a body of knowledge and a group of skilled people and working together to make something better—doing something different and interesting that is not the same as last year." Eicher thinks the best advancement leaders are self-confident and very self-aware. Good people-skills and an understanding of social interactions are also critical, and according to Eicher, their necessity goes without saying. "We work with a lot of really smart people in a lot of tricky and complex settings. Sometimes you have to have someone in the room stand up to the brilliant college president, dean, or professor and say, 'Look, what you're recommending is just not going to work.'" Standing up to powerful campus constituents can be tricky, but it's a necessary part of serving as a chief advancement officer. "If I manage everyone in my shop the same way, it will be a disaster," he says. "If I work with the volunteers the same way I work with faculty, I'll be ineffective. So I value flexibility along with savvy people-skills. You often have to change styles based on the audience, and then roll with the punches."

Finally, Eicher says chief advancement officers must have a dogged determination to keep moving things forward. Setbacks are inevitable, but it's important to be able to recover and keep going.

Leadership Competencies Most Difficult to Carry Out

Looking at it from a somewhat different perspective, Eicher believes it's most challenging to identify chief advancement officers with a balanced portfolio based on the competencies discussed above. These competencies are all challenging and difficult to carry out since the nature of serving in a leadership position is certainly a challenging endeavor, but for Eicher, the complete package is important and logically the most difficult to find. "You might identify someone who is very creative and flexible but who cannot walk into a room and get a quick and accurate read on what is really happening."

According to Eicher, developing future leaders is an important leadership competency, but one of the most difficult to bring to life day-to-day. "The thing I am most proud of in my career as a leader is developing people on my staff into future leaders themselves," he says. "For instance, Peter Hayashida worked for me for several years at UCLA and he became the vice chancellor of UC, Riverside, shortly after I left. The fact that I had a hand in helping him become a leader was fulfilling."

Focusing on long-term strategies and outcomes is also important for Eicher. However, he understands it's often difficult to keep a future-focused frame of mind within the context of fast-paced advancement organizations. One solution is to hire the right people.

Who, other than the Chief Advancement Officer, Is Responsible for Leading Advancement Organizations?

Eicher believes in the team approach to advancement leadership. He says it's hard for a chief advancement officer to be successful unless the chief academic officer, dean, faculty members, and volunteers have the same understanding of the process and time commitment necessary to raise funds. Academics must set the vision, direction, and priorities, but must concurrently value the chief advancement officer's input and strategy. Without this integrated partnership, advancement staff cannot be successful. Eicher says this about the importance of volunteer leadership:

> I think there has been an ebb and flow over the years regarding the role of volunteers. Fundraising in higher education used to be very volunteer-driven, but is much more staff-driven today. There is a lot of ongoing discussion about the need to get back to a better balance. Volunteers are critical partners, and we've spent a lot of time making sure they have ownership of our fundraising process and campaign strategies. Whether it is key volunteers or trustees, they are critically important to our success.

What Competencies Make You an Effective Leader?

Eicher strives to achieve mastery over the competencies he values, such as strategic thinking, flexibility, and developing staff, but he understands that mastering anything is elusive. "I think I'm flexible, strategic, and work with people in ways to try and build their confidence and self-worth"—all things he is convinced fall under leadership. And if you ask him if he is more comfortable managing or leading, he is quick to point to leadership.

> I think I'm a good manager, but managing at the fine details of the budget, spreadsheets, and that operational stuff is often delegated to my staff. I hire people who I know want to be held accountable for those sorts of things. These people help me to be a good manager. But if I hire well, I can spend more of my time leading the organization and less time managing.

He consistently describes a strategic approach to his work that he believes is his most notable strength.

> If you talk to any of my subordinates, current or previous, they would likely mention the strategic imperative. People who work with me know that they shouldn't bring in an idea or a piece of paper that doesn't start with goals, objectives, and why we should do what they propose doing. I can't read the rest of the plan unless I understand what it is we're trying to do. People who work closest with me understand this concept. My subordinates would also say that I push them to a level of discomfort. I push them to do things they may have thought they could not do. I try to push them beyond their comfort zone, and I'm sure I annoy them in the process!

Eicher's previous experience at the YMCA and his father's influence shaped his professional values and strategic approach to management, leadership, and problem solving. However, he also attributes his experience working with UCLA's chancellor, Al Carnesale, as transformational. Carnesale had been provost at Harvard and is an internationally renowned expert in the control of nuclear weapons, international energy issues, and the effects of technological change on foreign and defense policy. He is highly experienced in negotiations, and he taught Eicher to think about problems from multiple perspectives. "He taught me that no matter how good my idea was, I had to consider it from the perspective of the other party," he recalls. "Like most good negotiators, he wanted to be able to argue his opponent's side better than he or she could. It's a really important skill, as long as it doesn't paralyze you." Eicher learned to anticipate objections and to develop strategies around potential objections. He believes it's a craft advancement professionals must sharpen when communicating with faculty, deans, and other academic constituents, and he pushes his staff to think in this way. "People get annoyed with this process because they believe it slows things down, but they eventually appreciate the exercise and skill set once they have success with it."

Eicher has been described by previous and current subordinates as a visionary and thoughtful leader who has integrity, political acumen, and a sense for making good decisions. In addition, he has been praised for his orientation toward data, motivational and coaching skills, follow-through, accountability, and attention to detail. One of Eicher's former managers from UCLA, Peter Hayashida, said this about Eicher:

> Mike's leadership style is firm but fair, highly strategic and motivational. He works hard to position his subordinates with campus leadership and key volunteers. He pushes his employees to do and be more than they imagined they could do and be, and gently encourages them to stretch their wings and grow.

He inspires great loyalty among his team members and creates a rich, fertile culture for professional development, distributed decision-making with appropriate accountability, and overall organizational effectiveness. Most of who I am as a leader I can trace back to lessons I learned from Mike. I'm sure his style doesn't work for everyone, but it was perfect for me and allowed me to accelerate my own professional growth at a rate that I couldn't have imagined when I started working for him. The most compelling aspect of Mike as a leader is that his leadership philosophy is very values-based. He doesn't lie. He treats others with respect. He is humble about his accomplishments, but quick to give praise to others. He is patient in the face of foolishness, but pushes hard to ensure that everyone is doing the best work they can. He doesn't say much in group settings, but everything he says is deliberate, valuable, and insightful. He has only enough ego as required to do a job at his level, balanced with humility and humor that make him a lot of fun to grab a beer with. I'm hardly an objective source of information—I wouldn't be a vice chancellor today but for my 5.5 years working for Mike—but I watched him build a team that would follow him off a cliff and resulted in one of the most respected and admired advancement programs in the nation.

Leadership Development and the Future of Advancement Leaders

There is a reflective calmness about Eicher that combines with an aggressive confidence likely rooted in his deep leadership experience at both UCLA and Johns Hopkins University. His beliefs and philosophies of leadership are inspirational. But mastering leadership specifically is not something on which Eicher is focused. Rather, he is a lifelong learner who studies concepts and ideas from thought-leaders and experts. In short, he says, "I just read a lot!" For his own professional development, he observes current leaders, both good and bad, within the context of his own leadership position. "I watch other leaders and how they assess and develop plans to change culture, if necessary. I observe the positive and negative aspects of their leadership and identify strategies I can emulate, and also those I should stay away from."

Existing Professional Development Programs for Chief Advancement Officers

The influence of his father and his own experience at the YMCA was for Eicher his own professional leadership development program. He learned how to work collaboratively in teams, manage volunteers, develop staff, and cultivate the many other important competencies necessary for success in managing and leading large organizations. However, Eicher thinks there is a lack of existing training and development programs for aspiring leaders in higher education advancement. Most programs are not very substantive or comprehensive, and as Eicher points out, it is tough to change someone in few days or a week of classes. "You can sensitize people, but if they go back into the same environment with the same stresses and they don't have support to be successful, then it's difficult." Eicher is convinced the best way to develop as a leader is to work for a boss who is a good leader. But once these skills are observed, new professionals must test and refine them through practice and real-world scenarios.

> Just as you can't learn how to ride a bike by reading a book on cycling, you can't learn leadership by reading a book on leading. But you can pick up clues and ideas that you can try out and practice. I think you can learn leadership, but I don't think you can learn how to be a good leader by reading a book. I think you have to be in the trenches and you have to have somebody along the way coaching and mentoring, saying things like "You're thinking too short-term; You're not being very strategic; That was a good idea but it didn't work because of X, Y, and Z." You have to work for someone who is going to be honest with you and give you specific feedback.

One of Eicher's best pieces of advice for future advancement leaders is to pick your boss very carefully. "It's not just about liking your boss, but sharing the same values with your boss and determining if this is a person who is going to help you grow and prepare you for the next stage of your career." Taking a long-term view and not losing sight of the end goal is important.

The Future of Leadership Development and Training

From a practical standpoint, leadership development is a topic Eicher and some of his close colleagues think about often. That is, can the higher education advancement industry develop a quality leadership development program with measurable results and outcomes that has a real impact on the development of future advancement leaders? Eicher thinks it is possible and is working on a curriculum internally in partnership with a peer institution that he thinks will develop better managers and leaders over time, increase retention, help with succession planning, and ultimately generate more revenue for their institutions. The nine-month program, with experiences on both the East and West coasts, is currently in the pilot phase, but he is hopeful it will contribute substantially to the pressing leadership development need in the advancement industry such that other institutions may be able to either join as partners or model similar programs on their own campuses. He believes strongly that the future of advancement leadership training and development will only happen if current leaders take charge and address the issue.

Challenges Facing Chief Advancement Officers

The talent shortage of competent fundraising and advancement professionals has been well documented and is a big concern for Eicher. "I'm not sure how long salaries can keep going up," he laments. "When I think about our profession ten or fifteen years down the road, I wonder if the pressure on salaries will ease. If salaries keep going up at the rate they've been going, we're all in trouble. Our organizations will not be able to sustain the increases."

In addition, culture management and culture change are big concerns. Johns Hopkins University is currently in the process of planning their next campaign, and preparing for this is a concern for Eicher. Hopkins raised over $3.7 billion during their last campaign, which was considered a tremendous success. However, Eicher's challenge is to build on what made Hopkins so successful. For Eicher, it is about focusing on continuous improvement and always getting better, which can be challenging at a place like Hopkins, an already highly successful institution.

Eicher finds the stresses of today, such as finding talent, managing up, dealing with the day-to-day issues inherent in a large operation, working with multiple constituents, and managing the ongoing pressure to raise funds, very similar to those he faced in the 1980s when he entered the higher education advancement field. He believes many challenges of the past and present will persist well into the future.

Positive Aspects of Serving as a Chief Advancement Officer

You get a sense from speaking with Eicher that he truly loves the advancement profession. It's a job that satisfies both his intellect and curiosity. He draws energy and excitement from applying strategic thinking to big problems and creativity toward generating big ideas. It is the academic environment he loves most.

> Academia is a great environment. What I absolutely enjoy the most is regularly coming into contact with some of the best and brightest people in the world. And I'm not talking just about faculty, but our donors and our volunteers. These are some of the world's most accomplished, fascinating, and interesting people. For me, that's the fun of this profession. Experiences like walking through the Pentagon with someone who is a national expert on strategic arms like Chancellor Carnesale; or visiting central Africa with Peter Agre who was awarded a Nobel Prize in 2003, and seeing places where we are actually changing lives by preventing malaria. These are wonderful and amazing experiences. I don't think there is another job where I could experience so much with so many interesting people.

Preparation for Newcomers and Future Leaders in Advancement

As noted, Eicher thinks it's fundamental for advancement professionals at any level to pick their boss well. A poor boss can discourage new professionals and derail a potentially fulfilling career. It's a critically important point to remember when searching for a new position or promotional opportunity. In addition, he believes advancement professionals often leave their positions too soon. Rather than develop, grow, and learn the basics of fundraising, advancement professionals leave for more pay and larger titles. It can be seductive when an organization offers an increased salary with greater responsibilities. However, Eicher thinks there are many lessons to be learned from working through dynamic projects, building a program over time, and facing the variety of challenges that only longevity in one position can provide.

6

Susan K. Feagin: An Ivy Lifer

SUSAN K. FEAGIN SPENT THE MAJORITY of her dynamic career at two of the most prestigious private institutions in the world: Columbia and Harvard. Although she also led the development operation at one of the nation's top public institutions, the University of Michigan, her fundraising roots are grounded firmly in the Ivy League.

Feagin came to Columbia in 1968 when she was just nineteen years old and recently married to a Columbia undergraduate. She began working part-time as an administrative assistant making $95 a week for an alumnus employed in the university's central administration—a somewhat nontraditional start. Her parents thought she was "throwing her life away" by marrying so young rather than putting her education and career first. But her husband was attending school full-time, making Feagin's salary the sole income. She gladly accepted the role of primary earner, yet she too attended school on a part-time basis. Within Feagin's first year of employment at Columbia, her boss was asked by the institution's president to move into the president's office to serve as the campus ombudsman. Feagin followed, gaining high-level administrative exposure and the opportunity to begin what would eventually become a highly successful and productive administrative career in higher education advancement.

Feagin was exposed to the highest levels of university administration, a remarkable opportunity for a twenty-year-old. With less than one year of professional experience, she typed acknowledgement letters, interacted with the president, and later managed what faculty would tell her was the most powerful responsibility on campus: assigning faculty parking. Feagin finished her BA at Columbia in 1974, graduating with honors from the School of General Studies, and had the opportunity to become Columbia's first full-time prospect researcher. As she states, "My career in advancement was no more deliberate than that. I had the opportunity to move from an administrative assistant to a full-time professional-track position, and I took it."

At the time, and like those of most other institutions around the country, Columbia's development operation was very small. Peter Buchanan, an early mentor and "a great person to work for," was Columbia's director of campus development. He gave Feagin the opportunity to wear many hats early in her career, including those of event planner, prospect researcher, and coordinator of various development support functions. She had a bird's-eye view of central development support operations and was also assigned to assist the dean of the School of International Affairs in organizing a new development program. This gave Feagin important, unit-based fundraising exposure and would serve her well later in her career when she had to work with deans more as a peer than as a subordinate.

Feagin's early years at Columbia were formative. But in 1975, her husband decided to pursue a doctorate at Harvard University, so she moved to Cambridge and was offered a position as assistant coordinator of development in the Kennedy School of Government. This proved to be a turning point in her career, as she discovered development was more of a passion for her and a more fulfilling profession than just another job. After transitioning to a central development role where she helped plan Harvard's $350 million fundraising campaign—significant at the time but small by today's standards—development became, as she describes it, "a career choice rather than a career accident."

From 1978 through 1982, Feagin worked for another great mentor and major gifts strategist, Bill Boardman, and was given the opportunity to take on a variety of progressively more responsible positions at Harvard. She helped direct a $1.5 million campaign for Harvard's Center for Italian Renaissance Studies in Florence, Italy; administered the major gifts component of Harvard's $350 million campaign; oversaw regional fundraising for over five hundred top-rated prospects in New York; and directed all fundraising activities for the dean of the Faculty of Arts and Sciences. Boardman taught Feagin how to develop strategies for large gifts and was very generous in his support of her professional development by sharing and teaching his knowledge of major gift fundraising, allowing her to gain hands-on experience in high-level development work. During this time, Peter Buchanan, her mentor at Columbia who had spent time as vice president of development at Wellesley College, ended up back at Columbia as chief development officer for the institution. Buchanan, recognizing Feagin's skills as a fundraiser and administrator, soon recruited her back to Columbia to run a campaign for the arts and sciences schools and their twenty-eight departments, with a total goal of $177 million. Feagin eventually assumed a much broader role at Columbia, with direct oversight of major gifts, gift administration, and the National Campaign Committee, comprised of 175 volunteers.

After a change in the leadership in arts and sciences, Feagin went back to Harvard for a second tenure toward the end of 1987 to help plan Harvard's second and more-ambitious campaign, becoming the first-ever associate dean for development in the Faculty of Arts and Sciences. She continued advancing her career, assuming progressively more responsibility, and in 1996 was named director of university development, a position in which she coordinated fundraising activities for the entire institution, overseeing a $2.1 billion university-wide campaign and managing a development staff of over 150.

She flourished under Harvard's leadership, which landed her squarely on the radar of Lee Bollinger, president of the University of Michigan. As Feagin describes it, "I loved the job at Harvard and was in no way looking to leave. However, President Bollinger contacted me in 1997 and invited me to lunch. I knew who Lee Bollinger was, but hadn't met him personally. Of course, I couldn't say no to lunch with a university president, so I agreed to meet with him." It wasn't long thereafter that Bollinger convinced Feagin to join his team, and in 1998 she accepted the position of vice president for development at the University of Michigan, her first senior executive leadership post reporting directly to the institution's president. Three years later, President Bollinger became entangled with the elected regents at Michigan and, coincidentally, accepted the top post at Columbia where Feagin had spent many years in development before. Feagin recognized it would be difficult to stay at Michigan once Bollinger left, so returning to Columbia in 2002 with him for her third and final tenure there was an unexpected opportunity.

Feagin attributes her success to multiple variables. First, she was willing to leave Columbia and explore opportunities at both Harvard and Michigan. As she acknowledges, "It would have been very hard for me as a woman in development in the 1980s and early 1990s to have risen to a top position if I had stayed in the same place." She knew most of the players at both Harvard and Columbia since she had served each institution multiple times, but it was her willingness to take on stretch assignments and new roles that helped her grow and become a competent development and advancement professional. Second, Feagin jokes that growing up as a woman in the South was a big plus. She learned not to put her own ego ahead of others, and she learned that shrillness was not accepted. "You were taught to give other people credit and recognition for success, regardless of your role," says Feagin. "One must be willing to give the president, boards, trustees, volunteers, staff, and everyone else involved in the process public credit for successful development outcomes." It was a way of life in the South, which she believes served her well in her development and advancement career. She also believes that her ability to make decisions and get things done impacted her rise to a leadership position. She was a doer, and people simply liked working for her because of it. While Feagin does point to mentors for impacting her professional development, she also recognizes that there was a lack of senior female mentors in advancement. "In terms of women professional fundraisers, there were not very many back then. Remember, Harvard and Columbia undergraduate schools were not coed at the time, so it was very difficult to identify female professionals that influenced my rise to leadership positions," she recalls. Finally, it was a dearth of good managers that ultimately had a profound impact on her career ascension and leadership philosophy:

> I saw a lot of poor management throughout my career. People were not willing to hold staff members accountable to the idea that high performance is going to be rewarded more than poor performance. I have good memories of the first time I had to fire someone. It was actually a positive experience because there was someone on my staff who really needed to be fired, and this individual was surprised I had the chutzpah to do it. It turned out to be a real defining moment in my career.

For Feagin, it was an understanding that good management and leadership are a "constant slog." In order to be successful, you must realize that you have to constantly work on making your organization better, which often entails making tough decisions along the way.

Perspectives on Leadership

Feagin believes leadership is being able to inspire or encourage people to do absolutely their best work. It involves a lot of other things too, including setting clear expectations and getting out of the way, as a boss, to let them do the work. It's about motivating a team to realize that what they are doing is bigger than just a job. Feagin thinks the key is to build a community of professionals where people feel very strongly about the mission of the institution, what they are doing, and the impact they are having. This, in Feagin's mind, takes very strong leadership.

Leadership versus Management

According to Feagin, you cannot have good leadership without good management, and if you don't hold people accountable, leadership and vision become an empty phenomenon, or "empty picture." She observed this with deans who have a compelling vision, but who can't figure out a plan to carry out that vision. One must understand the concepts, systems, and processes needed to set the vision in motion, which often entails hiring strong managers as a starting point. Good leadership is closely correlated with good management:

> I had a very strong number two in my organization at Columbia, Fred Van Sickle. We worked together at both Harvard and Michigan. When I returned to Columbia, he came with me and we inherited a dysfunctional community that forced us to start from scratch. At our first planning retreat, we didn't realize people would come up to the microphone and begin crying. It was literally an environment where staff did not feel safe or respected. From that point forward, we decided to put a premium on, and emphasize the value of, quality management. We invested in management training and coaching and identified a consulting company to help us. They trained our trainers to coach our supervisors on quality management strategies and tactics that we could implement immediately. Our entire development and alumni unit bought into the concept, so now every new manager goes through this training, which reinforces our commitment to quality management. It's a process that teaches strategies for how to give feedback, engage in difficult conversations, and transition from being more hands-on to stepping back and letting staff carry out the work.

Feagin recognized she needed to shed staff who did not buy into the new culture and hire new people who would. However, once the new people came onboard, a mechanism was needed to offer career and professional development opportunities within and keep them from leaving. She and Van Sickle implemented a program called Your Columbia Career to address this issue. Results from a survey showed that the most important variable in employee satisfaction was their relationship with their manager. By providing professional development and coaching for managers, Feagin saw a significant increase in healthy employee-supervisor relationships. The executive coaching, combined with Your Columbia Career, led to a significant increase in retention throughout the advancement unit. Feagin explains the relationship between good management and good leadership this way:

> Management training helps people become better leaders by promoting ways in which a manager can sit with staff and be encouraging about their careers, while also telling them what they need to work on in a way they can handle; it's both management and leadership.

While Feagin was savvy enough to realize she needed to implement programs to fix an organization that some might refer to as broken, a lingering management issue continued to gnaw at her. "It's a constant struggle that management not become bureaucratized and overly processed; it's a constant re-balance where we make sure we are not having people do so many reports, and so many meetings, and not out doing fundraising." She keeps a watchful eye on this issue and encourages her managers to make sure the organization's high-performing fundraisers are enabled to spend the majority of their time fundraising.

Leadership Competencies Necessary for Success

Feagin first and foremost points to the importance of understanding one's own strengths and weaknesses as an important leadership competency necessary for success. For Feagin, it was an inventory called the IDI, or Individual Directions Inventory, that helped her figure out what factors were important for success in her daily work. Most of her indicators fell in the middle range of the scale; however, winning, maneuverability, and astuteness in university and human politics were areas in which she scored high. This relates to her strong ability, as she puts it, "to figure out how to maneuver to get things done." From a winning perspective, Feagin wants to have the best alumni and development operation in the country, and perhaps the world, which she says plays out in results. She tries to translate this winning attitude into inspiration rather than rely on "beating people with a stick" to get things done and to raise more money. It's about inspiring and motivating people to perform at their highest, most productive levels, which ultimately leads to effective and successful outcomes.

Feagin also believes it is important to be a competent *delegator*. She says it's the people as well as the structures that are important. Therefore, recruiting competent people and then leveraging the strengths of the staff through delegating is critical. She says,

> I'm able to let other people do things, accomplish things, and take the credit. What fascinates me are people who feel threatened by giving other people credit. I find the more I give other people credit for success, the more credit I receive for the organization's success, which I ultimately built and am responsible for. I almost feel guilty because it all comes back to me in the end. Many people, who I would describe as poor leaders, feel insecure about giving other people credit for success. They are worried it will diminish them in some way, although it's simply not true.

Leadership Competencies Most Difficult to Carry Out

Feagin believes one of the most difficult aspects of serving in a senior leadership position is buffering the staff from the negative "tough stuff" going on throughout the organization. It's necessary as a leader to keep morale high; therefore, communicating strategically is important. Leadership involves translating a positive outlook from the organization's highest levels to the staff below. If a leader projects negativity, it causes frustration, poor productivity, lack of motivation, and low morale, which ultimately leads to increased turnover.

This leadership dynamic appeared more clearly to Feagin when she arrived at Michigan. "Once I got to Michigan and had a seat at the president's cabinet, I realized this had been done for me in my more junior positions," she says. "At Harvard, before Michigan, I had a senior position but there were a lot of political issues going on at the institution that I didn't have to get involved with." Feagin began to understand that as chief advancement officer, you are privy to a lot of information throughout the entire university that can be demoralizing if the information is spread. She says, "You become aware of deans not doing their jobs, personnel issues, and other things that are demoralizing and would be equally demoralizing to the staff if they knew all the issues." Conversely, Feagin does not think one can be a Pollyanna because many people within the organization will have a good sense of what's going on. An important balance must be struck in which the leader provides just enough information to keep people informed, while maintaining a positive attitude and promoting high spirits among staff.

One way to maintain balance is to have confidants who are not immediately part of the organization. Feagin contends that you need a network of colleagues to turn to as a buffer, consultant, and coach. "It helps to have a coach to dump on and talk through the issues," she contends. "It also saves the spouse from hearing about work problems all the time. One cannot afford not to have a coach, if not for any other reason than to maintain harmony at home!" However, Feagin also recognizes the importance of having strong spousal support. Feagin's second and current husband, John Brown, who has his own fundraising consulting firm, serves as an important confidant and is a key ingredient to Feagin's success. She believes that without adequate spousal support, serving as a chief advancement officer would be much more difficult.

Finally, she recognizes the importance of perception, appearance, and the way leaders carry themselves professionally. She thinks leaders must react consistently to problems and challenges so people are not afraid to approach them about issues that come up. Understanding the issues and coming up with solutions is a necessary requirement of serving in a leadership position. Maintaining composure, reflecting on information, and following up with helpful feedback provides a level of stability that is important for promoting high performance and outcomes throughout an organization.

Who, other than the Chief Advancement Officer, Is Responsible for Leading Advancement Organizations?

Outside of the chief advancement officer, Feagin believes the institution's president serves an important role in leading the advancement enterprise. At Michigan, Feagin saw how important the development and alumni relations function was to President Bollinger. He respected its place and purpose in the overall success of the institution. Although he did not particularly like asking people for money, he realized that in order to be successful and to move the institution forward toward his vision, development was an important part of this process. Feagin says Bollinger finds development intellectually intriguing and a set of activities worth looking at and appreciating because of the human and psychological element of the process. As she elaborates, "He understands that this isn't about some manipulative process, but rather an interesting dynamic of human nature."

While the chief advancement officer and institution's president serve important leadership roles, volunteers and people on the board are also important. "At Columbia, it's the president and half a dozen trustees who have stepped up as big donors and big volunteer leaders for the campaign."

What Competencies Make You an Effective Leader?

Reflecting on her own career, Feagin repeats a familiar line regarding her strengths and effectiveness as an advancement leader:

> When I left Harvard, they appreciated my ability to make a decision and move things ahead. Many people want to think things over, but it wasn't my nature to be indecisive. It wasn't like I was impulsive, but I was able to move things along.

For her, it all comes down to getting things done, which has enhanced her reputation as an effective leader. It comes instinctively for Feagin. She also believes a leader must be proficient at delegating in order to move an organization forward both efficiently and productively. Reflecting on how her staff might describe her as a leader, she says,

> You'll hear a lot about how I delegate and try to give people the space they need to show what they can do. What might be telling is that I take all my vacation. I believe this is important. Fred, my number two at Columbia, would joke about how very well I delegated! I have had this great staff that made me feel I didn't have to do everything. One thing I learned the first time I worked with a coach at Michigan was that I have a tendency to try to motivate my staff to "step up" versus being nurturing and warm. My number two at the time was also this way. So when we brought a senior development officer from the

law school to the central office who was seen as more nurturing, that helped balance us a little. We also worked to change the way we interacted with staff. Being warm and fuzzy is not a natural part of who I am, but I'm aware of this and have tried to identify people around me who can balance me in this way. I also don't ask people much about their private lives. I try to keep it professional in a friendly way. I just don't have the bandwidth to take in every aspect of my staff's personal lives. It's more about my general make-up, who I am as a person. I also don't expect people to ask too many questions about my own personal life either, so it goes both ways. My staff might say they don't know me very well, but I believe it's important to keep professional lives and personal lives separate to some degree.

One of Feagin's direct reports suggested that she has incredible emotional intelligence. "She has the ability to establish an environment where all who interact with her experience being listened to and heard. She's also highly effective in earning the respect and confidence of other leaders." This individual went further, saying,

Susan cares deeply about the institutions she serves. She respects their essential nature as she understands their idiosyncrasies. Her leadership style is to focus on the highest impact strategies to drive results and earn the confidence of top leaders. She then translates those relationships into deep involvement and investment on behalf of the organization. She shares operational responsibility with others and uses her time strategically on prospect strategy and leveraging leadership capacity. Susan also lives out values of organizational excellence, such as respect for others, working at one's highest capacity, and involving alumni and volunteers at the highest level. She walks the talk of partnership, mutual respect, and excellence.

Leadership Development and the Future of Advancement Leaders

Susan Feagin exudes confidence, yet she possesses self-awareness and a reflective nature that has helped her grow as an advancement leader. With over thirty-six years of experience in higher education advancement—thirteen of those years serving as a chief advancement officer—Feagin is comfortable in a leadership role. When asked how she might improve upon her leadership skills to become a more effective leader, Feagin pointed to refining her ability to demonstrate more positive reinforcement to staff. As she laments, "I have to be deliberate about this, which can be difficult and often overlooked. It doesn't come naturally to me." She also understands that self-preservation is necessary for leaders. That is, not getting burned out and letting the job take over your life. Important to Feagin is recognizing when it's appropriate to pass the baton. "I'm very committed to passing the baton before people start asking, 'Is she gone yet?'"

Perhaps foreshadowing her departure, Feagin stepped down at Columbia shortly after this interview in 2010. Columbia's campaign was winding down, and Feagin was concurrently committed to winding down her own career. She said this about succession planning:

> I know that if I got hit by a Mack truck tomorrow, there are probably three people in my organization today that could step in and do my job. However, the key is to know how to deal with this. That is, to make it a positive and smooth transition and knowing when to let go as a leader. Not being in one place for my entire career makes it easier for me. I know colleagues that have been at one place their entire career and have noticed how hard it is for them to know when it's time to leave. For me, I started using my time differently. I let my number two take on more of the management and day-to-day pieces, while I focused more on the principal gift work. By doing this, succession planning is much more seamless. It is important as a leader to establish this kind of environment. If you leave, you do not want the organization to fall apart.

Existing Professional Development Programs for Chief Advancement Officers

As for most current leaders in the profession, there were few leadership development programs available to Feagin early in her career. As a young manager she was active with the CASE Winter Institute, but she came to feel that in a need to be inclusive to all sorts and sizes of educational institutions, CASE was less relevant and available to big universities. She found more support in the Ivy+ development group, which met annually. When she became a vice president at Columbia, she was invited to join a group of private-university vice presidents, which also meets annually, to share and perpetuate best practices and advancement values and philosophies. "Our problem is that we are all so busy we don't have the time to participate fully in these groups."

Feagin also points to executive leadership development programs that exist at Harvard and other institutions that add value to aspiring advancement leaders. However, she is not aware of leadership development programs specific to the advancement industry, other than those mentioned above.

The Future of Leadership Development and Training

Feagin argues that leadership development programs for higher education advancement professionals need to stay fresh and offer practical approaches for today's complex organizations:

Just because you knew how to do something in advancement twenty years ago doesn't mean you still know how to do it today. Advancement organizations need to keep being recreated. A common problem is that many organizations have a really strong group, people leave, retire and go away, a new group comes in, and there is no continuity of training and indoctrinating. It becomes a terribly inefficient system where new people come in and have to continually recreate the wheel.

She provides examples like Advancement Resources, Eduventures, Certified Fund Raising Executive, and CASE as offering a selection of various programs, but each has its pros and cons from a leadership development perspective.

In the future, Feagin believes it would be useful to have a program where techniques and philosophies of leadership are shared, including discussion of how they were developed and their effectiveness at different organizations. "If I found a good program that I respected that was a week long, or multiple times throughout the year, I would send my managers and leaders to attend," she says. "There are a lot of companies and organizations, like Eduventures, that share best practices, but they don't necessarily offer leadership training and development."

Challenges Facing Chief Advancement Officers

Advancement organizations have experienced tremendous change over the past few decades as they increase in complexity, sophistication, and importance to their institutions. Feagin laments that one of the biggest challenges of serving as a modern-day chief advancement officer is allocating time effectively and focusing on what's most important:

There is this sense of intensity, and the fact that we don't have any time. Chief advancement officers must constantly calibrate and balance their work, and that can be challenging. The expectations have become so outsized and supersized regarding what development can do. There is a lot of pressure around that, and chief advancement officers must help institutions manage expectations accordingly. There is a big disconnect between expectations and the investment it takes to meet those expectations. I also worry that as we become more professionalized and learn how to use data more effectively, we are losing the philosophy of relationship-building among our fundraisers. It's becoming more transactional, and we're hiring more people to manage transactions rather than build relationships. Fundraisers are often spending too much time doing reports, and if they are good, that becomes a problem.

Forecasting the future, Feagin believes many of these problems will continue through the next five to ten years, if not become even more significant and challenging. She points to increased expectations as the most difficult challenge to manage, but she also sees an increase in how institutions will approach their own philanthropy. Fundraising and development have become an institution-wide responsibility. Feagin believes organizations of the future will be forced to improve upon their own systems and processes in an effort to make the student experience more enjoyable. This, in turn, could have a profound impact and effect on gift size and overall participation rates of alumni giving. As higher education institutions adjust their systems and processes, additional pressure will be placed on advancement units to realize a return on investment and raise more funds in the future. She elaborates:

> Universities have such an advantage with our built-in alumni communities. I recently had an experience with a family member in a prominent hospital. The physicians, nurses, and staff were wonderful, but the systems were all messed up. We had to wait for hours for various services. At one point, I had this Aha! moment and realized that so many of our alumni think the same way about our universities. We have such wonderful faculty and students but very antiquated ways with our systems and processes. It's crazy, but people still give to colleges and universities because they are so great. Everyone is so wonderful and generous because we are doing things that will shape the future of our nation and world.

Positive Aspects of Serving as a Chief Advancement Officer

Feagin's dynamic career and the enjoyment she gets from serving in the higher education advancement industry have changed over time. As she puts it, "What I'm most proud of and what I enjoy doing most are two very different things. I didn't always enjoy the process of achieving the things I'm most proud of." But what stands out most for Feagin are the relationships she has built with trustees, faculty, deans, and staff, achieving results and successes together as a team. For example, she particularly enjoys interacting and working with trustees, building relationships with them, and helping them in the decision-making process of making a gift to Columbia. To Feagin, the entire process is fulfilling, meaningful, and, frankly, a lot of fun.

However, as with many senior-level administrators, she does not characterize the majority of her work as a chief advancement officer at Columbia as fun. "I'm currently working to close a $100 million gift, and it is invigorating and energizing; however, keeping it all together and moving forward is not necessarily fun." For Feagin, it's the results and outcomes of working in advancement that are most enjoyable, not the process. However, working together with colleagues in a creative way to bring the fun back into the process is something, she believes, that is an important responsibility of the chief advancement officer.

Preparation for Newcomers and Future Leaders in Advancement

According to Feagin, the chief advancement officer position is not for the faint of heart. It takes a certain kind of person with certain qualities, like persistence and tenacity, to thrive in this industry, especially if the newcomer has an interest in rising to a top leadership position. However, as Feagin points out, not all professionals with the potential to become a vice president take that route:

> I tell people to be really sure that this is in fact what they want to do with their career. I think a lot of people believe they have to continually work their way up and eventually become a leader in this field. However, I know many successful people in the higher education advancement industry who could have been vice presidents but chose not to go down that path. And, frankly, I think some of them have charmed lives because of this choice. Some close colleagues I know decided to go into principal gifts and focus completely on fundraising and working with high-level donors, volunteers, and trustees. I think being the top advancement person in a university is very hard and should not be taken lightly as a career path.

Feagin also believes that advancement professionals should strongly consider matriculating through a graduate program and get a master's degree so that it does not become an issue later in their career. She thinks a graduate degree will not necessarily prepare advancement professionals for their career, but it's a credential that shows they have the wherewithal to follow through on a major undertaking.

Feagin herself does not have a graduate degree. "By the time I finished my BA going part-time, I had had enough of work and school together. But in a world where status is driven by your highest degree, it would have been a little easier if I had an MBA or other respected master's degree."

There are several unanswered questions in Feagin's mind regarding advancement and its legitimacy as a profession. On the one hand, if advancement is a profession, then there should be the codes of conduct, standards of practice, and professional schools for training found in other occupations. As she observes, there are numerous fundraising tracks housed within extension programs around the country, but they suffer in quality and credibility. And as she rightly notes, there is a dearth of leadership training opportunities for advancement professionals generally. Feagin values what CASE offers, but as noted, she believes CASE, in an effort to cater to smaller institutions, has caused many large institutions to remain largely disengaged. "We have a lot of work still to do to figure this out for the advancement field."

7

Patricia P. Jackson:
A Natural-Born Advancement Leader

T HERE ARE MANY STUDENTS who enter their undergraduate years with an intense focus on one day attending a professional school for law, medicine,
or business. They study majors like premed, political science, or economics and work diligently to score high on academic tests and participate in
extracurricular activities to impress admissions committees. Another group
enters with an exploratory frame of mind, considering multiple options while
changing majors from time to time. Academically focused while discovering
the advancement profession during her undergraduate years, Patricia "Trish"
Jackson falls somewhere in between.

Today, the advancement career track is gaining more attention from undergraduate and graduate students. As parent programs and senior-class campaigns grow in popularity and phone-a-thons become more sophisticated,
students are exposed to development work much earlier. More and more
institutions are considering academic tracks with a focus on development
and advancement. In addition, many of today's students gain front-line experience through internships and graduate assistantships, thus making them
more marketable for early-career advancement positions. It is great news for
a profession that has historically lacked a robust pipeline of qualified professionals to fill existing and future vacancies.

When Trish Jackson attended school, it was much less common, and in
fact very rare, for students to go directly from graduation to a career in advancement. But that is exactly what she did. She says, "I am unusual for a
person my age. I graduated from college pretty much knowing that I wanted

to go into development and advancement. It happens more frequently now, but not when I graduated from school." Jackson attended Scripps College, a small, private, and highly selective liberal arts institution for women. While she matriculated, Scripps was undergoing a major renovation to restore seven residence halls to their original grandeur. With an interest in student government and leadership roles, Jackson was involved with much of the planning of the campaign around the project. "I had the opportunity to share meals with many alumnae and assure them that if they were to invest in this project, that we, the current students, would maintain the residence halls to a high level of restoration." As a result, she became friendly with the development staff and thought it seemed to be a fulfilling and generally fun job. "I thought, what an amazing job. People get paid to talk about how wonderful Scripps College is. Sign me up!"

What initially began as an interest in volunteering for her institution through various leadership and student government roles transformed into a future career. During her undergraduate years, Jackson was asked to serve on the search committee for a new vice president, which provided her with an up-close look at the roles and responsibilities of the chief advancement officer for Scripps College. It was an intriguing experience, and one that would lead to her return to campus upon graduation. "I went to work for a telephone company for one year as part of a management training program," she recalls. "I had worked for the business the summer between my junior and senior year. But one year later, the new vice president whom I helped recruit to Scripps recruited me back to campus to start a paid, student phone-a-thon program and a parents program." It was a turning point in Jackson's career. She knew that if she was going to have a career in higher education advancement, this was her opportunity, so she accepted the position.

Her title was assistant director of annual giving, and she was only twenty-three, but age did not hinder her success. She established the Scripps Association of Families to support admissions, career services, and fundraising. It was a fairly revolutionary concept at the time. In the mid-1980s, she eventually transferred to a sister campus of the Claremont Consortium and spent four years coordinating campaign activities and corporate fundraising for Claremont McKenna College. Recounting her early career experiences, Jackson says,

> My career path itself looks significantly more intentional than it ever was supposed to be. I started in annual giving and was grateful for that foundation. I really do think it's the cornerstone of philanthropy for most programs, especially at traditional residential liberal arts colleges. The vice president who hired me at Claremont McKenna hired three young people at the same time, and whenever he thought we were getting bored, he would switch our jobs around. As a result,

we all gained wonderful generalist backgrounds. As I look back on my career, I am really struck by what a pivotal moment it was when I was first hired at CMC. My title was Coordinator of Campaign and Related Activities, which has to be my favorite title of all time. But what the job really entailed was providing administrative support for the campaign at all levels. My first two weeks on the job, I traveled with a member of the first graduating class of CMC, who had worked for the college his entire professional life. He was the founding vice president for development. He knew the entire constituency, and I traveled with him for screening purposes. It was an incredible opportunity to see him interact with donors. He knew everybody. The other opportunity I had in that job was to sit in on senior staff meetings related to the campaign with the president, vice president for advancement, treasurer, dean of faculty, and the dean of students. Sure, I was there taking notes, but I got to hear how an institution operates and how a campaign fits into an entire institutional culture. I have since come to recognize, especially in leadership roles, what an incredible opportunity that was in understanding and navigating institutional culture.

Jackson recognized that sitting in a room with high-level campus leadership was a privilege. It wasn't just the exposure to campaign strategies that was most beneficial, rather, it was the opportunity to absorb conversations regarding institutional culture and begin to understand its importance to successful leadership. She was still maturing as a professional, but it shaped her own potential for leadership in ways she would not fully appreciate until she became a vice president herself. In fact, Jackson's early experiences motivated her so much that she knew she wanted to be a vice president. "It never occurred to me that I wouldn't be," she says. "If I stayed in this career long enough, I knew I would be a vice president someday."

In 1988, Jackson left Claremont McKenna College to head east and accept the position of director of major and leadership gifts at Mount Holyoke College. As she describes it, the opportunity at Mount Holyoke expanded her skills by giving her broad management responsibilities over both regional fundraising and planned giving programs. Her move was intentional, as she thought her management skills were slightly stronger than her front-line fundraising skills. "I was a good fundraiser, but a much better manager. From that point forward, I consciously chose the management path within development as opposed to the major gifts route." Shortly thereafter, Jackson took a position as director of development at Wheaton College in Norton, Massachusetts, where she was responsible for coordinating the $65 million Campaign for Wheaton, a fundraising effort that exceeded its goal by over $25 million. She remained there from 1991 through 1998. At Wheaton, she worked with a vice president whom she describes as "wonderful." But not long after she started, she began questioning her career ambitions. "I manage up really well, and I manage down really well. But most of all, I love serving as the 'stage manager' and making all the pieces fit together," she says. "I also love hiring. At that point, I was not convinced I needed to be in the top position because I was more interested in being where all the action is. The number-two position was a great fit for me."

Jackson had a successful run at Wheaton, but after seven years and an almost-finished campaign under her belt, she began thinking about her future. She was offered a generous package to work for an advancement consulting firm, but during the interview process she learned something very important about her passion for higher education. She discovered that working within an institution was a critical part of her success. Institutions build her up rather than drag her down. As she describes it, she finds such environments uplifting. They uphold her values both professionally and personally. Once she realized this, she promptly turned down the consulting offer and instead accepted a job opportunity with CASE. She says,

> I had been fairly involved with CASE throughout my career and saw this as an opportunity to give back to an organization for which I cared. In some ways, I knew that CASE was hiring me because of my network, but I also realized going to work for CASE would enhance my network in ways I couldn't even begin to imagine. I loved my time at CASE. The international development effort was just beginning, and I got to live in Washington, DC, where ministers of education talked to us weekly. I really enjoyed working at the macro level, but knew I would need to get back on a campus at some point in my life. I remember an experience early on that had a big impact on me. I was interviewing a conference coordinator and I asked her about her long-term career goals. She replied, "Well, I'm definitely on an association management career track." She was currently working at the Grocers Association, and I thought to myself, there is this whole world of association management that I am a part of and I have no idea what it is all about. In a sense, I felt like I had left the advancement profession and yet was surrounded by people in the advancement profession. It was a complicated juxtaposition.

After Jackson had been three years at CASE, Carrie Pelzel, vice president of development at Dartmouth College, offered her the opportunity to serve as associate vice president for individual and organizational giving. It was the type of position Jackson missed and an opportunity to serve as second-in-command for a development unit on a university campus. As she recalls, "I knew that I wanted to be involved with undergraduate students, which Dartmouth offered. The impact we have on students is certainly one of the fundamental reasons that I do what I do." The Dartmouth position provided Jackson with an added layer of complexity that she thought would be interesting, having always worked at small residential colleges. She would supervise all giving operations and be responsible for building a campaign staff. But during the interview process, personnel challenges were candidly conveyed. There were two units that would likely require leadership changes early in her tenure. But Jackson took the position anyway. It was all management, which she enjoyed, and mostly personnel management, not only within development but also with respect to how development personnel worked across the institution. She had staff members who worked directly for the dean of students, the dean of faculty, and the professional schools, so the job provided opportunities to work both vertically within development and horizontally across campus.

Once again, Jackson enjoyed her role as a number-two development professional. The vice president ambitions she had had in her twenties and thirties waned. "I realized I wasn't eager to be in the top spot anymore. I didn't have to become a vice president to feel like I was successful in my career." But after four years at Dartmouth, she got a call from Smith College that would not only change her mind, but also tease out her true strengths and passions. She remembers the phone call like this:

> I was at a bank in downtown Hanover and got a call from a search firm telling me they thought they had a job I was interested in. It was the chief advancement officer position at Smith. I thought, oh my, the first time during my career that Smith advertised for a chief advancement officer had been about fifteen years earlier. Many of the seven sister institutions still had independent alumnae associations, and Mount Holyoke, where I worked previously, did as well. I swore that I would never work for a place with an independent alumnae association again. So, the first time that Smith recruited for the position, in the mid-90s, they were going to bring the annual fund into the development office. I had people who knew nothing about the institution call me after reading the posting in the *Chronicle* and say, "Who would want this job?" So I told the search firm that I was not ready to be a vice president yet. I felt confident that whoever held the position first would be a scapegoat, and I didn't want to be a scapegoat in my first vice presidency. I didn't think it was going to be a great opportunity the second time either, so I told them to call me the third time. It was a completely different search firm, but it was the third time. Be careful what you ask for, right? At that point, I had thoughts about being a vice president again. It was such a natural capstone for my career, and I already knew everyone on the leadership team who would be reporting to me; I knew the constituency well; and I had many friends who were Smith alumnae. There were all sorts of reasons, personal and professional, for why it made a lot of sense. The big question was whether or not I would have good chemistry with the president. I did, so the opportunity fell in place, and I assumed the position fairly quickly. I've now been there for over five years.

Jackson attributes her rise to leadership to a conscious effort in her late twenties to early thirties to choose a management career track over a major gift track. She recognized early that these two tracks would become more and more distinct from each other as the advancement field professionalized. "When I interviewed at Smith, I was very upfront with them," she says. "I told them I was a good fundraiser and enjoyed being out there with the constituents, but that if they wanted an individual contributor as a fundraiser who only works with the very top of the pyramid, I'm not your person." She was confident yet she understood her own strengths and weaknesses, which Smith liked.

Looking back on her career, Jackson says she has observed both positive and negative role models. She was able to distinguish productive leadership strategies and tactics from unproductive ones, and she tried to adopt the former. Jackson, unlike the other chief advancement officers profiled here, was uniquely influenced by her experience at an all women's college. She describes it this way:

> I graduated with a fair amount of confidence and, although I'm not proud of this, a fair amount of bravado at a young age. Scripps instilled in me that I would be a leader in whatever I did. I didn't know exactly what I would be doing, but I came to view myself as a person with strong leadership qualities who had a responsibility to use them wisely and well.

For Jackson, Scripps College gave her a relevant lens and context through which to view herself as a leader. She learned that whatever she did with her career, she needed to do it well, with competent people, and for meaningful organizations. This was an important lesson she carried with her throughout her career. She is highly motivated by making a difference in the world, which has played a significant role in her job selections.

Perspectives on Leadership

Jackson thinks leadership is an ability to inspire action for a common cause among diverse groups of people. Inspiring others is the key to success, which she observed during her undergraduate years at Scripps College.

Regardless of her position in an organization, Jackson believes no job is too big or too small. She practices what she preaches and is not afraid to roll up her sleeves and get her hands dirty. "People know that I wouldn't ask them to do something I wouldn't do myself." It is that type of inspirational behavior that resonates with her staff. But outside of perseverance and hard work, she also keeps her job and role as a leader in perspective. She works hard, but laughs even harder. "All of my job descriptions have language noting we require a good sense of humor, including an ability to laugh at oneself." Part of this means that effective leaders must have a balance of ambition and humility.

Leadership versus Management

Jackson differentiates leadership from management by describing leadership as more inspirational, or a higher calling to action, and management as the implementation of that call to action. But she argues that management is a significant component of a leader's job. "To be honest, when I wondered about becoming a vice president myself, I questioned whether I'm a better manager than leader. I often wonder if I have what it takes to be visionary," she acknowledges. "I am really good at implementing a vision, but I think about the concept of management versus leadership a lot and how it relates to my role as the chief advancement officer."

Leadership Competencies Necessary for Success

Jackson contends that effective leaders must have a passion for the cause. They must have a sense of purpose and commitment to the organization to motivate followers to be productive and to perform at high levels. This is partly achieved by understanding institutional culture. As noted, she also thinks effective leaders balance ambition with humility. Chief advancement officers often need to step forward and lead as ambassadors of the institution, but at other times they need to step back and lead from behind the scenes. She refers to this as "institutional schizophrenia"; that is, knowing what action to execute based on the situation and environment. As part of this, Jackson also believes leaders must be flexible, resilient, and able to maintain perspective and laugh from time to time.

Leadership Competencies Most Difficult to Carry Out

Chief advancement officers have notoriously busy schedules, and Jackson's is no different. One of the most significant challenges for her as a leader is to set aside time for thinking. She says,

> I am a person who likes to act. I've had to work very hard at recognizing the importance of setting time aside for reflection and thought. Percolating time is really important, and part of what I get paid to do. We should not feel guilty about taking the time to think.

She believes advancement leaders should continually assess the effectiveness of the organization. "When a system or process works well, it's easy to become dependent on it," she laments. "However, advancement leaders need to step back once in awhile, in good times and in bad, and evaluate if adjustments are needed." Moreover, Jackson thinks it's important to separate "the important from the urgent." Most issues that ascend to the chief advancement officer's desk are often perceived as urgent. Learning how to tune out the noise and focus on what's truly important, both in the short term and long term, is necessary for chief advancement officers to be effective.

Who, other than the Chief Advancement Officer, Is Responsible for Leading Advancement Organizations?

According to Jackson, presidential and volunteer board leadership are critical to the success of higher education advancement and fundraising. Without their engagement and support, chief advancement officers could not be successful. She also points to academic leaders such as deans, department chairs, and high-profile faculty as important within the context of setting institutional priorities. However, she contends that the chief advancement officer is primarily responsible for ensuring priorities are indeed being set and for further engaging important stakeholders in the process. "I see the chief advancement officer as being responsible for bringing the right people to the table," she says. "Regardless if they are leading the discussion, it is important to make sure conversations are taking place, goals and priorities are being set, and the fundraising process is moving forward."

What Competencies Make You an Effective Leader?

Advancement is a taxing profession. Late nights, long weekends, and a demanding group of constituents, including donors, volunteers, and even academic leaders, put strain and pressure on chief advancement officers. But Jackson says she has stamina and "a delusional sense of optimism" that keep her going and maintaining effectiveness as a leader. "I believe people generally like me, and I've come to realize it's not something to take for granted." One of her more effective abilities is remembering people's names. She says,

> Learning people's names is important. When I left Dartmouth, they gave me a beautiful scrapbook from my time there, and it was signed by my colleagues. One person wrote, "I learned an important lesson from you . . . learn people's names and use them." In every job I've had, people throughout the organization have noted this strength in me.

Jackson describes herself as accessible, committed, and hard-working. She takes time to laugh, is open to new ideas, and is willing to tackle any job, regardless of how big or small it is. One of her direct reports at Smith gave a detailed account of how Jackson has evolved from a strong manager, which was needed when she first arrived, into a more broadly focused and inspirational leader:

In the time that I have worked with Trish, I have witnessed and supported her shift in focus from internal manager of the advancement operation, which was her well-developed and honed skill set when she arrived at Smith, to a more-balanced chief advancement officer, working more directly with key donors and volunteer leaders. After arriving at Smith and for her first several years, Trish was brilliant in assessing the strengths and weaknesses within our operation and repositioning personnel. She was able to gently, yet indubitably, make radical changes in the division's top leadership and mid-management leadership that have allowed us to reach a new level of functionality and talent while vastly improving the day-to-day morale. Now that we are in active campaign mode, Trish has shifted her attention to primarily managing up with the president, other senior staff, the board, and key donors. Trish is usually able to modulate expectations on the part of both internal and external constituents. She inspires confidence in those around her, particularly the president, which makes the work of the rest of the staff that much more effective. Trish is boundlessly optimistic, which when taken to an extreme is one of the few faults one can find with her. In addition, she is a "super-connector." She knows a truly amazing number and range of people not only in the field of advancement, but also in just about every other leadership capacity there is. She actively uses her network to both her own and her contacts' advantage. She never looks over the shoulder of her direct reports but lets us know that she is with us every step of the way. She then leaves it to our discretion if we need to check in every few feet or every hundred miles. Trish is passionate about professional development and makes it a priority, keeping enthusiasm high and expertise fresh. She never flinches from making a decision, yet remains open to feedback. As mentioned above, Trish's natural strengths are on the human resources side. She thinks about people first, whether they be alumnae, faculty, senior staff members, members of her own staff, or even potential staff members, as she views just about every colleague in the profession that she encounters as a potential staff member. While she is extraordinarily dedicated to her job, our leaders, our donors, and her staff members, Trish never takes herself, her role, or indeed the institution itself too self-importantly. This quality makes her an absolute delight to work with. While lofty in her ambitions for Smith and her staff, she is delightfully down to earth with an occasionally earthy sense of humor.

Jackson's knack for instilling loyalty among her direct reports is unquestionable. She creates a positive and productive work environment, inspires people around her, and is clearly a competent and effective chief advancement officer.

Leadership Development and the Future of Advancement Leaders

A noticeable characteristic emerged during Jackson's interview. She's comfortable with who she is as a professional, and she recognizes her own strengths and weaknesses as a leader, which is supported by feedback from her colleagues. For instance, Jackson thinks she needs to improve upon her listening skills and reflect longer before making decisions. Her self-awareness helps her leverage her own strengths while giving her the wherewithal to hire staff who complement her weaknesses or blind spots.

Existing Professional Development Programs for Chief Advancement Officers

Jackson credits CASE with having a profound impact on her rise to leadership positions, mainly because of the networking it has provided. "Certainly when I'm facing a situation that I haven't faced before, I'm going to call my closest network of colleagues and ask for advice and support," she says. Having an informal network of advisors is important for support and counsel when tough issues arise. But she also points to her master's degree in business administration as equally important:

> I'm glad I have an MBA. It is with an emphasis in nonprofit management. I'm not 100 percent sure it provided me with any specific skills or ways of thinking, but it did increase my credibility. It likely would have been different if I had done it in a more traditional way rather than over many years while I worked full-time, but it was still very helpful in my career.

Perhaps most importantly, Jackson believes it is important to seek out existing professional and career development on an individual's home campus. She has the unique responsibility of overseeing Smith's executive education unit, which is the only all-woman executive education program in the country. Since the unit reports to her, she attends sessions regularly and also encourages her staff to do so. Furthermore, she sends at least two staff members per year to the unit's Premier Consortia Program, a two-week curriculum focused on strategies and tactics for mid-management. She is also passionate about partnering with her campus's human resources department. "I use them as partners and try to identify resources they have that we can incorporate in strategic ways."

Like many of the leaders profiled in this book, Jackson is an avid reader. She participates in book groups focused on Smith authors or work-related texts. She also uses professional coaches, encourages best practicing with peer institutions, and engages campus constituents, like donors and volunteers, to provide professional development opportunities, which she thinks is an underutilized strategy.

> At Dartmouth, we did great things in our professional development program by using our donors as teachers. It served a dual purpose, as it was a great cultivation tool for the donor as well as wonderful learning opportunity for our staff. For one of the first ones, we asked a banker to come and talk about the history of banking with an emphasis in Dartmouth's role in it. His father had been a history professor, and he provided a most incredible overview of the banking industry. He loved it, and then to make it Dartmouth specific was a real treat as well. At Smith, the executive director of human relations of the Ford Foundation is on our board. She gave a presentation about giving and receiving feedback—content that people have heard many times. But everybody loves her, so it was like gospel truth in a way they had never heard before. It was a win-win, as she loved presenting, and the staff heard the message loud and clear. I think there are real opportunities to think creatively in ways we often overlook. Chief advancement officers need to utilize resources that are right in front of us more often.

The Future of Leadership Development and Training

Jackson thinks the future of leadership development starts with engaging human resources professionals as partners with advancement. During a recent interview for an article for CASE, she said, "I talked about the importance of collaborating with HR. The author told me I was the first person who said that. Apparently everyone else said to work around HR and ignore them." Jackson believes it is much easier and considerably more effective when human resources professionals are on your side. In every position, she says, she has made it a point to establish strong working relationships with the human resources team.

Leveraging relationships with donors and volunteers is also an effective professional development strategy for Jackson. "I like the idea of understanding more about the work that our donors do and the worlds in which they live," she says. "Whether it's spending time shadowing them or asking them to help educate us, these opportunities can be very beneficial to our staff."

Challenges Facing Chief Advancement Officers

Jackson believes that chief advancement officers spend a great deal of time managing board logistics and volunteer relations. "You are the only person on the senior staff—except the president—who has both committee responsibilities and the need to develop individual relationships with each trustee, she says. You basically serve as the prospect manager for the entire board, which can be time consuming, in addition to other duties in a chief advancement officer's portfolio." On one hand, the time commitment was surprising to her when she first assumed the chief advancement officer role. But on the other, she now relishes the close relationships she's formed with board members over the years. "I'm very much an extrovert and get a lot of energy from being with people."

For the future, Jackson questions the current model of philanthropy and whether it is sustainable. In light of current budget challenges and commitment to access, institutions are recruiting more and more international students, who often pay the full price of tuition. This could have major fundraising implications, as foreign-born alumni may not support higher education institutions at the same level domestic graduates have. As Jackson describes it, "We have a huge cultural advantage compared to our counterparts outside of this country. It will be a major issue at Smith going forward." She notes, "We hired our first director of international advancement recently, and it has been a very good move for us."

Conversely, women's colleges like Smith might benefit from the changing demographics associated with wealth accumulation and control. Jackson believes that as women control more and more of the country's and the world's wealth, and continue to live longer than men, schools like Smith will be in a better position to leverage larger donations, since their alumnae constituency is primarily female.

Furthermore, Jackson thinks the lines of advancement responsibilities will change significantly in the future. Private funding will not merely refer to philanthropy, but will involve other types of revenue generation as well.

> It is an iterative process regarding who owns the advancement operation. I think we are going to see the advancement chief sitting at tables talking about broad institutional priorities, not just those that have donor appeal. When I was at CASE, we talked a lot about the evolution of the profession and the notion that revenue generation for the advancement office will include a myriad of external, non-tuition dollars, not just philanthropy. Many people are talking about this. I often wonder if we will we see a new position emerge at major research institutions, perhaps a chief operating officer who oversees everything but the academic enterprise. It would be a position I think I would enjoy.

Positive Aspects of Serving as a Chief Advancement Officer

Jackson was born for this profession. She is unique from the standpoint of identifying advancement as a professional career choice as an undergraduate student. She doesn't regret her decision, and she enjoys many aspects of the profession:

> Every day is different. When I see students, I know immediately why I'm in this profession. I feel like I'm able to make a positive difference in the world. In this job, some days I have moral dilemmas and question if I'm making the best decision for the organization and the students. But most of the time I never question what I'm doing in the grand scheme of things. It is that sense of fulfillment that I'm indeed making an impact that motivates me each day.

She also says she enjoys meeting and working with extraordinary individuals, including donors, volunteers, and constituents who are among the most successful people at what they do. "I get to have access to some very amazing and distinguished people. I feel fortunate to have that opportunity."

Preparation for Newcomers and Future Leaders in Advancement

When Jackson meets with students or young professionals interested in an advancement career, she usually outlines a list of important points to consider. But the overarching theme of her advice is to listen and learn as much as possible:

> I always say commitment to cause and passion for what you are doing are critical. It's equally important to have excellent listening skills. Put yourself in situations where you can listen and absorb as much information about the advancement profession as possible. Talk to people who currently work in advancement. I don't know anyone in the industry who has turned down an informational interview with someone. So reach out and network with professionals frequently. Identify people from whom you can learn new things. Develop a network of mentors. And once established in the field, be open to new opportunities as they present themselves.

Jackson laments that current chief advancement officers haven't done enough to prepare the next generation of advancement leaders. She thinks chief advancement officers need to have a greater presence on campus by getting in front of more students and promoting the profession. Outside of work-study programs, phone-a-thons, and senior-class campaigns, most students don't know what advancement is. "I do part of the broader campus leadership training program with students every year. But frankly, I should be doing more and think other members of our staff should be doing more as well."

She also thinks advancement leaders have failed at building a diverse pipeline of future advancement professionals. "When people say they don't have any good applicants for fundraising positions, I say look at what admissions has done. We're so far behind, and we need to do better," she acknowledges. "We need to figure out what needs to be done, and do it." As a professional growing up through CASE, she winces at comments from her senior colleagues suggesting CASE doesn't provide meaningful professional development programming for them. "That is irrelevant in my opinion," she argues. "As chief advancement officers, we're sitting on the other end of the curve. It's our responsibility to give back to the profession."

8

Connie Kravas: The Academician

S OME FACULTY MEMBERS consider development a less-than-noble profession,
wanting nothing to do with raising funds for their institutions. Entertain-
ing donors at luncheons, groundbreakings, and private dinners is anathema
as it pulls them away from their mission of teaching, research, and service,
and in their mind it is unrelated to scholarly endeavors. And then there is
Connie Kravas. Kravas, who earned a PhD in educational leadership and
entered higher education as a tenure-track professor on a career path toward
what she envisioned as an intellectually fulfilling academic lifestyle, began
her faculty career in the College of Education at Washington State University
(WSU). She was on an upward trajectory, laddering through the tenure-track
process and eventually landing in a joint position as associate professor of education and assistant director of grant and research development. In this dual
role, she maintained a full academic load while shepherding faculty colleagues
through federal grant applications and other funding requests. "I attended a
conference in 1977 which I thought was focused on research development, as
in the transfer of research into product development, and low and behold it
was a fundraising conference!" She was instantly captivated.

Large-scale fundraising programs at major research institutions were nothing new, but Kravas was new to the industry. The mid-70s was a period of
professionalization within the advancement industry, with private donations
growing exponentially. Kravas was eager to learn more about philanthropy at
WSU and discovered they had already developed a strategic fundraising plan,
which culminated in the hiring of the school's first director of development.
Once the new development director was on board, Kravas served as a key

partner in building the program, and her advancement career was officially launched. "By that time I was an associate professor and unsure if I wanted to give up the tenure-track career path I had so diligently pursued, yet I was very intrigued with the fundraising profession and loved the work."

As she continued working with the director of development, Kravas and her husband, who also worked in academia, were granted a six-month sabbatical at the University of California, Berkeley, exposing her to the other side of higher education governance: administration. The experience was inspiring, motivating, and perhaps most importantly, eye-opening. So much so, in fact, that she decided that upon her return to WSU she would give up her tenure-track position and assume a full-time fundraising role. "Then, out of the blue, a week before we returned to Pullman, the director of development at WSU called me to say he was leaving immediately." I came back to a position for which I was very ill prepared, with a lot of hope, excitement, and gumption, but very little knowledge." Fortunately for Kravas, it was an institution that was willing to take a chance on her, and she's never looked back since.

Washington State University took what she describes as a "leap of faith" by hiring her into the development role. It was a significant step in professional responsibility, and one she thinks would be unlikely in today's complex advancement environments. But Kravas took on the role with a newfound excitement, slowly and methodically building what would eventually become a sophisticated advancement program.

As one of very few women in her CASE district when she began her advancement career, Kravas spent a total of twenty-seven years at WSU and steadily rose through multiple promotions, becoming vice president for university advancement in 1997. She also served as president of the WSU Foundation from 1981 through 1999. A member of the president's executive planning group, Kravas provided leadership and support for volunteers and staff within a comprehensive, university-wide advancement program. She worked across the university to identify fundraising goals and other goals representative of the institution's highest priorities. She was also responsible for leading the university through its first comprehensive campaign, generating over $275 million and achieving an alumni participation rate of over 50 percent, one of the highest alumni giving rates in the country at the time. Her success did not go unnoticed, as she was recognized with numerous awards, including the Major Gift Laureate award presented by the Institute of Charitable Giving in recognition of lifetime achievement in major gift fundraising and remarkable contribution to the profession. She was also honored as the Washington State University Woman of the Year in 1996, one of four awards presented by WSU in the program's inaugural year.

Kravas left WSU to become vice chancellor of advancement at the University of California, Riverside, and later returned to the Pacific Northwest to assume the top advancement post at the University of Washington. There she was at the epicenter of a fundraising campaign that raised $2.7 billion by its end in 2008. In total, she has spent over thirty-four years in the advancement profession, and she can point to three "revolutions" impacting her professional and career development:

Simplistically, I think of our work as consisting of three *I*-words: building insiders; institutionalizing fund-raising; and integrating advancement. The first thing that I needed to understand and learn about this wonderful work of development is that it is a people business, and that developing enduring, genuine relationships is the most important thing of all. To jump-start the engagement process at WSU, we created a 501-c-3 foundation with a phenomenal board of trustees bonded together with institutional leadership to do something that we all felt was critical for the success and quality of the institution we were serving. This model in those years was pretty common, and it may work well at some institutions today. It's a model of semi-autonomous foundations where the emphasis tends to be on unrestricted gifts. In this scenario, there usually is an awards process whereby the foundation leadership distributes grants back to the institution. Ours was a highly centralized organization in those days, and we did attract some amazing, caring, and thoughtful volunteer leaders to join hands with us. It was an exhilarating time.

For Kravas, this is the period she refers to as the first *I* of her professional development. That is, she believed her role was "to make insiders out of outsiders." But shortly thereafter, the thinking and philosophy evolved at WSU and development work became more *institutionalized*, a period she refers to as the second *I*:

The institution was experiencing stress between development, alumni relations, and communications, and we all acknowledged that having these programs reporting to separate parts of the university's organization chart was counterproductive. For the first time, a vice president for university relations was hired to pull all three programs together. Naturally, when our new boss arrived, he asked each of us to describe our respective programs. I'll never forget his reaction to learning about the one that I was overseeing—our institutionally related foundation. He said, flat-out, "What you have built here is a house of cards." I'm sure I reacted defensively at that moment, but, you know, he was absolutely right. In fact, he was just spot on. To be honest, the board and I already knew that there was something missing from that first model. So it was strangely comforting to admit that we could do better.

In this second phase of her career, Kravas set out to *institutionalize* fundraising by building a hybrid model focusing both on central and decentralized partnerships across campus and encouraging all parts of the university to become involved. This model involved close working relationships with the deans, who became, as she describes them, "incredibly strong partners." Changing the culture was not easy, but Kravas eventually began hiring staff members who had a joint reporting line to both the development office centrally and the academic units peripherally. Kravas and her team not only worked with external constituents to make outsiders feel like insiders, they effectively stewarded internal stakeholders to make them feel like they owned the fundraising process. To increase private philanthropy, Kravas focused more on restricted versus unrestricted gifts, which had long been the practice. "Every school, college, and department identified its own greatest needs and aspirations, and we helped align donor passions with unit priorities rather than pushing for unrestricted gifts. As important as unrestricted gifts are, too much emphasis on them tends to suppress philanthropic opportunities," she posits. "I also believe it doesn't build trust or ownership with your academic partners, which are so important for success."

Finally, when Kravas arrived at the University of Washington, she experienced the third *I* of her professional development. At this point, she worked within both centralized and decentralized models of advancement, but it wasn't until she was at the University of Washington that she learned the true meaning of advancement *integration*:

> Here is a visual picture of how we used to think about the advancement pyramid. We envisioned marketing and communications at the base—our broadest way of opening doors of understanding and awareness about the institution. At the next tier, we placed the alumni association and annual giving—programs designed to get people and constituents involved in some way. At the top of the pyramid, we would place major gift development. This kind of stratification might have been useful as a conceptual planning tool, but it was counterproductive to our goal of building a *truly* strong advancement team and, ultimately, I would argue, to serving the university as effectively as possible. For example, we used to have three different teams working on web design, and now we have them all integrated. It doesn't mean that you do away with specific goals or roles in alumni and constituency relations, or your philanthropy program, or your communication and marketing program. But they collaborate around functional responsibilities and the whole truly does become more than the sum of the parts, if you will pardon the hackneyed expression. There is great synergistic energy from their ability to look at each other and truly understand, believe, and recognize that we are working for the same cause. I think if you were to talk to anybody here at the University of Washington today, they would say that they are truly part of an integrated culture.

As Kravas reflects on the diverse stages of her career, she points to many experiences and influences that have shaped her philosophy on leadership. For example, the following question posed in a book impacted her significantly: If you have a son or daughter who is ready to enter the workforce, would you be thrilled if he or she as a young professional became part of your organization? "I thought as honestly and deeply about this question as I have about anything in my career, and I will tell you the answer I arrived at was 'I don't think so.'" What she came to realize was that employees are motivated by much more than salary. It's the intangible benefits that are often tough to define but cannot be ignored, benefits like roles, responsibilities, and organizational values. Kravas believes employees want to work for a cause or organization that meets three basic criteria. First, employees must have faith in the cause or organization's mission. Mission is motivating and stimulates personal fulfillment, job satisfaction, and productivity. Second, employees need to feel they are contributing in a meaningful way. They want responsibilities that contribute to the overarching mission of the cause or organization and its ultimate success. And finally, employees want their role and contributions respected and appreciated within the greater organizational structure. Salary and benefits are important, but they typically fall below these other key intangibles. As Kravas laments, "There is no excuse not to provide for these three requisites for high employee satisfaction. The first criterion can be daunting for some companies, but not for us in higher education. We have this incredible opportunity to work for amazing institutions that change lives and serve the greater good."

Early in her career, Kravas focused more on the "to dos" rather than the "whos" of the organization. But now she is much more focused on the big picture of motivating staff, fostering shared-vision, developing a healthy culture, and creating values that are consistent with the needs of staff. "I've always been respectful and fascinated by this wondrous opportunity to learn and build lifelong relationships with the people I had the privilege of working with outside the institution," she says. "However, I was less thoughtful and appreciative about the important, authentic qualities of relationships inside the institution." Kravas thinks leaders must be effective at not only making outsiders feel like insiders, but also at making insiders feel like insiders. "It's my role to help everyone at every level feel like they are an important part of the organization and that they have an opportunity to be successful."

Perspectives on Leadership

Kravas draws inspiration from observing successful leaders. For instance, she quotes Jeff Bezos, founder and CEO of amazon.com, who said, "Your brand

is what people say about you when you are not around." It was an insightful statement that she thinks about often. "I have to say that my definition
of leadership follows the same premise," she contends. "I'm not sure how
people would describe my leadership abilities when I'm not around. But what
I do know is that leadership is *not* some prescribed set of traits." She believes
important leadership qualities include competence, purpose and passion,
and self-discipline. "I don't think anyone can be a good leader by emulat-
ing someone else, or by following a prescribed recipe of leadership." Rather
Kravas thinks one's leadership brand must be authentic and consistent with a
substantive core set of values. She says,

> Leadership is very idiosyncratic. There are some very fundamental aspects of it,
> but most importantly we should try not to make it overly prescriptive. If we do,
> it might encourage people to look outside of who they really are, rather than
> within. One of the things I enjoy the most is working with colleagues who follow
> their own instinctive paths. They are formidable leaders and they are very differ-
> ent from me and one another. Yet we hold each other in the highest regard. That
> kind of diversity of talent, background, and commitment to one another creates
> a very rewarding, high-performance, and joyous workplace.

Kravas is aware that what she says and does as the chief advancement officer matters to her staff. She believes it's important to set the tone and cultural
expectations by making it a priority to meet with all new hires during their
orientation process. She calls it an "educable moment," and shares with them
the values important to the advancement team. Kravas and her colleagues
look for people who are smart, hardworking, and caring. "You can't teach
these characteristics," she suggests. "Candidates have to possess them when
they join our organization." Those are the same kinds of attributes that are
needed in good leaders.

When Kravas says *smart*, she's not simply referring to high IQs, but rather
to people who are curious, eager to learn new things, and equipped with good
judgment. "We have all worked in environments where one person who is not
at the same speed or going in the same direction can ruin the working environment for everybody else," she says. "It only takes one negative person to
make the office a miserable place." She defines hardworking people as those
who pull their own weight, maintain a balanced lifestyle, and have an innate
desire to pour themselves into the institutions they serve. However, the most
important characteristic for Kravas is caring. People who care are secure,
comfortable in their own skin, empathetic toward others, and trusting. They
exude a win-win attitude and embrace diverse viewpoints. They generally
follow the Golden Rule, which is a behavior Kravas says she didn't faithfully
practice early in her career. "I finally came to realize that I expected this from

others, but it wasn't something I necessarily focused on myself. I did not always lead by example. Once I acknowledged that, I realized that I was not proud of this and had to change."

Leadership versus Management

Rather than differentiating between management and leadership, Kravas views good management as one aspect of a leader's overall responsibilities. To Kravas, good leaders manage in a way that focuses on broader organizational themes and goals. It is more about managing the culture than people themselves. "As managers, we should set the tone for the kind of culture that people deserve to work in." She thinks organizations and the people within them succeed if good structures, sound policies, savvy budgeting, and overall accountability are in place. Good leaders should focus on hiring the right people and allowing them to use their best judgment by insisting they contribute in a way they think can make the greatest difference. Supervisors should also allow subordinates room for mistakes. "We need to get over thinking that everybody should be perfect. I don't know anyone who bats 1000. I sure don't bat at that level." In fact, Kravas keeps a bowl in her office with a crow on it because, she says, her staff says she has to eat crow often:

> We keep track of some funny moments when we have really blown it. But as long as you hire well and you have the attitude that you are getting better together, then it becomes less about managing people and more about building an environment that fosters learning and encourages people to manage themselves and contribute in a meaningful way.

Leadership Competencies Necessary for Success

The Pacific Northwest is full of successful entrepreneurs and businesses, including Boeing, Microsoft, Nordstrom, and Starbucks. In her role, Kravas has had the opportunity to work with many successful leaders within these organizations, and she credits their influence with how she thinks about leadership and important competencies necessary for success.

> We work in an incredible environment here in Seattle because we have so many gifted and wise organizational leaders who I learn from every day. Whether you're a Starbucks consumer or not, as a company, Starbucks has done a phenomenal job. There is a book about leadership influenced by the Starbucks culture called *It's Not about the Coffee: Leadership Principles from a Life at Starbucks*, written by Howard Behar. One of their former executives, Mr. Behar explains how important it was to create a positive culture among baristas. If baristas

didn't support each other, they would be less effective in communicating with the customers. Of course, there are other things about Starbucks that are admirable, like the benefits package and the healthcare insurance provided. But employees know they will be evaluated every year on how much they contribute toward the culture of their workplace. They know that they have the choice of either contributing positively to that culture or they should find a different workplace that fits their needs.

Kravas believes advancement is very similar. Outside of the fundamentals, she thinks organizations should hire people who fit the culture and possess values important for success within the culture. "This is a service profession. We are fortunate to be part of this particular service profession, and we need to remember that." So for Kravas, the most important competency necessary for leaders to be successful in advancement is the ability to develop a culture that focuses on the institution and its success. "This is not about raising the most money, or having the most alumni memberships, or having the greatest brand if the brand isn't true to the institution. It is really about serving the institution first and foremost," she says, "then understanding that advancement must pull together and determine how we can best contribute to advancing the institution."

Leadership Competencies Most Difficult to Carry Out

By their very structure, universities operate within a complex matrix that, at some institutions, has devolved into a conglomerate of individual units competing with each other across disciplines, often at the expense of broader organizational goals. As Kravas has observed throughout her career, advancement sometimes gets entangled in academic competitiveness. It can become especially contentious when large interdisciplinary gifts are at stake. How will the gift be counted? Who will have expenditure authority? Working across academic units on interdisciplinary funding projects is perhaps one of the most challenging aspects of serving as a chief advancement officer, yet it is becoming increasingly more important. "I personally believe that cross-institutional work is going to be more and more important as we try to solve some of the world's most intransigent problems."

Who, other than the Chief Advancement Officer, Is Responsible for Leading Advancement Organizations?

Advancement is a unit that transcends every corner of an institution's campus, and Kravas understands her success rests largely on the shoulders of others. She thinks volunteers provide a type of leadership she simply cannot provide:

We have volunteers here who I would walk to the ends of the earth with. They don't just say they are willing to chair a campaign, but rather, they roll up their sleeves and do some of the heavy lifting themselves. For example, in the case of our former campaign chair, he was very busy as cochair of the largest foundation in the world, but he rolled up his sleeves every single day of our campaign and thought through issues with us. He was part of our team, and we even had an office here for him. He would make calls that no one else in our organization could make because he always knew how to find a donor's passion. Having the chance to work with someone like that makes you more effective at your work and feel better as a human being.

Kravas has also been fortunate to work for some of the country's most outstanding presidents, chancellors, provosts, and vice presidents, and she values the opportunity she's had to learn from their wisdom. They provide outstanding leadership for advancement on multiple levels.

What Competencies Make You an Effective Leader?

Kravas doesn't take her job lightly; she recognizes the weight of her responsibilities, especially as it relates to staff development and productivity. In many ways, she epitomizes the selfless leader and works tirelessly to develop a culture of empowerment. She says,

> A long time ago it hit me like a thunderbolt. This job is not about me but rather everyone else in the organization. To be an effective leader, it's my responsibility to empower and support my staff in a way that removes obstacles and allows them to be productive and accomplish great work.

She says building a supportive culture is a primary key to her success. "When I say I work with incredible colleagues, I truly mean it. Anyone of them could have my job. There is a great deal of confidence in our program here, but mostly it is confidence in one another." Developing a culture of shared values across the advancement organization is important for high performance and successful outcomes, but it's taking these shared values one step further and instilling trust and confidence among staff that counts. Once this happens, organizations perform at truly high levels, achieving lofty goals and outcomes along the way.

Kravas thinks her staff would say she is enthusiastic, fair, caring, empowering, empathetic, and fun. She maintains a healthy sense of humor and tries not to take herself too seriously—a common theme among many effective leaders. But perhaps most importantly, she strives to be a good listener.

> People ask me frequently if I get nervous making cold calls. And one thing I learned a long time ago is that if you go into a cold call thinking about yourself,

you've already made it an uncomfortable situation. I approach it by telling my-self I'm going to listen more than I'm going to speak, and we're both going to feel good about our interaction by the end of this first meeting. It's all about the process and the moment rather than a means to an end. If you approach it that way, it ruins the communication.

Kravas projects a sense of self-awareness. She describes her own leadership strengths consistently with how others perceive her. One of Kravas's direct reports said this about her:

Connie is good at hiring and does not hire clones that are just like her. Instead, she is very good a filling her own competency gaps with people who compliment her weaknesses. She's compassionate to a fault, cares deeply about the mission of higher education, and is highly skilled at dealing with difficult people. She also has a PhD, which adds credibility. Connie believes in empowering everyone to be their best self. She's very strong on teamwork, talks a good game of work-life balance, and is unstinting with praise and recognition. She's got great values, and they manifest daily in a variety of ways. She makes us all look good and motivates us to want to be better.

Words like *caring, empowerment, values,* and *passion for higher education* are consistent themes articulated by both Kravas and her staff. A colleague who's worked with Kravas for many years described her leadership like this:

Empowerment is the first word that comes to mind. As Connie will tell you, she has hired people with greater knowledge and broader skills than she possesses, and when she does, she provides them with the tools and resources to be suc-cessful. She empowers them to lead their own effort. In all of our employees, we want bright people who possess a questioning intelligence. We also want them to be hard working but with balance in their lives. Finally, they should be caring. Caring in the sense of understanding that our business is built on trust-based relationships and you can't get to a trust-based relationship unless you care enough to listen. Connie lives all of these values in her work-life, and that is why she is such an exceptional leader and colleague. Additionally, she is dauntless when it comes to engaging our key constituents. If someone feels they have been mistreated, she steps up and eats crow with the best of them by acknowledging we were wrong and listening to ways we can rectify this situation. This allows her to diffuse situations in a more positive manner and shift the conversation to finding a solution rather than drawing lines in the sand. It creates an atmo-sphere among our team of being solution-oriented. Furthermore, she engenders loyalty. I have been her number two for over eighteen years, and we have been professional colleagues for over thirty-five years. I know that she is my strongest advocate and supporter and would endorse my candidacy for any vice president position outside of the University of Washington. But what I have come to understand is that we make a great team and successful teams are not self-centered or self-promotional. It is not about us or me, it is about our role in making a great university better, together.

It is clear Kravas has an uncanny ability to communicate a consistent vision and tone throughout an organization, and this is supported by the people who have worked for her. When everyone is reading from the same page of the same chapter of the same book, successful organizational outcomes are sure to follow.

Leadership Development and the Future of Advancement Leaders

Like most of our leaders, Kravas has enjoyed a long, successful career in higher education advancement. She is reflective about her role as an advancement leader and acknowledges past mistakes. A seasoned administrator who commands a loyal following, she recognizes her responsibility to develop the next generation of advancement leaders. Those who have had the pleasure of working for her describe her as a supportive leader who is deeply caring. But Kravas acknowledges imperfections and always strives for improvement. For her own professional development, she says, "It's important that I practice what I preach. I try very hard, but I don't always listen as much as I should." She continues, "It's important that I listen to what the needs of the institution are and figure out strategies for people to find their own passions and express them through gifts and endowments that can make a big, big difference to the institution that we serve."

Existing Professional Development Programs for Chief Advancement Officers

Kravas follows the philosophy that every experience provides an opportunity for learning and professional development, whether it is a meeting with a donor, attending a conference, or merely speaking with a colleague. She thinks some of the most educational moments are often missed. It is a mindset; that is, making it a priority to deliberately seek out ways to improve and leverage the experiences of everyday life in a way that provides growth and development. She says,

> My husband and I recently returned from California where we stayed with a wonderful couple. They are both personal friends as well as cherished donors. While there, we listened to them describe a gift they had made that absolutely transformed their feelings about themselves. While doing some research with

their church, they had discovered that the widows of pastors were often forgotten and left with nothing after their husbands had passed away. So they created a national endowment program which has already provided modest incomes and, more importantly, dignity to over one hundred of these widows. As we listened to them tell their story, you could hear in their voices that something had caught fire within them. They have supported many generous causes for other organizations, but nothing has been as personally meaningful to them. I feel that moments like this provide learning moments that will last a lifetime. For instance, in this case I learned that it wasn't only the joy they felt about helping a worthy purpose through this gift, but how it made the donors feel about themselves that was most important.

Kravas cherishes these interactions. "Rather than always asking for money, I sometimes reach out to donors to ask them how we can better serve their needs as philanthropists," she says. "I cannot tell you how much donors appreciate this approach. You wouldn't think of an experience like that as professional development, but it truly is an opportunity where you learn something from a donor that can change an organization fundamentally." Kravas also says she makes it a priority to learn from her colleagues regardless of context, location, or environment:

> Whether it's a big or small conference, I have a personal philosophy that I'm going to learn something. It's just that simple. There have been times when I have attended conferences and people say, "There is just nothing for me to learn here." To me, that attitude creates a self-fulfilling prophecy.

Kravas and her colleagues sometimes bring outside consultants and education programs to campus for internal training because it is both more economical and substantial. There is also a successful program offered at the University of Washington, developed about five years ago by one of her colleagues: the Advancement Leadership Class. Offered only to advancement professionals, it is a prestigious program focused more on higher education than advancement specifically in which participants must be nominated to fill the twenty program slots each year. In one session, a former president might teach participants what it is like to lead a major public institution. They might hear directly from a regent and learn what a regent's responsibilities are all about. They talk to people who run the physical facilities. In general, they get a broad education on higher education organizations and how they operate, which is often missed in the development of early-career advancement professionals. "Our former president was just remarkable at explaining the feudal system out of which higher education evolved, which leads to this almost guild approach to the professorship and the tenure process," she remarks. "They really learn and grasp the totality of higher education. It really gets under their skin in a powerful way." The program culminates with an end-of-year project focused on improving something meaningful at the University of Washington. This project is typically steeped in advancement, and as Kravas points out, the projects are usually on the mark. "Each year we wish we could implement every single one of them, and we do implement many of them as our budget allows."

The Future of Leadership Development and Training

Kravas recommends that more institutions implement advancement leadership training programs internally for their staff much like the leadership class offered at the University of Washington. She believes advancement leaders have an obligation to look at their undergraduate and graduate students as potential interns, focusing on diversity and engaging them in supportive learning environments. At the University of Washington, paid interns spend time in prospect research, communications and marketing, and front-line development environments in specific units. By the time they leave, almost all of them go into the advancement profession. She contends,

> We have an obligation to be leaders in developing a pipeline of new professionals. As we do this, advancement also has the opportunity to lead their campuses in terms of diversity. We have more women in the profession today, which is great, but I also see us growing in terms of all forms of diversity. There is an urgent need for well-trained, diverse advancement professionals. It's exciting to help launch so many bright careers.

Challenges Facing Chief Advancement Officers

The stakes have become increasingly higher for today's chief advancement professionals. And according to Kravas, this is the result of the field's professionalization. Advancement is becoming "everyone's business," garnering a level of respect on campus and in the community that was lacking in the past. As a result, chief advancement officers are expected to help their institution create a vision that inspires philanthropy. "You don't want the timing of a campaign or the annual schedule of fundraising to drive the academic mission. Yet there is something about the work we do that is helpful in the campus's planning process," she says. No longer can the chief advancement officer sit back and wait for the campus to develop a strategic plan. Chief advancement officers must roll up their sleeves and significantly contribute to the process. This process is not only about advocating for individual college and interdisciplinary goals and objectives but actually realizing outcomes that advance and solve society's most pressing problems.

Budgeting issues are also a challenge. Due to the "Great Recession," Kravas had to cut her advancement budget by nearly 25 percent, which meant cutting her workforce by the same amount. "All the stages of grief were experienced, not only by me, but by everybody in the organization. We had wonderful people lose their jobs. How do you ever feel anything but angst and heartache when that occurs?"

Beyond immediate challenges, Kravas finds the ever-progressive environment of larger campaign goals both exciting and concerning. "Because there have been so many billion-dollar campaigns, I worry that newly ensconced administrators at all levels will think advancement is just about setting a number goal rather than having the prospect base, strategic plan, vision, and organizational strength, both internally and externally, to deliver those big, big goals." She thinks there must be more deliberate reality-checking in the future to ensure advancement units face achievable goals.

Finally, the integration of all aspects of advancement, from communications and marketing to alumni relations and development, will be critical to the effectiveness of advancement in the future, Kravas believes. She sees these functions less as separate professions but rather as different tracks with complimentary reward structures. "You can't say that you really believe every unit within advancement is of equal value and then pay so differentially. We need to be very thoughtful about how we approach this issue."

Positive Aspects of Serving as a Chief Advancement Officer

Kravas seems to recognize she has been gifted a unique opportunity to fulfill a career that leverages both her professional strengths and personal interests. She consistently refers to her colleagues as "bright" and "talented" people who allow her to rest peacefully and worry less about the organization's success. "People think I must be really anxious, but I'm not. I have so much confidence in my team." But more than anything else, she draws energy and excitement from interacting with so many interesting people both internal and external to the institution.

> There are times when I've left an interaction with someone where I felt like there is no reason in the world I should be paid to do this work. It is so much fun and brings so much joy that I feel great about the work I do. For example, one of my colleagues who I've worked with at a couple of other institutions came in the other day and stunned me by presenting this wonderful orchid and saying he just wanted me to know it was our twentieth anniversary. This kind of genuine affection is shown all the time around here. I can tell you with total honesty that we love and respect each other and that's very special to me.

Preparation for Newcomers and Future Leaders in Advancement

Kravas thinks new advancement professionals should worry less about their resume and focus more on learning the profession, working hard, and being authentic and kind. The human element is so important, and by following these principles, she thinks opportunities will come. Leadership does not occur singularly at the top of an organization, but at every level. She says new professionals should live values that promote and encourage leadership within them and strive to always improve. "I watch for leaders at every level, and we are very thoughtful about ensuring we don't somehow create a revolving door. We want people of great capacity to find a path for career advancement right here." Capacity and high performance flourishes in a stable environment with multiple learning opportunities where employees are empowered to develop their skills. Kravas describes it like this:

> Today's professionals are so much better prepared than I ever was. Between the structured programs at CASE and some of the wonderful consulting firms, I think we're starting to understand donor motivation much better, which is helping us be more successful and raise more funds. But we really need to help develop the kind of professionals who are comfortable in their own skins so that they can really work well with one another, inspire a team effort, and become future leaders in the industry. It has to happen on a more personal level. We talk a lot about these principles here, and whether it really helps people develop their own authentic leadership style, I don't really know. As I shared with you previously, I did have an Aha! moment where I didn't like what I saw in my own self. I have shared that personal history with a few colleagues when I thought that perhaps they were not being the kind of leaders they wanted to be, and I've seen some rather dramatic changes. I used to think that people couldn't fundamentally change. But sometimes those Aha! moments can really have an impact. What it all comes down to is having the self-awareness and self-reflection to be able to change.

9

Jerry A. May: Leadership from the Big Ten

FOUNDED IN 1817, the University of Michigan is one of America's most highly regarded postsecondary institutions. It holds many distinctions among public and private universities. It has one of the largest alumni constituencies in the world, a multi-billion-dollar endowment, ninety-five academic programs ranked in the top ten nationally, and a storied tradition of athletics excellence. In addition, Michigan enrolls over forty thousand students, making it one of the biggest postsecondary institutions in the world, and is a founding member of the Association of American Universities. This is merely a snapshot of the school's distinguished profile, as its accolades span an incredibly wide spectrum.

Jerry A. May has served as vice president of development at the University of Michigan since February 2003. In advancement circles, he is considered one of the foremost higher education development experts of his time, leading two of the most prestigious public institutions in higher education, the University of Michigan and Ohio State University, to unprecedented fundraising heights. May knows firsthand the blueprint of academic excellence. He understands the organizational complexities and dynamic funding models involved in running a multi-billion-dollar educational enterprise. And he is keenly aware of the passionate and powerful constituent groups (e.g., alumni) who impact and influence the decision-making process at institutions like Michigan and Ohio State, thus resulting in a challenging political operating environment. But in spite of this, May's adeptness and competence have guided him through a long and productive advancement career unlike many others.

May did not deliberately chart out a career path in higher education. Born and raised in Grand Rapids, Michigan, about thirty miles from Hope College, his undergraduate alma mater, May recalls, "I didn't make any big moves initially in my life. I went to Hope College because some of my friends were going there, and at the time I thought it was a really great thing to do and a pretty good reason for going." But he was always drawn to leadership roles, even early in his life. "I was secretary of the student council in sixth grade and president in my senior year, and I knew how to organize and motivate people. I never knew that I would be an educational executive, but it just sort of evolved."

At Hope College, May majored in English but was motivated by a lingering interest and curiosity in what the dean of students was doing. As a student at a small, four-year, liberal arts institution, he interacted with the dean on a regular basis. May says,

> I asked the dean one day, who was one of my earlier mentors, how did you become a student affairs professional? He talked about his career path and education, which included a PhD from Michigan State, and he was inspiring.

From that point forward, May wanted a career in higher education and took appropriate steps to achieve his professional goals.

Upon graduating from Hope College, May considered attending law school. But instead, he enrolled in a master's program in higher education and student personnel at the University of Vermont. Once finished, he secured a position at New England College in Henniker, New Hampshire. There he eventually rose to the position of dean of students, following closely in his mentor's footsteps. But something happened during his tenure at New England College that put May on a completely different career track: he was exposed to fundraising. Most development programs back then were not formalized, so many people across the organization took part in raising private funds. "While I was in student affairs at New England College, they took me to New York frequently," May says. "I started speaking to wealthy parents in the city about the change process their kids were going through from a student development theory perspective. This was my first real exposure to fundraising."

A short time later, May moved to Michigan and enrolled in a PhD program at the Center for the Study of Higher and Postsecondary Education at the University of Michigan. He knew the potential impact a terminal degree might have on his career, but shortly thereafter he was encouraged to look at an entry-level position in annual giving. As he laments,

I was working on my literature review and had every intention of finishing my PhD. But I got the job so fast, it was totally unexpected. I never finished my PhD, and looking back, because of my background and experience, I would have likely had the opportunity to be a college president many years ago had I finished.

May worked in annual giving for about a year, but his talents gained him recognition across campus as he assumed progressively more responsible positions in foundation relations, major gifts, campaign management, and principal gifts. For over thirteen years, May worked in the development operation both centrally and peripherally, laying the foundation for future leadership positions that would stretch his knowledge, skills, and leadership capacity to their full potential. He describes his time at Michigan like this:

I was lucky to be at Michigan because Michigan is so big and has so many positions. My first two jobs in annual giving and foundation relations paved the way for future development opportunities. People at the business school said they needed someone to run their campaign. They only needed about $15 million, but in those days, which were the early 1980s, it was a lot of money. So I went over and ran the business school campaign to raise funds for a couple of buildings. In that position, I felt like I really connected with the work. The business school was a good fit for me. Later, a man by the name of Jon Cosovich came to Michigan from Stanford to work in the central office, and he was impressed with what I was doing at the business school. So one day, he and Associate Vice President Roy Muir asked me if I would leave the business school and rejoin the central office. My campaign piece at the business school was ending, and they asked if I would work as the associate director of the university campaign, which was $160 million at the time.

Working on the university-wide campaign was a significant professional milestone and a launching pad for May's career. He had the opportunity to develop campaign strategy, work with Marts and Lundy campaign counsel, and serve as the coordinating manager responsible for campaign preparation across the entire institution. The position gave him invaluable experience and exposure, which led to future positions as director of major gifts and director of principal gifts. May was viewed as an up-and-coming advancement professional, and other institutions soon recognized his current success and future potential.

In 1992, with May as a relatively young professional in his early forties, Ohio State University approached him and asked him to consider their top fundraising position: vice president of development and president of the Ohio State University Foundation. Michigan had prepared May for a large, complex institution like Ohio State. As he describes it, "The good thing about

Michigan was that they always had something new for me. I got numerous promotions and was frequently rewarded with more money." But the incredible opportunity and general lure of Ohio State was tough to resist, so he accepted the position, despite competitive retention offers from Michigan for both May and his wife, who was an executive in Michigan's student affairs division. While it was a great career step for May, the transition resulted in a significant pay cut for their household. He recounts,

> What ultimately led to the decision was the counsel and advice I received from a couple of my mentors. They said I really couldn't turn down the Ohio State job. I was scared, of course, because it was a leap. Gordon Gee was president, and he told me this was a high-risk, high-reward position. He thought I was a great fit, and he wanted me to take on the challenge. At the same time, my wife said she did not want to work anymore, so this presented a good opportunity for our family. But when Deb decided not to work—our son was eight years old at the time—we took about a $70,000 cut in pay. But it would have been very difficult for her to work because she supported me tremendously in my job at Ohio State.

Ohio State elevated May's career. It tested his knowledge, skills, and abilities like never before, and exposed him to the most sophisticated levels of public higher education administration. He credits his move to Ohio State as the best professional growth decision of his life. The interview itself forced him to think and speak about development and advancement in a way that gave him confidence in his ability to do the job. "I interviewed with the search committee for an hour, and my wife, Deborah, asked how it went," May recalls. "I told her that it was fun and that I didn't realize how much I knew about development." He credits Michigan for providing him with the practical experience he needed to be successful at a place like Ohio State. As he explains, "Michigan trained me so well that the transition was just not very difficult."

May served ten years at Ohio State. In his role there, he led a comprehensive development program responsible for all fundraising activities across the university, including policy formation, strategic planning, and program implementation. He successfully planned and implemented the second university-wide fundraising campaign in Ohio State's history, surpassing its $1 billion goal to ultimately raise $1.23 billion. In addition, he staffed and provided leadership to the institution's president, chair of the foundation, board of trustees, and the cochairs of the campaign. It was a stretch position that challenged his professional acumen and political will, but he succeeded, leading with confidence and competence.

However, May never lost his passion for the University of Michigan. His roots were planted firmly in the state and institution, so when Michigan's senior development position opened up in 2003, he returned.

May has worked nearly twenty years as a chief development officer at two of the largest, most complex academically and athletically distinguished campuses in the world. He possesses an illustrious pedigree unlike many in the industry. Reflecting on his personal leadership style and philosophy, May says he experienced many negative situations and worked with some negative people early in his career who forced him to think about his own leadership potential. He says,

> I can give you a long list of incredible role models for me in my life, but I worked with a couple people in particular at this little college in New Hampshire very early in my career that gave me lessons of how not to do things. It was the period in my career when I served as dean of students. I was smart enough to observe and learn that what they were doing was not effective. There was also a guy decades ago at Michigan who was in a senior leadership position, and I watched the way he manipulated people, played political games, and was not at all transparent. I was a nice young guy, so he latched on to me. I was young and energetic, but I watched him and I thought to myself, if I ever get to a higher leadership role, I will behave a lot differently than he does. These experiences and interactions had a profound impact on my future leadership style and philosophies.

But he also recalls individuals who had a positive impact on his career, and he credits them with having a more significant impact on his leadership style and philosophy than the negative professionals he observed early on:

> I learned an enormous amount during my time in student affairs. I worked with a guy by the name of Keith Miser, who became a vice president of student affairs at three different schools. He was my master's thesis advisor and was someone who impacted me in my twenties. Another individual who I mentioned earlier, Jon Cosovich, was an enormous influence from a fundraising skills perspective. There was also a guy by the name of Wilbur Pierpont, who was a retired chief financial officer. He taught me a lot about management. I would see him every week for about five years. So it was Pierpont who positively influenced me from a management perspective, and Cosovich from a fundraising perspective.

May's philosophy and approach to leadership took on new meaning when he worked for President Gee at Ohio State University, and then later for President Mary Sue Coleman at Michigan. As he acknowledges, he has had the true fortune of working for and learning from two of the most dynamic and successful college presidents in the country. In President Gee, he observed someone who took public speaking to an entirely new level. "Gordon was a master of public relations and communications. He knew how to spin things. He was great on his feet and always had a wild sense of humor," May says. "Gordon was responsible for teaching me how to take my own public speaking to a higher level." In addition, Mary Sue Coleman taught May how to tackle challenging problems, stick his neck out on issues, and make tough decisions. "I was a people pleaser as a kid. I'm an only child, and I learned quickly how to win people over, which is a great skill," he concedes. "But if your whole thing is about being popular, then eventually you will fail." By observing Gee and Coleman, May realized how tough decision-making can also be inspirational. He believes people who sit on the fence and are not willing to make tough decisions are less motivational than those who take a more confident position.

As May progressed in his career, he quickly realized that senior leadership positions in higher education, especially those in advancement, come with a lot more responsibility than authority. At Michigan, a highly decentralized institution, he is sometimes blamed for things out of his control. "Somebody once sent me a letter about how they were really mishandled in a little department in the medical center, but the medical center staff didn't report to me." What Michigan did for May was toughen him up in a way that enabled him to withstand criticism. "I went into meetings with a few academic leaders and knew that I had to be prepared or I wouldn't succeed. It was the territoriality of Michigan that made me realize I had to come into meetings with strong arguments." He goes on to say, "I had to be articulate. I had to make a point of view because a nice smile was not going to be enough." Michigan prepared May for what was waiting at Ohio State. He was competent and had the credibility and confidence to stand up to powerful people. As he describes it,

> This is going to be a really arrogant thing for me to say, but somebody actually gave me feedback that I kind of took the place by storm. I went in there tough. I knew how to do my homework, and I knew how to run a campaign. They didn't have anyone that knew how to run a campaign. I immediately laid out the plan and outlined what we were going to do. And Gordon wanted to start immediately, so we got into a campaign. Ohio State raised more money than they had ever raised before, and because of that I was acknowledged for strong leadership that, frankly, Ohio State should have had years before. But they just didn't. I was the first guy there to do it in a more professional way. I give an enormous amount of credit for my success to the experiences I had in the four or five jobs at Michigan. It was the discipline I gained from the high expectations of the people around me who worked in a very competitive environment like the University of Michigan.

Perspectives on Leadership

At minimum, May defines leadership as taking responsibility. But he also says there are different levels of leadership, and people demonstrate effective leadership in different ways. "I think that leadership is not only about taking responsibility, but it is taking an organization, team, or program to a new level of performance." For May, leadership moves an organization beyond just the people and their innate talents toward larger goals and objectives. He believes there are three types of leadership. The first is leading by position. "Everybody knows you have to be the leader, and everyone has to accept that you are going to lead by nature of your position." The second type is leading by facilitating. "You're not necessarily the guy out in front charging on the horse with your sword, but you're the person who is out there helping other people develop their leadership skills and putting them in positions geared toward their strengths." The third type of leadership involves a scenario where the leader has little control or ability to facilitate. May calls this "stimulating" leadership:

> These are situations where a leader has no control, no leverage. Sometimes these are in fiefdoms or with difficult people. This is when I call on benchmarking studies, outside consultants, special strategy sessions, or even outside volunteers to get involved to stimulate some reflection or change.

He has thought a lot about leadership and has come to the conclusion that there is not one specific kind that works. He thinks the three outlined above are most relevant to chief advancement officers, but he also recognizes there may be other approaches that are equally relevant depending on the person, situation, environment, or context.

Leadership versus Management

For May, good managers articulate clear expectations and goals. He says management is working toward a purpose, providing support, evaluating people, and then letting them carry out the work. However, it is also about providing inspiration, motivation, and direction. It is about engaging people and helping them feel like they have a meaningful role in the organization, sharing the spotlight, and bringing people along toward shared success. He thinks leadership is taking an organization to a higher level of performance where it takes on a life of its own and grows. "I think it takes motivation by the leader to get people to that level. Without motivation, people just do their jobs and go home."

Leadership Competencies Necessary for Success

In an environment where chief advancement officers have little control, May still believes that accepting responsibility is a key attribute for success. "I look around the table at Mary Sue Coleman's executive officer team with ten vice presidents, and there is not one person in that group who does not accept full responsibility for everything in their area and everything peripheral to their area," he says. Accepting responsibility is fundamental. He also says that chief advancement officers must focus on high performance, provide leadership on critical issues, be innovative, and continue focusing on sustained excellence. They must have an inner competitive drive, organizational skills, strong interpersonal skills, sophistication, intellectual curiosity, a focus on lifelong learning, and good delegation skills. Good leaders must also be willing to accept feedback, reflect, and adjust if necessary. It is not just about evaluating others, May states, but having a willingness to be evaluated as a leader. Good leaders must also take initiative and, as he describes it, "wake up every day to your own alarm clock." But for May, a passion for lifelong learning is perhaps the most important competency necessary for leadership success:

> The thing I feel most appreciative about in my life is that I developed what a number of executives have, which is a constant curiosity. I was in Key West recently, and while I know how to lay on a beach, drive a jet ski, snorkel, and all those kinds of fun things, what really motivated me was an intellectual experience I had with my family. One of our friends told me I needed to go visit the house where Harry Truman lived. So I went over to the Truman Little White House one afternoon, and I took my family, and we took a private tour. I was fascinated by the place and the important events in Truman's life there. I have been lucky from the sense that I enjoy learning. I'm motivated by learning new things. I think the reason that I'm such a great fit in higher education is because I love what higher learning is all about.

Delegation is also important to May. He thinks that people who rise to leadership positions too soon struggle to overcome an aversion toward delegation. "I was fortunate and actually knew how to delegate when I became the director of major gifts at Michigan. I learned this when I was the dean of students at New England College years before. I had six people that worked for me, in a little tiny operation of thirty people," he says. "I often wanted to do things myself, and I probably made some mistakes where I tried to do too much myself." But May believes if you're observant and intellectually curious, you eventually realize delegation is an important component of successful leadership.

From a fundraising perspective, May says good development professionals need to be willing to go after goals. "When I recruit, I try to find fundraisers who are tenacious. I think tenacity in fundraising is one of the great gifts. Being tenacious and never giving up." He also knows the warning signs to listen for if someone isn't cut out for the job. "When I hear a young development officer conclude that a donor just doesn't want to give, I know that person either needs more mentoring, or they should get out of the profession because almost nobody means no," he says. "Everyone can get involved in some capacity."

Leadership Competencies Most Difficult to Carry Out

May points to motivating staff as one of the most difficult competencies to develop. He also believes people who fail are usually those who do not know their own strengths and weaknesses. Good fundraisers are sometimes poor managers and vice versa. According to May, it is important for leaders to recognize how and when to delegate and to ensure they hire enough smart people to get work done in areas where they are weak. For example, May says,

> I remember when I was taking a higher education course at Michigan with a social sciences professor. I was so fascinated by some of her work that showed that some of the most creative people in the world fail because they can't manage and can't move a project forward. They succeed when they match up with an implementer. I think identifying people who have both fundraising and managerial qualities is very hard. What we find in higher education is that there are not a lot of people who have a mix or blend of both of these qualities.

Who, other than the Chief Advancement Officer, Is Responsible for Leading Advancement Organizations?

May believes the chief advancement officer is ultimately responsible, and must be responsible, for leading a campus's advancement initiative. "Once, I did not go to work for the president of another university because he said he saw himself as the chief advancement officer," May recalls. "I thought to myself that I did not want to work for this person because that's *my* job. He is the president and I am going to be there to serve the president," May says. "I need him to be the leader of the university and not the leader of the fundraising program." May thinks a president should provide the inspiration, direction, and academic leadership, but the chief advancement officer should facilitate the advancement process and overall fundraising program. "My job is to bring the president in to build a relationship and solicit when necessary, but I think the head of development or advancement has to be the leader of the process."

However, volunteers are also a key constituency that May believes provide leadership in a way the chief advancement officer cannot. He says public institutions are not as experienced as private ones at engaging volunteers, but volunteers serve an important function in moving advancement strategies forward. As May describes it, the volunteer structures of private and public institutions are often very different, but whatever the situation, he tries to position volunteers as leaders as much as possible:

> I try to get as many volunteers as possible out there to serve as leaders. We feature them in publications; we get them out there speaking; we publish their testimonials. But I haven't found an abundance of volunteers that are really great at asking. About 10 to 20 percent are really skilled at asking for gifts, but the rest are better at hosting events, identifying prospects, giving testimonials, and telling their philanthropic stories. In spite of this, the vice president for development has to make sure volunteers are out in front and are given enormous credit for the organization's success. They have tremendous influence.

What Competencies Make You an Effective Leader?

May is an enthusiastic, highly competent leader with a deep knowledge of advancement, likely the result of his experience at two of the largest public higher education institutions in the world. He comes across as calm and deliberate, yet his passion for advancement is always near the surface. "I get very enthusiastic when asked about my profession, and I'm lucky that I'm the type of person who belongs in sales"—a loose reference to the development profession. "I don't think I could work very well or very long for an organization that I didn't believe in. But when I believe in something, I am told my positive attitude and enthusiasm is infectious."

May thinks his strengths relate to his passion for higher education and for the work he is doing. He is also particularly good at recognizing when to lead and when to take a back seat to other people in his organization. "Later in my career, I started nurturing my staff more. I am very much a generative person because I realize that if you don't grow the talent in your own organization, you leave it flat or even in a vacuum." May also says he tries to be innovative in his leadership development strategies:

> Many years ago, I started various kinds of prospect strategy meetings with groups of development staff that I use, frankly, as tutorial sessions for some of the younger professionals. Letting the younger staff see the senior people working on a complex prospect strategy is an invaluable learning experience.

He describes himself as a consensus builder and takes pride in his ability to manage change, while constantly striving to make the organization better:

> I use my management team, especially our head of talent management and development operations, and others to help with the change process. Chrissi Rawak is actually one of the strongest change management people that I have

had on my team. Jefferson Porter, our associate vice president, is just really good at understanding how people are going to respond. In terms of my own leadership style, I think it is really important to listen to people. You have got to be a good listener in this business. At the same time, after you've listened to all sides, you have to be willing to take a stand. You've got to be out there making your case, but it has to be based on a lot of input from a lot of people rather than just saying, I believe this because I believe this.

May also says he tries to draw on the wisdom and expertise of other people inside and outside the organization and then articulate their thoughts back to them. He points to Gordon Gee and President Bill Clinton as two people with very good listening skills from whom he has drawn inspiration. "Gordon Gee is a master at listening to people, making them feel good about being listened to, and then feeding it back to them later." On Clinton, he says,

> When Bill Clinton came to Michigan a couple of years ago to give the commencement speech, he actually picked out people in the crowd who were there that day and did some homework on them. He talked specifically about their stories and things he learned from them, and by the time he was done, he had captivated the audience.

This quality makes people feel like they have ownership in the organization. For May, that is an important part of a leader's job.

May says his staff would describe him as aggressive. "I push hard for my goals, but I am also reasonably fair-minded." He also thinks they would say he takes stands on issues and is respectful of people. "It's one thing I worry about. As a society, we've become so critical about everybody and everything that when I say something constructive, or tell people I need them to do something better, I always make sure I'm telling people good things they do as well." According to May, most people likely think he is hard-driving but also inspirational. He tries to be as open and transparent with his staff as possible so they will be open and transparent in return. "I like to disclose things. Once in a while I will tell people mistakes I have made, and why I made that mistake. Owning mistakes seems to relax people and give them courage to take risks."

One of May's professional leaders, Chrissi Rawak, describes him as a confident leader who is empowering, creative, internally and externally focused, and a relationship builder. She also thinks he is positive, optimistic, and focused on building a team-oriented environment. She says,

> He's generally a supportive leader who articulates high expectations. But he's supportive in a way that helps me be successful. He's given me the opportunity to gain exposure across all levels of the university, which has been invaluable to my success.

Leadership Development and the Future of Advancement Leaders

For his own professional development, May says he sometimes asks his senior people for direct feedback to help him become more effective as a leader. While he does not go so far as to fully subscribe to the 360-degree method of evaluation, he does value feedback from his staff in a less formal way. "When I feel somebody isn't with me or doesn't agree with me, I'll probe further and ask more questions because I want them to tell me how they really feel." In addition, he looks to his immediate supervisor for specific feedback:

> Every year I ask my boss how I've done on certain projects. I usually give my current boss, President Coleman, some examples and ask specifically if I met her objectives. Some of my colleagues will also give me feedback that I exaggerated something, or I was being too nice—whatever the situation is. Fundraising volunteers also give feedback, often unsolicited. You learn from your boss, you learn from your peers, you learn from your volunteers, and you learn from your management team. So in a sense, this is 360-degree feedback, but it is received and listened to in a more informal way.

May is more relaxed as a leader today than he was twenty years ago. "Many years ago I got an award from the University of Vermont, and part of what they wrote up in the student affairs division said something about having grace under pressure," he recalls. "I just laughed because I am too emotional to have grace under pressure." He thinks his leadership style has evolved over the course of his career, and adds, "I always wished when I was younger that I was more like the Marlboro man as a leader—calm, confident, unrattled. But I've calmed down since then," he acknowledges. "Today, I'm much better in tense and difficult situations, often when other people are losing their heads." Restraint has been a cornerstone of May's leadership style and an important quality that has helped him be successful and get things done, but having grace under pressure is a focus of his own professional development. He elaborates:

> My management style is not always as elegant as I would like it to be, or as gracious. But I've actually worked hard at being more gracious. A former CEO of Bank One was a wonderful mentor for me. He was a volunteer, John McCoy, who died recently in his nineties. I watched how gracious he was for the ten years I worked at Ohio State University. I worked hard to emulate him because I loved his gracious and kind qualities. I pick people out when I see qualities I respect, and I try to emulate those qualities. That's how I learned to ski. I started following really good skiers down the ski slope when I was young. They inspired me.

Existing Professional Development Programs for Chief Advancement Officers

May says he attends the traditional programs and conferences available for most chief advancement officers, but questions their overall effectiveness for developing leaders. He enjoys interacting with colleagues and sharing best practices at conferences hosted by the Association of Governing Boards (AGB), CASE, and others. He has also chaired the Big Ten Fundraising Institute, which, he points out, is a great place to learn from colleagues and other vice presidents. But generally, he's concerned about future leadership training and development for the advancement profession as a whole. "I don't know if I have ever attended something very effective, outside of the Big Ten Fundraising Institute," he laments. "I learn mostly by watching other successful leaders. There is not enough leadership development training in our profession."

The Future of Leadership Development and Training

A lack of skill among current professionals in the areas of management and strategic planning is among May's primary concerns. He believes the advancement industry should develop programs to teach strategic planning from a leadership perspective and that organizations should make it a priority internally:

> I think as a profession, we can do much better in training and professional development, which is why I have a talent management team focused on these skills. They really understand what is needed and put together meaningful training programs.

Secondly, May thinks we need more programs focused on generational communication issues. It is important for leaders to understand how different generations think, approach their work, and view the world. He expands,

> I am reading a book right now about the millennial generation. I am reading it because it is a different group of people. They really think differently, and I need to understand it in order to be more effective with this group as a leader. Generation Y thinks much differently than generation X. I also think I need to learn more about social media. It is appalling how little I know about social media. I don't believe social media is necessarily the only answer to communicating better with younger generations, but I also think that if I don't learn it pretty quickly, I am going to fall behind.

May believes future advancement leaders must be more competent at displaying leadership behaviors. They must constantly compare notes with colleagues and have common discussions about their effectiveness as advancement and fundraising professionals. Current donors are much more sophisticated about the fundraising process than those of past generations. Therefore, he asks, "How do you motivate people in the future when they start getting cynical about the fundraising process in general?" For example, May says,

> I met with a donor for breakfast in New York the other day, and he basically preempted me. He literally said, "Okay now that your son is graduated from college and you previously made a two million-dollar gift, you probably feel like it would be really nice to put a capstone on the impact that you've had on the university." We had a good laugh because those were exactly the words I was thinking! I think we have to get better. If we don't freshen up our fundraising strategies they could become stale and ineffective.

Challenges Facing Chief Advancement Officers

According to May, chief advancement officers have one of the most interesting positions on campus, but also one of the most challenging. With faculty independence, shared governance, and a web of units operating both dependently and independently, chief advancement officers must work within an organizational structure that can be difficult to navigate. "In both public and private institutions, the decentralized nature of universities is a blessing and a curse, a strength and a weakness." Learning how to manage decentralized organizations is very important because the customer (i.e., the donor) often becomes confused. "There are far too many development officers who don't have the necessary management skills to be successful at the next level," May says. "We need to find better ways to train them."

Another challenge for May is keeping intimacy within his organization. "I always say to my staff the world is getting more and more impersonal, yet interpersonal relationships are one of the fundamental human needs we have." There is a competitive advantage for fundraisers to build close personal relationships, but as organizations get bigger and chief advancement officers have more demands placed on their time, it's difficult for leaders to provide a high level of personal attention to everyone who needs it. "From a management point of view, I need a deep pool of talented people around me who the volunteers like as well as, if not better than, me," he says. "That personal touch is so important." Finally, May thinks there is a real problem with presidential turnover at many universities and its impact on fundraising and advancement. "Presidential turnover is hard on an institution, especially if there is no succession plan in place, or depth among senior management. Relationships take time to build, especially at the presidential level." From a fundraising perspective, May contends there is an unknown and unquantifiable cost to rebuilding relationships with institutional representatives as people leave.

Positive Aspects of Serving as a Chief Advancement Officer

May's career has truly been defined by leadership. From his first experience as dean of students when he was in his twenties to his ascent to the position of chief advancement officer in his early forties at one of the world's largest and most complex institutions of higher learning, May has been no stranger to the concepts, theories, and practice of leadership. Leadership came naturally to May at an early age, and thus his leadership skills and abilities have been recognized at every stage of his career.

There are two specific things May says he enjoys most about serving as a chief advancement officer in higher education: forming close relationships, and the external component of the job. "I just love those aspects. Whenever I need to pump myself up a little bit, all I have to do is go on the road and meet with donors," he says. "Nine times out of ten, I feel so lucky to be in this position which has enabled me to meet so many interesting people and to help them with their philanthropic vision." His passion stems from a deep interest in fulfilling the needs and interests of higher education institutions. "When I was the dean of students, I loved discovering what I could do to help the institution as a whole. I would ask myself how I could make the entire college better, not just student affairs." This level of thinking stayed with May as he transitioned to leadership positions in development and advancement later in his career. "When I sit around the table with the president of the university, I love thinking about issues that go well beyond fundraising, such as the quality of our recreational facilities, sustainability issues, and public service," he says. "I enjoy having that platform and being part of the team addressing these issues. Sometimes I'm just a very small piece of the conversation, but it's still very fun."

Preparation for Newcomers and Future Leaders in Advancement

May's advice for newcomers is to stay focused on the job and learn how to be a high-performing fundraiser. Good fundraisers understand how to build confidence in the people they work with, both internally and externally, and it is one of the most important qualities necessary for success. "You have to keep gaining confidence throughout your career, and it gets harder and harder as you move up the ladder," he contends. "Standards get higher as you move up, but at the same time, there are more and more things out of your direct control." May believes it is important for advancement professionals to make a good first impression. "You only have a couple of minutes in that first meeting with a donor to gain their trust and confidence. So you have to do your homework and figure out how to engage them."

He also thinks advancement professionals need to keep their head down and stay out of institutional politics, refine their skills early in their career, and learn how to work through tough problems and challenging situations:

> There are so many fundraisers who want to quit when times get tough. There are always jobs, so when faced with a tough environment and lousy boss, rather than learning from the experience, development officers sometimes run from the problem. Advancement professionals need to toughen up a bit and learn better coping skills.

May doesn't suggest staying in a bad environment that becomes untenable, but he believes that learning how to work through problems and deal with difficult people is an important skill necessary to being successful.

May also believes development professionals need to learn the big picture of a college or university and not just view it through the lens of a small unit. Learning the big picture, taking a broader perspective, and understanding that you are part of a bigger organization adds to an advancement professional's growth and development.

May counsels new professionals to put salary on the bottom of the list when considering early career choices. "It should be the last factor in a new professional's decision," he says, and he suggests it is more important to focus on *who* you work for. For May, finding a boss who will serve as a mentor and role model and provide constructive feedback is invaluable. It is important to learn by doing, and perhaps even more important, to be open to feedback. He explains,

> The good thing about generation Y is that they are always asking me for feedback. They want my job tomorrow, but they also want to know what they could do to be better. You learn by doing and, therefore, you cannot be afraid to receive feedback. That's how you get better and improve your skills. The people who don't grow are the ones who don't look for feedback on how to improve.

At Michigan, May frequently asks the question, How do we make our organization better while addressing the talent shortage of competent fundraisers? The answer is never simple, but he deployed one of his senior managers to tackle it, which led to the creation of a highly successful internship program, which has gained national attention:

We just love the internship program. Do I think it's the answer? Not entirely, but if we can get other institutions to develop similar programs, then we can all start hiring from a reliable pool of well-prepared and well-trained interns from campuses throughout the country.

But May believes the profession needs to do a better job of exposing more students to philanthropy in general. "We wrestle with how to do more with students in the next campaign. We already engage them in traditional ways by featuring them in front of people, having them speak in front of donors, and sitting them at table next to donors at events," he says. "But I think we need to get students participating more in the fundraising process, in addition to the phone-a-thon." He argues that organizations need to leverage social media in a more creative way, which may be one way to engage future generations. But the real opportunities start in the classroom:

I think we can train students earlier and expose them more often to philanthropy. Every year I visit three classes in three different colleges at Michigan where they have a place in their learning plans for undergraduate students to learn about fundraising. One class is for graduate students. When I talk, I have kids come up to me afterwards and say, "How did you get into this business?" There is a sense among the students that they're really interested in what fundraisers do. So I think we have to inspire our students more to want to go into the fundraising business. I think we have to give them a real taste of it through experiences with donors, volunteers, and in the classroom. I think if we get to them in their early twenties, we can educate them and perhaps show them how we work. I don't necessarily mean like a doctor, where they follow you around, but I think they need to be exposed and see what it takes to be successful, and as we know, it's not always glamorous. It takes hard work. It's about building meaningful relationships but it's also about developing a strategic plan and holding yourself accountable.

10

Sarah R. Pearson: The Creative Strategist

I T IS NO SECRET that the advancement industry attracts professionals with diverse backgrounds. Some have degrees in the humanities, and others in the hard sciences. A few have master's and professional degrees (like MBAs), and even fewer have matriculated through doctorate programs. Development professionals come from industries such as marketing, communications, and public relations, but just as many have worked as journalists, business professionals, teachers, and professors. Although it is slowly shifting, there has never been a specific degree or academic program necessary for entry into advancement and fundraising. Furthermore, there is no clear path within advancement that leads to the chief advancement officer position. Many, if not most, chief advancement officers have experience in development, but today more and more rise through the ranks of advancement administration, alumni relations, marketing, and even government relations.

Sarah R. Pearson's path to the chief advancement officer position was, in a sense, both traditional and nontraditional. She describes her entry into the profession as "rather unusual." But since most people identify with a nontraditional entry into the profession, her path is certainly not unique. A theater major as both an undergraduate (Bates College) and graduate (Brandeis University), Pearson moved to New York in the late 1970s to pursue an acting career. Like many young artists, she did not find the struggle of life in the theater rewarding or productive. It was a difficult period, especially in light of the recession sweeping across the country. In an effort to earn an income, Pearson worked for AT&T alongside over one thousand other artists, writers, and performers on the Department of Justice antitrust lawsuit against AT&T. It was her first experience in business and led to her first supervisory position. To supplement her income, she also did part-time bookkeeping for a small Wall Street firm. She was fascinated by the business environment and embraced the variety of experiences the work provided. However, in the early 1980s, she returned to Cambridge for personal reasons, which led to an entirely new career. As she recalls, after she had applied for a few jobs in Cambridge,

> Harvard offered me the position of gift processing supervisor in the university development office, and my advancement career was underway. My path is somewhat unique in that I learned development from the operations side: gift acceptance, record keeping, data entry, acknowledgement processes, steward-ship, and how these processes supported and enabled the fundraising teams across the university. I had no previous knowledge of the profession, but I found the work fascinating. And what good fortune to learn under strong manage-ment. Tom Reardon was the director of university development; the team also included Dick and Bill Boardman, Joe Donovan, John Hanselman—and so many others. It was a great team and an eye-opening experience for me. I was asked to reshape the gift processing function into a more modern configura-tion. What was most motivating to me was the planning I observed. My team was housed close to Joe Donovan's group, and in the hallway between our two offices was a massive planning calendar. I walked by it daily and observed the blueprint for what a fundraising program and strategic plan looked like.

During this period at Harvard, the institution was undertaking a $250 million campaign. Pearson's advancement team designed a prospect manage-ment tracking system. It was a phenomenal opportunity for Pearson to learn the basics of what successful fundraising entailed, while improving opera-tional systems and processes. She acknowledges, "I just don't think I could have been luckier than to have had the chance to work behind the scenes and learn from an incredibly gifted leadership team." At Harvard, Pearson observed two important organizational nuances. The first was the joy and fun the leadership team demonstrated as they worked with staff to develop campaign strategy. And the second was the generosity exhibited by Tom and other senior managers as they invested in young professionals. Pearson de-scribes it this way:

> I had no experience in this field. Tom brought me in, gave me tremendous sup-port, and invested in my learning process. As a result of his mentorship, I got the start that I needed and believed I could make a contribution to the field. I am still in contact with Tom today. It was really an impactful experience.

Over time, Pearson felt she needed to expand her portfolio and gain front-line fundraising experience. In 1988, a fundraising position opened at the

American Repertory Theatre, a unit of Harvard, and she applied. "Robert Brustein was the artistic director. He was a risk taker and an interesting leader to learn from," she remembers. "He was incredibly dedicated to his staff. I worked at the ART for eight years, progressing to the position of director of development. I learned the business of development in a small-shop setting from a generalist perspective." Managing a team of three, Pearson had an opportunity to work in annual giving, corporate and foundation giving, special events, and government grants. The ART launched a small endowment campaign, and she learned the art of soliciting major gifts, stewarding donors, and building lasting relationships with individuals and families. As she recalls, "We were tiny as a team but incredibly committed to the theater within the greater context of the university. The combination of learning with a large central shop to a very tiny front-line operation was invaluable to me." This variety of fundraising experiences was just what she needed to boost her career.

It was a formative period. Pearson worked for a total of ten years at Harvard before transitioning to a new role at Boston University. She learned the basics of advancement at Harvard, but credits Boston University with teaching her an important professional lesson. "I went to Boston University for two years and took charge of their fundraising team at the Huntington Theatre. Unfortunately, I was not in lockstep with the leadership of the theater company," she laments. "It created a personal dilemma. It was the one time in my career where I felt like I should not be the lead fundraiser or the person out in front representing the theater company. There was something missing in my ability to proactively support the leadership, so I discussed the situation with the leadership and submitted my resignation."

Pearson worked for another year in the Boston arts scene but worried she was being professionally pigeon-holed as a performing arts fundraiser. So in the early 1990s, she began searching for a different type of higher education fundraising role, eventually landing at Cornell University in Ithaca, New York. "I was introduced to the Cornell development team by a very dear friend of mine from Bates College who was already working in development at Cornell. It turned out to be a huge turning point in my career. It was only a five-year period, but I would say it shaped my career and set me on the path to meeting my potential as a leader."

She first worked as the director of development for the College of Human Ecology, "a real underdog situation," she explains. But as Pearson reflects, professionally challenging situations often sharpen skills in profound ways that steady and predictable situations don't:

> The college had one of the smaller goals in the campaign, a small prospect pool, and a fifty-two-member alumnae campaign committee. It was an all-alumnae campaign committee at Cornell—this during a period when women's

philanthropy was emerging as an important national issue. I worked for Dean Francille Firebaugh, who was the only female dean at Cornell. She had a major impact on my career; to this day her photo remains in my office. Francille was a truly gifted leader: strong willed and tough, but was also very caring for the college and for her team. She was a master at working within the larger university community and making things happen for her under-resourced, under-endowed college. She had incredible integrity and compassion. As a leader, she constantly encouraged me to make improvements. If we succeeded at an event on any given evening, the next morning Francille would say, "Yes that was great, but how are we going to do it better next year?" Even though I worked with Dean Firebaugh for only two years, she had an impact on my career and my development as a focused, strategic, and caring manager and leader.

Pearson acknowledges she left her development position in Human Ecology a bit too quickly. But she was drawn to Cornell's central fundraising unit for the opportunity to work with development managers from a macro-perspective. A self-described annual fund junkie, she took on the role of director of the Cornell Fund and managed a staff of twenty-five people responsible for raising unrestricted gifts from undergraduate alumni. Her team raised over $15 million annually, providing central services to undergraduate schools and units through the strategic application of mail, phone, and personal solicitation programs. She also managed one of the most successful alumni reunion programs in the country. But perhaps most importantly, Pearson was part of a team of advancement leaders, developing campaign strategy and program plans that would impact the success of the organization. She says, "It was at Cornell that I finally got involved with big-picture strategy development."

When Pearson arrived, Cornell was preparing to go public with a $1.25 billion fundraising campaign, a lofty goal at the time (and even today for most institutions). She recalls a team of colleagues who were energized, creative, and "holistically focused" on success. As a newcomer and one of the few people hired from outside the university community, she was surrounded by colleagues who had worked for Cornell for many years, all sharing a deep passion for the university and the community. "The drive that they all shared to move the dial forward during the campaign was remarkable. The creativity they brought to the table was astonishing," she says. "We were encouraged to be activists and to find the best way to build up existing programs while creating new programs that would move Cornell forward." She credits two development leaders, Inge Reichenbach and Dave Dunlop, for having a significant influence on this period of her career. She states,

> Inge is a great strategist; she's a futurist. With Inge, the conversation always focused on where we should be in three years, or where we should be in five years. She would ask questions about trends, best practices, and what we needed to be

prepared for as trends emerged or gained momentum. She was an enormous influence on me because she helped me shift my focus from day-to-day to bigger-picture strategy. Inge was also a master at hiring talented managers and then setting them loose. The entire team was energized, creative; always seeking out possible future trends and opportunities. We were motivated and inspired, and we all felt the sky was the limit. It was an empowering environment that fostered productivity and success. Also, as I mentioned, Dave Dunlop was leading us with his relationship-building philosophy. Dave, as we all know, is one of the gurus of relationship-based fundraising. He was a generous mentor—always there to help us understand the importance of building nurturing, lifelong relationships; always putting the donor first.

Pearson describes her five years at Cornell as transformational. As happens with many successful professionals, however, personal circumstances intervened (her husband Don wished to live in a more urban setting), and Pearson moved to Chicago where she accepted the position of senior director of major gifts at the University of Chicago. Recruited by Dennis Barden, who served on the development leadership team at the time, Pearson worked her way up to the position of associate vice president for development. She reported to Randy Holgate, who served as another key role model. For seven years, she used her knowledge and experience gained from her time at Cornell to plan and help launch a $2 billion campaign. "I had an opportunity to exercise my strategic planning chops while working with Randy. Randy led development at the University of Chicago for over twenty years. Her commitment to the university was really unmatched," Pearson remembers. "Randy understood it all so well—the politics, the complexities, the people, and the players. She taught me what it meant to be a super citizen of the university and the community." Pearson says Holgate was a patient, flexible mentor who maintained a balanced approach to fundraising. "I would often rattle the cage about preparing for and resourcing the campaign. Randy was more deliberate and understood the campus's big-picture issues as they related to resources and financial pressures. She kept things in perspective for me." Most importantly, Holgate taught Pearson the true meaning of "super citizenry" and the significance of understanding the various pressures faced by the administration within a complex environment.

Pearson's work at the University of Chicago laid the foundation she needed to assume the role of chief advancement officer, a natural next step at this point in her career. Northwestern University was a neighboring institution and in 2002 was searching for a vice president. In and of itself, the position presented an attractive opportunity; however, it was the chance to work for the institution's visionary president, Henry Bienen, that sealed the deal. Pearson describes President Bienen as both a futurist and an opportunist who inspired Northwestern to aspire to new heights. As she reflects,

"Northwestern took some of its greatest leaps forward under Henry's leadership." When Pearson arrived on campus, Northwestern had recently finished a $1.5 billion fundraising campaign. As the campaign concluded, programs needed to be re-engineered and existing talent redeployed. "We had some very talented managers, but we also needed to get the right people sitting in the right chairs. We also needed to capitalize on senior team synergies and creative dynamics." Pearson brought the Alumni Relations team back under the umbrella of a larger and combined development unit. She also attracted talented new managers to her team, while building a culture of support and encouragement among existing staff. "Our goal was to create an environment where our staff believed that they had our full support to take on big challenges and aspire to best practices." It was an opportunity for Pearson to utilize her expertise and strengths, while capitalizing on the skills of her colleagues at Northwestern. She drew expertise from all areas of her background, including development operations from her time at Harvard, annual fund and strategic planning from Cornell, and organizational and campaign planning from Chicago. She was the right fit at the right time, successfully serving eight years as Northwestern's chief advancement officer.

As with many top positions, there is a time to move on, and Pearson's time came in early 2011. After fifteen years in the Chicago area, she was hired as the chief development officer for the Broad Institute at MIT and Harvard.

Pearson contends that leaders are typically visionary, strategic, and future-focused—qualities she observed in leaders she had the good fortune to work alongside. She says,

> There is certainly a strategy theme that impacted my formative professional years and eventual rise to leadership. At Harvard, I observed how strategy played out on charts, maps, and planning calendars. At Cornell, I learned strategy from a practical perspective, and I learned how to be a futurist. At Chicago, I exercised these skills daily while planning and preparing for a campaign. And at Northwestern, I took everything I learned to a whole new level and tried to develop best practices.

Pearson recognizes that true rewards await leaders who aspire to excellence, take occasional risks, and push themselves to new heights professionally, which is what she has tried to do time and time again throughout her career.

Perspectives on Leadership

Pearson describes leadership as the ability to set forth a vision for the future that encourages positive change and outcomes. Moreover, she thinks it is the ability to inspire and empower others to achieve at the highest levels of an organization. It is a leader's responsibility to motivate and inspire employees to be the very best they can be. An inspired team of employees typically turns in a high performance, bringing to life a vision of desired organizational outcomes.

Leadership versus Management

In defining leadership within the context of management, Pearson gets more specific. In addition to *vision, inspiration,* and *motivation,* she uses terms like *risk taker, mentor, super citizen, role model, great communicator,* and *confidence* to describe high-performing leaders. She also thinks effective leaders must be willing to take a bullet for the organization. "In moments of crisis, if and when things go awry, a great leader is willing to step up and take the hit for any team member."

Management, however, is much different. Pearson describes it as more task oriented, involving things like planning, directing, problem solving, delegating, stabilizing, pushing teams to meet goals, and tracking resources. Pearson argues that not all talented managers are talented leaders. But she does acknowledge that the lines between management and leadership are often blurred. Great leaders know when they need to manage or delegate important management duties. As some of our other chief advancement officers have stated, there is not always a clear delineation between the two concepts.

Leadership Competencies Necessary for Success

Pearson believes advancement leaders need to be nimble and to think in terms of change within the profession. "This is a field that is constantly moving and evolving," she says. "We're all dealing with the day-to-day stuff, but you also strive to be a visionary and keep your mind on the future." From Pearson's perspective, today's chief advancement officers need to better define the model of advancement for the twenty-first century and then consider leadership competencies that are important for that model. What will future advancement programs look like? How will they operate? And how do we ensure new generations of leaders receive adequate coaching to meet the future needs and demands of the profession?

In this respect, it will be more important than ever to draw on a deep domain of knowledge. Pearson says advancement leaders will likely rise more frequently through advancement positions and will need to know everything there is to know about the field. She also thinks motivation, on multiple levels, will continue to be critical:

> Chief advancement officers must be able to motivate and empower staff to do their very best. In addition, they must also be able to motivate campus colleagues,

who may or may not fully comprehend the advancement program—including budget officers, student-life colleagues, and communications professionals. And most important, the CAO must be particularly strong at building relationships with and motivating trustees, volunteers and donors, and their families.

Because nearly everyone involved with universities has a stake in advancement's success, motivating campus partners is crucial. In some ways, it's about influencing through motivation. And to be successful, chief advancement officers must be highly skilled communicators. Pearson laments, "I've seen people who motivate but don't really communicate well. That can work at times, but when I think about the real advancement superstars, they are highly effective communicators."

Another important competency to Pearson is optimism. "Great advancement leaders are endlessly optimistic. I'm not sure how you can work in this profession without being optimistic." She also believes honesty and integrity are essential—along with a thick skin and an unwavering commitment to the team. "Chief advancement officers have to be tough because ultimately they are responsible for the department. The CAO must stand tall and not be afraid to face criticism," she says. Finally, Pearson thinks great leaders must be good at building bridges, generous in spirit, and caring. Advancement work is ultimately about generosity of spirit and caring for an organization's constituents, including those who donate both their time and money to support the institution. Enjoying people—learning about them, listening to them, caring for them—is integral to any leader's ability to be successful. All of this makes it possible to help connect donor passion with institutional needs.

Leadership Competencies Most Difficult to Carry Out

The last few years have presented once-in-a-lifetime financial pressures for many institutions, including Northwestern. And as Pearson contends, it has been difficult for chief advancement officers to stay in "bridge-building" or "super-citizen" mode. "Units across the entire campus have all kinds of needs. Alumni Relations and Development is ultimately a service unit. You have to keep your doors and windows wide open and listen to everyone's needs and priorities. However, as the CAO, you know that you can't do everything and you can't deliver for everyone. This is challenging." She thinks that the chief advancement officer must maintain focus on the higher-level mission of the institution and the vision of the president, which can result in tension across campus. Under all these pressures, Pearson tries to stay positive. "An adversarial approach undermines the effectiveness of being a service-oriented unit. When we are all under pressure to raise money, hit our goals, and get cash in the door, it can be taxing to maintain the super-citizen exterior."

Who, other than the Chief Advancement Officer, Is Responsible for Leading Advancement Organizations?

Pearson contends that the chief advancement officer is not the only person who can effect change and demonstrate leadership in an organization. She points to her senior cabinet of associate vice presidents as exemplary leaders. For example, at Northwestern one of her direct reports managed fifteen fundraising teams at one time. "She had enormous pressure to both lead and manage the fundraising process. She was responsible to help propel these teams forward and unleash their talent. Her leadership and management skills had to stay very high in order to meet goals."

But Pearson thinks leadership can also manifest itself in a staff at every level. For example, those who manage and direct multi-unit projects have the ability to influence cross-functional team members in an effort to achieve broad organizational outcomes. People who are successful at getting programs to work and moving people toward shared goals and outcomes demonstrate all kinds of leadership in various ways. She says, "These are people throughout the organization who know how to influence people and take the program to the next level. And as they do that, they are influencing, motivating, and getting people excited to be successful as a team. I don't think leadership in this form has to come from a senior management chair alone."

Pearson notes that Northwestern's president, provost, and deans demonstrated tremendous leadership to the department and influenced the advancement effort:

> At Northwestern, we were always very careful to make sure that the president came to a full departmental meeting to inspire our advancement teams at the beginning of each year. We would also invite the provost and deans. It's a complex research university, and there are many people who interact with external constituents such as academic unit directors, the director of athletics, coaches, and others who demonstrate leadership in their own ways. This year, the "Thank You" campaign to annual fund donors began with a video clip that featured Pat Fitzgerald, Northwestern's head football coach, because he embodies what Northwestern is all about. To me, that's leadership. I think there are many leaders within a complex setting who can help influence outcomes that really optimize advancement.

What Competencies Make You an Effective Leader?

At this stage in her career, Pearson's deep knowledge of advancement contributes to her mastery of the profession and ability to develop a strategic roadmap for success. She describes herself as a super motivator and cheerleader. She thinks her staff would describe her as present and in the moment, invested in their future, a strong mentor, and clear and forthright. Over the years she has tempered some aspects of her style. "I am much more patient now," she reflects. "I am willing to say and deliver challenging messages in appropriate ways if I think it will help the operation and the university move forward. This often takes a patient approach to seeing through outcomes and objectives." She has been described as energetic, enthusiastic, and willing to do whatever it takes to get the job done. As an example, she offers the following story:

> Last October during reunion weekend at Northwestern, we had a tailgate party with over 1,500 people. We had a huge circus tent, and it had been raining for three days straight. No floor had been laid down so it turned into muddy pit. I have never seen such deep mud! But there was no other venue for the gathering, so we had to coax 1,500 people to come into this tent. I decided to get right in there and help lay down catering tables as flooring. It was quite a sight—trying to help alumni navigate the mess and have a great time while doing so. And though we were wet and muddy, it was a fabulous reunion celebration. I remember some of the younger staff looking at me like I was crazy, asking me why I was willing to struggle in the mud, and I explained this is what I love. If I'm going to ask my staff to work through the mess, then I'm going to do it too—and I'm going to make it fun. I think that's one way to express leadership: through action. And I believe it really motivates staff.

A testament to her ability to strategize and inspire, one of Pearson's direct reports described her as laser focused on priorities, articulating clear expectations and a vision related to specific goals from year to year. Pearson was also described as an "amazing teacher" who fosters an environment of continual self-improvement and overall improvement as a team:

> Sarah inspires her team about the value of their work through her own commitment to the cause. She's energetic and has an intelligent approach to the work she does. Her team knows she has their back at all times, which allows them to feel safe to discuss challenges. She also brings an intelligent sense of humor to the work.

Another direct report said this:

> Pearson possesses and exhibits excellent business and management skills. She encourages open and honest communication, empowerment, and a belief in professional behavior. Like most successful leaders, she has excellent oral and written communication skills.

Leadership Development and the Future of Advancement Leaders

Pearson is both a creative and strategic leader. Her educational background in theater and lengthy tenure working in the arts strengthened her innate creative drive. But her experience working in both advancement operations and front-line fundraising provided her with a solid foundation of skills and abilities for strategy development and implementation. Her unique pedigree has helped her be successful as both a manager and leader.

From a professional development perspective, Pearson focuses on continual improvement through a commitment to lifelong learning. "I think I can always learn more about best practices, understanding donor motivation and behavior, and learning more about how we can be the very best fundraisers possible." One way she learns is by observing other successful leaders:

> I like to study other leaders, especially vice presidents and presidents. I'm fortunate to be on the board of trustees at Bates College. This for me has been a huge learning experience. While it is a small liberal arts college setting, it provides me with the chance to observe high-performing leadership. Working alongside Elaine Hansen, the former president and a spectacular leader for Bates, helped me learn so much. She has a very special style and approach to leading a community. For me to come over into an environment where the financial dynamic and strains and stresses of a smaller institution are different meant that I could utilize this environment to continue to think about leadership challenges and opportunities. Observing different leaders in different environments helps me become a much better leader.

Existing Professional Development Programs for
Chief Advancement Officers

Like many chief advancement officers, Pearson credits CASE with offering a full spectrum of professional development and training conferences for early- to mid-career professionals. There are also a few programs on leadership and management for higher-level leaders. But the need for a meaningful leadership training and development program within the profession is an issue the CASE Philanthropy Commission discusses frequently. Pearson laments, "I don't think we have all of the programs that we need. We are trying to address it within the Philanthropy Commission. That is, what can we do as a profession to ensure we are preparing the next generation of advancement leaders?" Pearson notes that the majority of leadership development and training is home grown, through campus-specific programs. She says Northwestern has a leadership training program, as do many other campuses. Northwestern's program is very high level and intense, and is carried out over the course of a year. Each vice president nominates up to two candidates for the program. These candidates, if accepted, are asked to commit a number of days of work over the year to participate. "We found it very valuable for team managers," says Pearson. She also finds formal and informal peer networking groups valuable for sharing best practices and comparing notes. "Staff need to be encouraged to undertake ongoing self-assessment as well as have constructive, open dialogue with senior partners—these are key to building strengths as a leader," Pearson says. "We need to be fearless in seeking regular feedback so that personal potential can be developed."

The Future of Leadership Development and Training

Looking to the future, Pearson believes rigorous self-assessment, reflection, and a continual focus on learning are important keys to success for the next generation of advancement leaders. She states,

> There were periods in my career where I couldn't read enough about management and leadership. When I came to Northwestern, our senior management team participated in meaningful discussions about leadership and management. We read management books and took skill and strengths tests and talked regularly about the distinctions between leadership and management. I'm not sure I know of a program that instructs or helps us assess clearly what the differences are between management and leadership and how managers assess themselves appropriately.

But Pearson also believes leadership development and training programs need to focus more on refining communication skills:

> We don't do enough training in that area. I am lucky that I was trained in the theater arts. It's second nature to me to stand at a podium and think about ways to motivate an audience. I would say that most of our managers are not well trained in strategic communications. But if they want to be effective leaders, they have to learn this skill.

Challenges Facing Chief Advancement Officers

Pearson outlines a theme that seems pervasive among chief advancement officers: demands and expectations are continually escalating. She points to the ever-increasing appetite for higher fundraising results as one such pressure point. But as the profession evolves and becomes more sophisticated, other issues arise, such as the increased global reach of institutions. "Our leaders, including presidents, provosts, and deans, are continually trying to move higher education forward within a very challenging operating climate and environment," Pearson says. "They spend a tremendous amount of time thinking about financing higher education." Understanding these issues and supporting leaders as they deal with complexities present fascinating challenges. Pearson thinks the current higher education environment is as complex as it has been in many years. As a result, the chief advancement officer must work harder than ever to inspire and motivate staff, alumni, students, parents, volunteers, and donors in an effort to help the institution meet its full potential.

There is also the issue of the changing landscape of philanthropy itself. Pearson suggests that the appetite for campaigns will not subside. However, the donors themselves, their motivations, and how they think about philanthropy may change. Part of this change will be generational. "Motivations may remain the same—the desire to do good, give back, have an impact—but the way in which gifts are made is shifting; the expectations of our younger alumni and donors are heightened." These generational issues will influence how we shape our own activity and how we build relationships that last. Finally, growing and developing talent to address these challenges will be important. Like most chief advancement officers, Pearson recognizes this as a pressing issue that needs to be dealt with.

For the long term, Pearson says that public and government scrutiny will continue to persist, which could lead to increased reporting and compliance requirements for advancement organizations. Within this context, long-term financial models, including philanthropic models, for higher education in general will continue to evolve. "Financing higher education from the spectrum of the role of government to student tuition will be a major issue." And as more students study abroad and work abroad, global philanthropic strategies will need to be incorporated into business plans. Finally, transformational gifts, like those donated by Bill Gates and Warren Buffet to their own foundations, may cause advancement units to rethink their approach to fundraising. Pearson asks, "If some of the bigger foundations begin to add to their endowments by raising money for themselves, how will that change the landscape of how we approach our work?"

Positive Aspects of Serving as a Chief Advancement Officer

Pearson is most passionate about what she refers to as "seeing the future every day." She loves being around students and working with faculty to solve immediate problems that will have a positive impact on younger generations for years to come. But most importantly, she says,

> I love what higher education is about. It's my primary passion. Working with people who want to do good in the world. Working with donors and alumni who love their institutions, who want to uphold their values and work with people who have the capacity to give back philanthropically, that is where all of the joy comes from for me. I enjoy leading a team, but it is really the relationships with students, alumni, parents, friends, volunteers, and donors that inspire me to do as much as I can.

Preparation for Newcomers and Future Leaders in Advancement

Pearson thinks newcomers in the profession need to be self-reflective to the point where they can accurately assess their own strengths and weaknesses. They need to learn the higher education industry from A to Z and to have a deep understanding of the institution they serve. For professionals aspiring to become future chief advancement officers, she suggests studying current leaders and the competencies that make them effective, high performing, and successful. "You learn the most from observing a role model, working closely with a mentor, or partnering with an inspirational leader. I tried to learn everything I could from observing presidents as they worked with institutional boards. I also learned from trustees who were leaders in many fields." Pearson says she focused first on understanding her strengths and weaknesses, identifying the traits and characteristics of successful leaders she worked closely with, and then incorporating these whenever possible into her own work-life routines.

But beyond this, Pearson acknowledges that the industry needs to invest more in leadership preparation programs. "First of all, if you are leading a team of any shape or size and you identify others who have leadership potential, I think you have to personally invest in them," she says. "You have to encourage, mentor, and guide them, make sure they take courses, stay up on their readings, and encourage self-assessment. On the most basic of levels, we have to do that." She also considers it her responsibility to identify people with leadership potential and help them get to the next level professionally by guiding them through more and more complex situations where they get to exercise new skills. She recounts the following example to illustrate this point:

> I worked with a young manager at Northwestern who was head of our annual giving program. When Morty Schapiro arrived as our new president, our department was tasked with inaugural weekend, as well as all the coordination of introductory events around the country. This manager has unusual leadership skills, so I put her in charge of the inauguration planning. The inaugural committee was composed of faculty, deans, graduate students, undergraduate students, police, event managers, and many others. It was one of the most complicated cross-university teams we had assembled, and it was a wonderful opportunity to put her in a situation to lead a large, cross-functional team. It brought out her leadership skills and gave her incredible exposure. I believe chief advancement officers should be brave enough to give opportunities to potential leaders in the organization. They should provide experiences for promising staff to manage and lead within complicated situations and settings where they are challenged to work across different disciplines and functions.

Pearson also thinks current advancement leaders should encourage the next generation of leaders to travel to other institutions and observe their high-performing leaders. They should be supported to proactively seek out opportunities to participate in conferences. "Every time I am with a group of colleagues at another institution or at a conference, I learn." But Pearson laments that one of the biggest challenges for up-and-coming advancement leaders is finding time for leadership development within a busy environment with little time for reflection and thought. "We are so busy and consumed with our day-to-day challenges that we tend to focus our people on managing rather than leading," she says, adding, "We all have people with leadership potential, but we tend to say, 'Hurry, hurry, do this, and do that,' and the quiet time required to be really reflective is lacking." Pearson believes it is important for future advancement leaders to find a balance and to focus on strengths as they continue to develop vision for leadership. "We must commit to helping potential leaders and encourage them to expand their skills in various contexts. We have to be bold in our actions to ensure we are really pushing existing talent where it needs to go."

11

Carolyn A. Pelzel: An Entrepreneurial Advancement Leader

T O BE A SUCCESSFUL FUNDRAISER requires a certain level of comfort operating within an ambiguous and entrepreneurial environment, which often involves risk and uncertainty. Risks include those that are professional in nature, requiring careful steps in navigating one's career, but also organizational risks, such as strategically managing resource investments (i.e., costs) against anticipated fundraising outcomes. The academic budget cycle resets annually, and dollars raised start from zero. For schools accustomed to raising millions of dollars each year, it can be a daunting task to keep the pipeline of major gift donations fully primed on an ongoing basis.

Carolyn A. Pelzel is an advancement leader accustomed to taking risks. On the surface, her path to serving as a chief advancement officer followed what appears to be a mostly traditional route. However, a closer look reveals a professional who leveraged her strengths by assuming somewhat risky, yet strategic, career opportunities with significant reward potential.

An alumna of Trinity College in Hartford, Connecticut, Pelzel fully embraced a liberal arts undergraduate education. She focused less on her future career options than she did on her immediate interests, majoring in philosophy of religion and French language and literature as an undergraduate. Pelzel was a model student with an interest in attending graduate school, but she lacked supportive counseling from both Trinity College and her family. She also struggled financially, which made an advanced degree seem out of reach. It was a period of self-reflection and uncertainty. She considered law school, but decided to first experiment with a law career by working in the legal department of Etna Business Credit, located in Hartford, where she remained after graduation. As she recalls, "Clearly because of my training in philosophy I was attracted to the law and wanted to sample it. It really did light a fire, and I got very excited about the profession." She adds, "Not the type of business law I was doing, but law in general." The experience prompted Pelzel to chart a plan toward law school, but with student loans hanging over her head, she focused on earning an income instead. Her goal shifted to debt reduction, with law school to come later. However, her path did not exactly go as planned because Northfield Mount Hermon School, her secondary school alma mater, had other ideas.

Northfield Mount Hermon School, located in Northfield, Massachusetts, is a private boarding and day school. Today, it enrolls over six hundred coed students and boasts a low faculty-student ratio of 1:7. Graduates of Northfield attend some of the most prestigious institutions in the country, and are known for their high achievement. As Pelzel considered her options, Northfield reached out to her, explaining that they were looking for someone to develop their alumni relations program while simultaneously working in student recruitment. "I didn't know much about either of those areas," she remembers. "But I felt a great debt of gratitude to the school because I went on a very heavy scholarship. I thought it would be a wonderful opportunity to give back to an institution that gave so much to me, while earning an income so that I could pay off my student loans and go to law school." She accepted the position and promptly moved to western Massachusetts, where her advancement training began. She states,

> I loved the aspects of the academic community, and then one opportunity after the other was presented to me. After just one year, the school launched a capital campaign and the director of development came to me and said he wanted to hire a couple of young alumni to work on the campaign and asked if I knew anyone who would be interested. I told him *I* was interested, and he was excited to hear me say that. So I joined him on the campaign, which was probably the best training imaginable. It was literally boot camp. I went through this experience not only with the director of development but also with a consultant who became my mentor, a man named Burr Gibson, who for many years was chairman of Marts and Lundy. Burr trained me in the discipline of fundraising and in the art of philanthropy. I started to learn about the power of philanthropy and philanthropy as a form of leadership and became very engaged in the whole subject matter. Then the director of development left to become head of a school, and I was left to take on the campaign. I hired a team to lead the campaign to its finish, at which point I began to think about how to shape the program to raise a lot more money. So I presented the plan to the president and board of trustees, and as part of the plan, I ended up becoming the school's new director of development. Shortly thereafter, a couple years later, we had a change in leadership, and

I was asked to be the director of external affairs and take on alumni relations, development, and communications. By that time, I was hooked.

Through her early experiences at Northfield, Pelzel discovered an innate passion for education and a keen sense and love of business. It was this marriage of education and business coupled with the opportunity to meet extraordinary people across the full spectrum of life and professions that motivated her. But it was also the opportunity to work within an intellectual environment full of educational and learning opportunities. As she recalls, "I would meet with a business person one day, a lawyer another, a doctor the next, and so on. It was always different and always interesting, so the thought of law school was eventually dropped." Northfield provided Pelzel with a strong advancement foundation, and she remained there in progressively more responsible positions for over five years. Giving back in the form of professional service to her secondary school was fulfilling. However, Northfield eventually started to feel very small, and Pelzel sensed it was time to explore new opportunities.

In 1980, Pelzel was approached by the National Association of Independent Schools (NAIS) about an opening. They were seeking a field representative for their member schools and needed someone to work with school heads, trustees, and development officers to help them create their own school-based development programs. The combination of responsibilities was attractive, so she accepted the position and held it for three years. Pelzel traveled extensively, providing fundraising advice and support services to membership schools while also managing annual data-gathering and reporting programs for the association. As part of her portfolio, she installed a new information system for NAIS. "I was comfortable with technology, so after a couple of years the president of the association decided that it was time to computerize the organization and asked me to facilitate the process," she recalls. "We operated in the quill-pen era, so we hired a firm called the Williamson Group to come in and upgrade our technology." Pelzel was fascinated with the project and intellectually curious about the role of technology in education, both from an academic and an administrative perspective, making the job a great fit.

Pelzel's competence and professionalism were on display as she facilitated the technology project for NAIS, making an indelible impression on the Williamson Group. What she did not know at the time was that the founder of the Williamson Group was looking to hire someone to manage the company's daily operations, and he recognized the potential in Pelzel. Around this same time, she continued to contemplate graduate school. Although law school was off the table, her interest in business and success with project management convinced her she needed formal business training to take full advantage of future career opportunities. She describes it this way:

> I actually went to visit the Tuck School of Business. I was really interested in Tuck and found out there were very few people who attended Tuck who were interested in the not-for-profit sector. The admissions director said they really wanted me to come and that I would be good for diversity, but to be candid, she said, there were not many people interested in taking business school skills back into the not-for-profit sector.

Pelzel was at a fork in the road. The Williamson Group offered her a senior-level management position, but business school pulled on her academic interests and sensibilities. In the end, she decided to accept the position of executive vice president of the Williamson Group rather than apply to business school, closing the door on an advanced degree.

Pelzel says that her position at the Williamson Group taught her more about business than she could have ever learned in business school. As executive vice president, she led management, marketing, sales, and product development initiatives for the company, which offered fundraising and administrative computing systems for schools, colleges, museums, and hospitals. She refers to her experience at the Williamson Group as another "boot camp" learning opportunity. "It was a small, entrepreneurial venture. I don't know if it was the right decision, but I learned everything I could about running a business from the ground up." She learned what it took to be an entrepreneur and the interesting dynamics of assisting a small business through survival and growth. She describes the experience like this:

> I really learned about business. I worked for a man who shunned most management techniques, listened well to the needs of his customers, and was brilliant in producing user-friendly products. He dressed in cut-off blue jeans every day, as did everybody else in the firm. They didn't believe in policies or practices, or even meetings. At the end of each day, he would buy a six-pack of beer or two and a bag of Doritos and would yell down the hall to have everybody come sit in his office. They would walk in and sit on the floor and that's when they would talk about the company, its growth, our products, and where we were going. It struck me as disorganized. It is interesting because this method worked to the extent he was developing some pretty good products, but it didn't work because the company didn't have a business plan. There were some other competitors on the horizon, one of whom was eating our lunch. In my position, it seemed like every approach I took was hitting a dead end, and I was really frustrated. But I started reading some management books, looking for inspiration. I read one by Peter Drucker, and there was a kernel of wisdom in it that turned on a very bright bulb in my head that has

been a guiding light for my entire career since. It talked about the importance of being effective rather than being right.

This small bit of advice helped Pelzel navigate an entrepreneurial operating environment. In the early months, she projected a sense of what was right versus what was wrong, and most of the firm rejected her view of "right." As she read Drucker's book, passages about effective communication with supervisors resonated with her. For instance, does your boss like to talk quickly in passing, or does he or she prefer to have more meaningful, one-on-one conversations? Does your boss like to be involved in the germ of an idea, or does he or she like to be presented with a fairly well-developed concept for review and comment? Pelzel says, "After reading the book, I went out and bought a six-pack of beer, a bottle of wine, and a bag of Doritos and went into Jim's office, sat on the floor, and we talked. All of a sudden, the things that I knew needed to change started to change." It was a big lesson in leadership for Pelzel. She learned that leadership can come from any direction, or in this case, any location. It can come from behind a desk, in a hallway, or even from the floor. But most importantly, it starts with having a vision and the desire to be effective rather than right. Being or thinking you are the smartest person in the room is not as important as contributing. Once Pelzel got her head around these concepts, she did some great work for the Williamson Group. She discovered that by communicating in a way that fit her boss's style, she could help her ideas and concepts take hold and gain traction. It was not the ideas themselves that were the problem, it was how she presented them. Pelzel began focusing more on the process of communication rather than on the substance of the ideas, which resulted in more successful and effective outcomes.

Pelzel's experience at the Williamson Group was enlightening and educational, but she missed the learning environment of academia. "At the end of the day, it was really about selling computers and selling software," she laments. "Unfortunately, both the founder of the company and I were far more interested in technology and how it could be applied more effectively than anything else." The job at the Williamson Group had been a risky career move indeed. But Pelzel had a knack for the application of technology in educational resource development. For six years she served educational institutions externally as a consultant and through the delivery of technology application systems, while sharpening her project management skills internally. She developed a unique set of management skills that prepared her for the next chapter of her professional life.

Pelzel knew it was time for another change. She had worked at the Williamson Group for nearly six years when Harvard University presented her with a new challenge. "I got a call from a close colleague at Harvard, and he talked to me about a significant project to upgrade the computer system for the school's fundraising and alumni relations units," she recounts. "He said the project was over budget and late, and that he needed to hire someone who knows both fundraising and technology." There may not have been a person better equipped for the job than Pelzel. Up until this point, her career had been grounded in both front-line fundraising and the application of technology systems to increase fundraising results, so this was a unique opportunity for her. She was interested in getting reacquainted with educational philanthropy, and after flirting with the position, she accepted. "I joined the university in the central development office and took on not only the computer project but some other management problems as well," she says. "It took four years to get everything where I thought it needed to be and pass it on to others, and that's what I did." She managed a staff of sixty with an operating budget of $1.3 million and a capital budget of $7.5 million and installed a new computer system to manage data for the university's 370,000 constituents. It was a high-profile project attached to a large budget, and its success did not go unnoticed.

Around the time Pelzel completed the project, Harvard president Derek Bok expressed concern that the "poorer" schools at Harvard were not receiving enough fundraising attention. The schools of Design, Divinity, Education, Government, and Public Health lacked wealthy alumni. Rather than making futile attempts at soliciting alumni constituents who were proud graduates but had little financial capacity, President Bok determined those schools needed a fundraising strategy focused on wealthy, non-alumni who were attracted to their missions. At the time, it was an entrepreneurial approach to solving a very real fundraising problem. Pelzel was fascinated by the project and highly impressed with President Bok. Eventually, the director of university advancement asked her to take on the project, and she gladly accepted. She describes it this way:

> It was in effect trying to create a start-up within an established development organization. We did research and identified billionaires who had a passion for education, and we made cold calls. From that whole experience, I learned how hard it is to do something new and entrepreneurial in a very established environment. It is hard to connect Silicon Valley with a big established company, like Harvard, and that was kind of what I was doing. And I was doing it at a pretty young age in my career. It gave me access to the president of the institution and to the highest level of volunteers, but it also stimulated jealousies throughout the development organization. At the time, I didn't know how to manage my own career in that kind of environment. I ended up learning an entirely new set of lessons about professional risk-taking and the resulting consequences. You really have to understand and be aware about your own tolerance for risk-taking.

I have a pretty high tolerance, so I was willing to do it, but it wasn't without consequences related to jealousies and other tough interpersonal conflicts.

All challenges aside, Pelzel's experience at Harvard was career changing. She was given big projects and assignments and afforded the opportunity to participate in launching Harvard's university-wide fundraising campaign. As she puts it, "I was given the freedom to try different things, and I loved it." After eleven years at Harvard, however, she came to realize that her knowledge, skills, and abilities were refined and developed enough that she was ready for a leadership position. Her colleagues also noticed, and while Pelzel was attending an Ivy Plus development conference in the mid-1980s, she was approached by Dartmouth College regarding their senior development position, which was currently vacant. "I always told my husband that if I ever left Harvard, I wanted to move south to a warmer climate, so when I shared with him that I had some interest in this position at Dartmouth, he declared that my sense of geography was pathetic." It was an intriguing scenario for Pelzel, and it presented a wonderful career opportunity. Reporting to the vice president of development and alumni relations, she would oversee the entire development operation and build the framework for a future campaign. She accepted Dartmouth's offer and assumed her new role in January 1997.

Shortly thereafter, Dartmouth's president decided it was time to launch a campaign and put more resources into development. As a result, the president split the alumni relations and development functions into two units and promoted Pelzel into the position of vice president for development, a position she held for nine years. In June 2010, a new president arrived and asked Pelzel to take on all external functions, including alumni relations, development, communications, and management of the board of trustees. She willingly agreed and was promoted again to the position of senior vice president for advancement. "The irony is that I am doing the same job today that I was doing when I first started at Northfield Mount Hermon School. I really haven't progressed in my career very far at all!"

Pelzel says she is grounded by a keen sense of self-awareness and understanding of what it means to be a leader, shaped largely by her experiences and influences over the years. As she has matured, both personally and professionally, she has become motivated less by position, status, and title and more by making a difference in society and contributing to her organization. She describes three keys to leadership she has learned over the years, the first being staying focused on the impact you have on your environment and on society. "If you're primarily concerned with your standing, your influence, your stature, and what tables you're sitting at, I think it impedes your ability to lead," she contends. "People follow individuals who are passionate about making a difference. That is the first thing I would say about leading." Second, Pelzel thinks it's important to differentiate between work and family. At work, the primary goal of a leader is to maintain loyalty to an institution and the mission of an enterprise. It is essential to treat everyone with respect, but in a way that does not project or confuse work and family life as one. To avoid this, Pelzel says leaders should execute their mission effectively and draw a psychological line between their organization and their interpersonal relationships with colleagues. "In my own mind, it was an essential separation. You can and should mentor others, but your first responsibility must be to the enterprise. Along the way, effective leaders must make very tough decisions." Finally, the third key to leadership is understanding how it differs from management. Pelzel believes you cannot lead without managing, but you can manage without leading. Leadership involves inspiring people to reach far beyond what they .think is possible. "It relates to self-esteem. It's really about Maslow's hierarchy of needs. Touching people and giving them a sense of self-actualization is an art form that I think is critical to good leadership."

Perspectives on Leadership

Defining leadership, Pelzel says it involves harnessing human resources and generating momentum toward a higher goal. She thinks it involves a vision for the future and deciding where an organization needs to go. It is about seeing opportunities and having the courage to lead an organization toward something unknown that does not exist. Leadership requires visualizing opportunities and taking a leap of faith to embrace them. In contrast, she believes management is more about understanding resources and aligning them with institutional goals. Good managers identify strengths and weaknesses throughout an organization and develop systems and processes to leverage strengths while improving weaknesses. This involves stretching existing but often limited resources.

Leadership Competencies Necessary for Success

For Pelzel, successful leaders possess a keen interest in and desire for continuously learning. "Lifelong learning is important, not just about the advancement profession, but about the entire enterprise and senior leaders who work side by side with you." She also emphasizes the importance of flexibility and having a tolerance for ambiguity, something reinforced during her early experiences at the Williamson Group. "This relates to the idea I stated earlier about how it's more important to be effective rather than right." Pelzel describes the phenomenon like this:

I often see advancement professionals who project expertise in the work they do. They'll go in and meet with a new dean and have the urge to tell the dean how it should be done, not realizing that the most important thing is to go in and understand who that dean is, what they are good at, and what motivates and excites them. Our job is to motivate, not to tell people what to do. There has to be a willingness to adjust the means to get to the end goal. You have to have laser-like focus on your goals and then be flexible about how you get there. It takes courage because very often your team is going to want formulas; they are going to want clear paths and structure, and your job is to teach people how to be flexible and how to deal with ambiguity. It's often important not to be afraid to put yourself in a vulnerable situation and tailor your approach to the specific audience to be more effective. You have to be interested in what makes people tick. I don't think you need to be super gregarious. I have found that a lot of successful chief advancement officers are often INTJs [introversion, intuition, thinking, judgment types] on the Meyers-Briggs type indicator, which I think is interesting. It is the opposite of what you would think. The ability to ask strategic questions and be in inquiry mode all of the time is important. I think a lot of times leaders feel like they must be in charge when sitting at the conference table. They feel like they have to know everything. I think it's quite the opposite. I think effective leaders are those who ask all of the questions and are willing to put themselves in a position that shows they don't necessarily know the answer.

This is consistent with Pelzel's belief that it is important to be a critical thinker rather than have deep domain knowledge. Deep domain knowledge is essential at times, but knowing how to connect the dots and consolidate considerable amounts of information into strategic action is more essential for successful outcomes. "For example, if you don't have deep domain expertise in media relations, you must have excellent critical thinking and inquiry skills so that you can work your way through any problem, whether or not you have the knowledge." Pelzel says effective leaders should be good at dissecting issues, understanding what is important, and then making connections across the organization in a way that informs the decision-making process. Conversely, leaders can hire people who have deep domain expertise.

Pelzel believes leaders should take their work seriously but not take themselves too seriously. Working with high-level constituents, including campus leadership, wealthy donors, powerful volunteers, and elected officials can be stressful. Laughing at yourself helps you keep the responsibilities of a highly stressful chief advancement officer position in perspective.

Leadership Competencies Most Difficult to Carry Out

Most challenges for Pelzel center around human capital and talent management issues. She thinks it is incredibly difficult to make personnel decisions that, on the surface, do not make sense to the rest of the organization. Leaders have access to confidential information and knowledge about situations that simply cannot be shared at times. Withholding information about a specific personnel decision can be difficult. As she acknowledges, "It is possible to be 100 percent truthful to oneself, but one can't always share the truth with the entire organization, which can be tough." This phenomenon leads to a loneliness that is prevalent among most people in top positions. "Who you can or can't talk to about various situations and issues can be difficult," she laments. "As a leader it's important to be very careful about what you say, when you say it, how you say it, and to whom you say it."

Pelzel also says it is difficult to manage people who have grown within an organization from its infancy but who no longer possess the necessary skills to be effective in the larger, more complex, and more sophisticated organization that it has become. The challenge emerges when these people must be let go.

Beyond personnel issues, Pelzel cites a facility in high-level negotiations as one of the more challenging leadership competencies necessary for success. Whether you are dealing with donors, academic leaders, or volunteers, negotiation skills are vital. These skills often come to life when chief advancement officers are negotiating between the goals of the institution and the interests and motivations of donors. When these do not converge, however, it requires a level of savvy in the chief advancement officer to steer the organization away from a potentially negative public relations outcome.

Who, other than the Chief Advancement Officer, Is Responsible for Leading Advancement Organizations?

Pelzel firmly believes that the chief advancement officer is primarily responsible for leading advancement programs on campus. She even thinks colleges and universities often rely on the chief advancement officer to lead the campus's strategic planning process. She says,

> It is difficult for presidents, provosts, and deans to decide which departments get resources and which don't. Many academic leaders have turned to the chief advancement officer to help solve this issue by driving the strategic planning process. But it's a responsibility many people think should not be within the purview of a chief advancement officer. I think it makes our jobs a lot more interesting, but it often makes it more complex.

What Competencies Make You an Effective Leader?

Pelzel says she tries to work harder than everyone else, and never asks anyone on her staff to do something she would not do. She says others have described her as committed, fair, direct, forthright, trusting, and a good communicator with focus and a sense of direction. A current direct report said, regarding Pelzel's competencies, that leaders of advancement

> must understand the vision of their institution and advancement's role in achieving that institutional vision. They must be excellent strategic thinkers to create an advancement organization that is single-minded in all its individual goals of alumni relations, communications, and development, while at the same time collaborative in order to find those critical points of intersection and integration toward a greater accomplishment. And they must be tremendous communicators in order to lead senior administrators, academics, trustees, and staff toward that greater accomplishment. Carrie has all of the above, and she also has an amazing ability to ignore the minutia when the bigger vision or strategy is most critical while also paying close attention to the significant details that drive success. She consistently leads toward the priorities, always aware of what they are for herself and communicating priorities for her organization. This clarity is tremendously effective and provides the basis for a culture of accountability and achievement.

Pelzel says she tries to keep a distance between herself and her staff, which is sometimes perceived as a negative. She laments, "I think people would like me to be closer to them personally, more involved in their lives and more engaged with them in a social context. But I find it hard to engage more socially with my staff without seeing the potential downside." There is a cost to increased social interaction that, she says, would decrease her leadership effectiveness. Pelzel's loyalties are first and foremost to her institution as a whole and its overarching mission.

Leadership Development and the Future of Advancement Leaders

Professionally, Carrie Pelzel has entered a stage of career refinement. She has served as chief advancement officer at one of America's most prestigious institutions for a decade and has a deep understanding of the advancement profession. She is a competent leader who projects a sense of wisdom and astuteness. But she is also curious and a self-described lifelong learner. She recognizes that even though she has served as a chief advancement officer for many years, there is always more to learn. For her own professional development, Pelzel says she needs to carve out more time for thinking, reading, and strategy development. The intellectual components of her job are so important, yet they often get squeezed and pushed aside. However, she knows that hiring outstanding people and developing systems to hold them accountable in a productive manner allows her to reflect and focus on aspects of her job where she can make the most impact.

Existing Professional Development Programs for Chief Advancement Officers

Pelzel acknowledges there is a lack of existing leadership training and development programs for chief advancement officers, and those that do exist are not particularly effective. But she points to an aptitude testing program offered by the Johnson O'Connor Research Foundation as enlightening. The basic premise of the foundation and its testing service, which is based on comprehensive research conducted in the 1920s, is that people are happiest in their work-life when they draw upon their strongest aptitudes. Pelzel believes this kind of assessment would be useful for all current and future chief advancement officers. She describes her experience like this:

> I went to the Johnson O'Connor Research Foundation and participated in a day and a half of interesting and fun testing. They also give you a vocabulary test and an interest test. At the end of the sessions, a counselor sits down with you and discusses the results. They present an outline of your strongest aptitudes and the professions that draw upon those aptitudes. The key to a successful career is figuring out what your strongest aptitudes are, doing your very best to carve out a professional life that draws on those, and then hiring people to off-load work that would draw upon your weakest aptitudes. When I finished the last session, I walked out of there feeling reborn because for the first time in my life I realized that I didn't have to try to be good at everything. I didn't have to be down on myself because I was not good at everything. It was the most liberating experience I have ever had. I think some kind of leadership training associated with discovering our strongest aptitudes is what we should be offering to advancement professionals.

The Future of Leadership Development and Training

According to Pelzel, most professional development programs in advancement focus too heavily on content and process issues. For instance, CASE offers sessions on annual giving, major giving, phone-a-thons, and foundation and corporate relations, among many other topics. These sessions are good for newcomers, but they do not provide the deeper-level learning opportunities needed by seasoned professionals. Pelzel suggests that programs focused on wealth accumulation, wealth management, donor motivations and interests, and the psychology behind major gift donations would be useful. She thinks universities should provide institution-specific classes during the on-boarding process, as well as skill-based and functional training across disciplines. Advancement training can be "myopic and self-centered." In order to understand the advancement and fundraising business, we need to understand what motivates donors to invest their time and resources.

Challenges Facing Chief Advancement Officers

Pelzel sees a future with ever-increasing fundraising goals, crystallized within a higher education environment in which institutions have an insatiable need for more money. As she describes it, colleges and universities do not always make the necessary tough choices in the short run and end up adopting highly ineffective business practices along the way. She explains it this way:

> Our business model says, produce a world-class product, figure out the cost of it, discount it by 50 percent, and then set that as its price. Then for some people, discount it even more because you want to make sure they can actually take advantage of the product. So for 40 to 50 percent of its customers, institutions discount it again, and then you beg donors for money to make up the difference. Any way you look at it, it's a strange business model.

Peering into the future, Pelzel believes universities must evolve more aggressively with technology, especially as it relates to social media. "I feel everyday as though I am in this bubble, and there is a whole other world that has evolved around me," she says. "We are not connecting with that other world and transforming our business to fully exist productively and effectively in that world where our students exist." Within the context of advancement, she thinks schools need to be more nimble in how they communicate with alumni and other constituents. "The alumni office is the slowest moving part of advancement, and it is also usually the most under-resourced," she says. Furthermore, adopting the philosophy that if you do a good job of educating students, they'll be so grateful upon graduation that they'll donate later, Pelzel thinks more resources should go directly into the classroom. It's about creating a high-quality product and experience for students as they matriculate in the short run, which can be leveraged for future resources in the long run.

Finally, Pelzel thinks there is a significant culture of resistance toward marketing and sales in higher education. She thinks colleges and universities should implement more-sophisticated strategies around advertising, branding, and communications:

> In the next five to ten years, all of our institutions will need to dedicate more resources to presenting the strengths and distinctions of our institutions. It is happening now at my own institution. My president realized that we have to

invest more in thinking about what shapes the reputation of our institution. We have to bring in the very best people we can to manage the communications function. I think there is going to be quite a change in the kind of professional needed to do our work in the next five to ten years.

Positive Aspects of Serving as a Chief Advancement Officer

Pelzel loves everything about her profession. She loves the diversity of responsibilities, the continuous learning opportunities, the complexity of higher education institutions, and having the ability to apply problem-solving skills to challenges with very high stakes. And since the stakes continue to rise, the job becomes increasingly more interesting to Pelzel. She says,

> Higher education in the U.S. has always been admired worldwide, and we're still doing pretty well, but I think it could change within the next ten years. There could be quite a shakeup in U.S. higher education, meaning schools that are currently ranked in the top 10 might drop to the top 20 or 30, and other schools could move up. I also think we're going to see much greater competition from outside the U.S. The knowledge economy is highly competitive, which means some higher education institutions will be at risk.

Outside of the increasing pressures of the job, which seem to motivate Pelzel, she is constantly inspired by the volunteers, trustees, and donors who find meaning through their generosity. "What they do for students, education, and for the advancement of knowledge is truly inspirational."

Preparation for Newcomers and Future Leaders in Advancement

Newcomers should take great care in choosing their career path, Pelzel says. The work of advancement, especially development, requires a significant commitment of time and energy, and, therefore, one should consider the ramifications that come along with it. "This is a profession where you have to be at a lot of events, you have to be involved, and you have to be visible. It is often a seven-day-per-week job," she says. "One must be prepared for it to be a life, not a job." Pelzel also believes new professionals should get comfortable with managing across the organization (i.e., sideways management) and learning how to manage big expectations with little authority. An advancement professional's responsibilities can be ambiguous and unclear at times. Jobs are not always straight forward and well defined. Likewise, development professionals should be comfortable around money. "There are people who get into advancement work because they like people," she says. "But if you're going to be in this field, you have to be very comfortable with the fact that our job is to raise the maximum dollars possible for the priorities set forth by the administration. You have to be comfortable with money, both on the institutional side and talking about money with donors and other people."

To prepare for an advancement career, Pelzel urges professionals to consider business school. Advancement organizations have become so complex and so focused on business practices, including marketing, sales, communication, finance, and organizational development, that an MBA has become the must-have degree moving forward. Learning these skills on the job, as previous generations of advancement professionals did, is no longer sufficient. And regardless of education, skills like negotiation, management, presentation, and communication should be continuously refined and sharpened as they are absolutely critical for success in the advancement industry.

12

Martin Shell: The Optimist

I N SOME WAYS, MARTIN SHELL'S CAREER PATH is similar to those of the other chief advancement officers profiled in this book. He never set out to have a career in advancement but instead planned to be a journalist. A philosophy major, Shell attended a small liberal arts school, Hendrix College, in Conway, Arkansas, receiving his bachelor's degree in 1980. During school and for a year after graduation, he worked as a reporter for a local daily newspaper, the *Log Cabin Democrat*, where he covered political and government beats. He was building a solid foundation for what he thought would be a career in communications. In 1981, U.S. Representative Ed Bethune tapped Shell to become his press secretary in Washington, DC, where for two years Shell managed communications between the congressman and the national and state media. It is a familiar story indeed. Shell was a young, talented professional going down what appeared to be a successful career path in communications, unaware of what the future truly held.

In Shell's early years, the advancement industry was much less sophisticated than it is today. Some schools had a full complement of development and advancement staff, but there was little promotion of the profession, and the industry was still evolving. Regardless, if anyone was a good fit for the advancement industry, it was Shell. After two years in Washington, he was recruited back to his alma mater, Hendrix College, to serve as its alumni director. Shell's role at Hendrix included as much development and fundraising as it did alumni engagement. He spent half of his time engaging alumni prospects with giving strategies and the other half producing alumni outreach events and activities. This broad portfolio exposed him to many facets of the advancement profession. He truly loved the work and enjoyed the profession, but two years later Shell took a brief detour into the private sector. He accepted a job as assistant to the general manager of a large utility company, but, as he recalls, "I realized quickly it was not for me. I was not able to be myself." Despite this, his timing was impeccable. At Hendrix College, a search was underway for a director to manage their campaign and day-to-day development activities. Shell couldn't escape the lure of returning to his alma mater, so he accepted the position. Unlike his last move, this proved to be one of the best decisions of his career because shortly thereafter, he was promoted to vice president for development and college relations.

Hendrix College is an institution that has produced many leaders in both advancement and higher education circles. As Shell describes it,

> Hendrix College has a long history of good fundraising and seems to attract talented professionals. David Gearhart, who is currently the chancellor of the University of Arkansas, is a former vice president of Hendrix. Rock Jones later succeeded me at Hendrix, and he has moved on to be the president of Ohio Wesleyan University. I've also had a nice career since my time at Hendrix. It was a great place to have done advancement work.

Once he left Hendrix, Shell moved around with some frequency, joking that it's "harder to hit a moving target." But he also knew he couldn't stay in Arkansas. "My wife is also from Arkansas, and we eventually decided it was time to see a different part of the world. So I took a job as campaign director at Villanova University." In 1990 when Shell accepted the position, Villanova was in the planning stages of a campaign. It was a great learning experience for Shell. The position allowed Shell to work closely with counsel, develop strategies, and build the framework for a campus-wide fundraising campaign. Shortly thereafter, he was promoted to the position of associate vice president of development, where he managed the entire development operation, including the campaign. "In hindsight, it probably would have been better to remain in the campaign role for a while longer," he posits. "As associate vice president, I ended up doing a lot of managing. All of the major gift staff reported to me, which took up a lot of my time." Villanova is a much larger institution than Hendrix. It has multiple schools, academic units, and programs. It gave Shell the opportunity to work with deans in business, law, nursing, and engineering, as well as the arts and sciences.

After two years at Villanova, Shell decided it was time for a change. He'd always gravitated toward leadership roles, and this time was no different. Shell assumed the position of vice president of institutional advancement at the Pennsylvania College of Podiatric Medicine, which later merged with Temple University. There he was responsible for planning and implementing a college-wide fundraising campaign and overseeing public relations, marketing, communications, and government relations. He stayed long enough to get the program off the ground, but in 1995 he moved on to become assistant dean for development and alumni relations at the University of Pennsylvania Law School, serving as its chief advancement officer.

Penn Law was just concluding a successful capital campaign and laying the groundwork for a number of new initiatives. Shell was instrumental in providing key support to the dean during the development of the school's strategic plan. He also cochaired a university-wide task force charged with establishing guidelines and performance standards for major gift officers across the entire campus. The position allowed Shell to draw from his vast experience as a communications professional, fundraiser, and manager.

However, despite his success, Shell was still relatively young. He decided he wanted a new challenge to further his professional development. This time, Shell headed west. Stanford's law school was searching for a position in line with what Shell held at Penn. As one of the nation's top law schools, Stanford Law School has high standards when it comes to hiring, and Shell's experience was a perfect match. So in 1998, he headed west to assume the position of associate dean of external relations overseeing all advancement functions, including development, alumni relations, communications, and marketing. Two years later he became the law school's senior associate dean for external relations and chief operating officer, expanding his portfolio beyond advancement to include admissions, career services, facilities, financial aid, budgeting and finance, human resources, information systems, registrar, and student affairs. It was a big role with significant responsibilities as he managed a staff of over 150 and a budget of $35 million. Describing the promotion, Shell says, "To this day, I'm not sure I'm a great manager. I had not spent a lot of time in management training. I moved into that position to manage operations and help put some oversight in place, but I'm not sure it was the best fit for me. At the same time, it was an incredible opportunity and I learned a great deal about all facets of the academy."

After Shell's nearly four years of service at the law school, his competence as an administrator and leader was noticed across campus. His dynamic personality combined with broad development, management, and operational experience was attractive to the central development office. In addition, his experience at Stanford included working with significant principal gift prospects. The central office was in need of someone of Shell's caliber to both manage development staff and carry a portfolio of top prospects. So in 2003, he assumed the position of associate vice president of development, in which he provided direct and indirect management of central-office and school-based major gift staff, as well as the offices of campaign planning,

annual giving, planned giving, development operations, foundation relations, corporate relations, communications, marketing, finance, and human
resources. It was a large role indeed, but Shell was up to the challenge. As
typical throughout his career, just two years later he was promoted to vice
president of development, reporting directly to the university's president
and overseeing hundreds of millions of fundraising revenue each year. Reflecting on his time at Stanford, Shell says,

> Frankly, one of the reasons for leaving the law school for the central develop-
> ment office was that I was doing some major gift fundraising, working with
> some very high-end donors. Concurrently, I increasingly spent my time manag-
> ing staff and operations, making sure that the IT systems didn't blow up and fac-
> ulty members were getting what they needed, and helping with the admissions
> process or something in student affairs. I became concerned that if I was going
> to stay in the advancement profession, then I needed to refocus more fully on
> advancement work, not law school operations. That would mean staying more
> involved and engaged with managing prospects and donor activities. The central
> development office position allowed me to remain focused in advancement but
> also leverage my operational and management skills.

Shell believes there are certain skills and qualities that have made him an
effective leader, which include his ability to listen and his high emotional
intelligence. He expounds,

> In particular, I attribute my listening skills to my experience as a newspaper
> reporter. It was important to listen and decipher between the things people re-
> ally said and the things that they didn't say. I had to read between the lines. I
> have shared this story a lot with colleagues. I remember years ago when I was
> in the newspaper business covering a venue with a U.S. Senator who was giving
> a speech at a local event. I knew a lot of the people who attended the speech,
> and I remember chatting with some of them after the event. They were so
> overwhelmed by how great the speech was, noting that the Senator's talk was
> so moving and inspiring. I certainly experienced what they were describing, but
> when I went back to the newsroom that night and distilled the speech, I realized
> that its substance was pretty thin. It was one of those Ah-ha! moments. I real-
> ized that you have to listen on different levels. Many people were listening on an
> emotional level that night. The Senator was clearly using rhetoric and a style of
> speech to move people, which is an important leadership component and may
> have been intentional on his part. But what I took away from that experience is
> this: What you say and how you say it, and what people hear and how they hear
> it, are critically important to how you influence people.

Shell says he has made it a priority to develop a good set of listening skills
throughout his career. More important is his ability to listen with empathy.

"I try to understand what people say directly, but especially the things they say indirectly." Shell's sense of empathy helps him relate well to his staff and display a sense of caring and compassion. It allows him to connect on an emotional level, which in turn stimulates loyalty and productivity.

But perhaps most importantly, Shell has relied on what he refers to as "a healthy sense of optimism" throughout his career. He believes nearly everyone who ascends to the chief advancement officer position must be overly optimistic, especially in an environment in which widespread obstacles, challenges, and roadblocks are present. "I believe one must be positive and have a can-do attitude to be successful in our business." For example, he says,

> I was in a meeting this morning with the executive cabinet of the university. The meeting included the president, provost, deans, vice provosts, and other administrators. I jokingly told them I have decided to give myself the title of director of optimism, particularly after the last two and a half years when things have not been nearly as rosy as they have been in the past. I don't think you can be truly successful in this business, and certainly successful as a leader of a team, if there is not an optimistic bent to who you are and how you view the world. On most days, I am a pretty optimistic person.

Shell credits his career success to the people who have blazed a trail and laid the foundation before him, especially those who have served as his mentors. "I have been exceptionally fortunate to have worked with a great group of people who have directly or indirectly mentored me," he says. Furthermore, he has gained strength and confidence by observing leaders who have demonstrated success throughout his career. He seeks to embrace their positive attributes and style. For instance, his early years as a reporter at the small daily newspaper in Arkansas were highly influential. The newspaper's owner, Frank E. Robins III, ran the family-owned paper for years and made an impact on Shell. "I started working there when I was in high school, and there were a lot of things that I learned from Frank," Shell recalls. "There are a lot of things about business practices, operating procedures, and other professional nuances that I embraced from him. I still use many of those skills today." But Frank Robins was not Shell's only mentor. "I would say I've had mentors every step of the way. Oftentimes it has been the boss, but not always." At Stanford, Shell credits volunteers, trustees, faculty, senior university leadership, and other constituents engaged in the development process as particularly influential:

> I have learned an immense amount of knowledge from this group of individuals. When I was named vice president, in my first meeting with the development committee of the board of trustees, I jokingly said to them, "I'm not sure I've had an original thought in my life."

Shell's selflessness and deprecating humor is not only endearing to trustees and volunteers—it also creates a sense of approachableness among staff and subordinates. It stimulates a culture of collaboration and promotes innovation from the ground up. Shell eliminates the fear of failure by remaining open to feedback and new ideas, which directly relates to his lasting sense of optimism.

Perspectives on Leadership

Shell thinks leadership is a blend of administration and inspiration. It is the ability to inspire and motivate direct reports, as well as non-direct reports, which is important in higher education. As Shell describes it, "Sitting down with a group of volunteers to discuss a plan or idea and accomplishing a desired end result requires a lot of influence." With direct reports, a command often works, but one cannot command constituents in other units. They require influence and persuasion to accomplish goals and objectives.

Leadership versus Management

For Shell, management is more of an internal process. As he describes it, you can be the most effective and persuasive speaker in the world and have wonderful fundraising instincts, but without an ability to "make the trains run on time" and "ensure others are making the trains run on time," your credibility and effectiveness suffer. He believes management is more about the "nuts and bolts" of running the organization. It is a more rudimentary and direct process carried out by middle and senior managers.

On the other hand, leadership has more of an inspirational feel to it. Shell describes it this way: "In our line of work, we don't sell widgets. We are asking people to invest in our institutions, the faculty, staff, and students who populate them, and the ideas and innovations that result." Therefore, to be an effective leader and deliver a compelling message for support requires a high degree of inspiration, motivation, and vision, according to Shell. As discussed earlier, it also requires a dose of optimism, which is important for encouraging subordinates and staff to remain positive.

Leadership Competencies Necessary for Success

Number one on Shell's list of competencies important for leadership success is knowledge. It is not necessarily general knowledge but rather specific knowledge of an institution and how to run advancement units within that institution. Shell believes it is critical to understand institutional culture and the intangible flare that makes one institution different from another. In addition, effective leaders must be able to "walk the talk." Chief advancement officers must know how to work with donors and prospects, engage them in conversations about giving, and close major gifts. "At Stanford, the last three chief advancement officers have been expected to be intimately involved in the donor cultivation process," Shell says. Shell has lived in every aspect of advancement, from alumni relations and development to communications and advancement operations. He thinks having a broad perspective is important when leading from the top.

From a more traditional view, and consistent with most of our advancement leaders, Shell says oral and written communication skills are equally important:

> In our line of work, you present yourself to a very well-educated population, whether it is speaking to the faculty senate or meeting with a group of alumni. At Stanford, we produce a very bright, highly motivated, and sophisticated alumni, parent, and donor constituency. Being able to communicate effectively verbally and in a cogently written form is very important.

Shell further contends that chief advancement officers should understand the nuances of accepting a gift and the administrative process involved. While this appears more management related, Shell argues that knowing how to deal with gift acceptance issues can help smooth over donor relations problems as they arise. Donors should have confidence in a leader's ability to know and understand the gift administration process, especially with principal gifts. Shell says,

> In hindsight, the law school job was really important for my professional development, but I didn't see it that way at the time. I gained a better understanding of advancement operations in general and how it relates to the overall operation of the school. For example, I also gained a better understanding of admissions and how our alumni feel when their kids are going through the exceptionally competitive application process. It is an emotional experience for them. Having lived in that area professionally allows me to empathize and communicate with alumni in more meaningful ways.

As with most successful leaders, recruiting and retaining the very best and brightest talent is important to Shell. However, recruited talent also must be given sufficient opportunity to be successful. Shell believes effective leaders should not micromanage or constantly question the decisions of their staff.

Leadership Competencies Most Difficult to Carry Out

Shell contends that the most difficult component of a chief advancement officer's position is the ability to operate within a complex organization—a description that epitomizes higher education—and to successfully juggle a wide spectrum of responsibilities touching nearly every aspect of the institution. It is a balancing act of significant magnitude.

According to Shell, leaders must know when to step back and let their staff carry out their jobs in a way that is effective for them. As he describes it, this is often easier said than done:

> Letting staff accomplish goals in a way that may or may not be your way is still one of the most difficult challenges of what we do as leaders. When I moved into the chief operations role at the law school, I was supposed to make the trains run on time. When I left to come over to the university development office, for the first year and a half I effectively did the same thing. But now, I'm in a different position. I serve as the leader rather than the manager. Particularly for someone who has moved up within an organization, one of the real challenges is to let go of the old things that you did while holding on to the pieces that are still important in your new job. It can be challenging to give new direct reports the ability to do things their way. A good leader must not be so ego-invested to believe their way is the only way.

Shell acknowledges that most leaders who sit in the corner office have a well-cultivated ego. However, he tries to focus his attention on his organization's collective success rather than personal gain. A leader's ability to succeed, he says, is diminished if he or she focuses inward rather than outward. It would be easy to accept praise and commendation for Stanford's success, but Shell resists:

> We raised $911 million dollars in fiscal year 2006, and for the past decade, Stanford has been among the top universities in the nation in fundraising success. I mention this because it underscores something to which we pay attention. The year we raised $911 million dollars, I kept saying, "It takes a village to raise a gift." I had maintained that belief long before 2006, and nothing has dissuaded me of it since. Development is a team sport, and frankly, it is a contact sport. If you are going to be an advancement leader, you have to take a team approach. We have great individual contributors, but by themselves, they cannot achieve the kinds of results we have achieved and continue to achieve as a team. It is a leader's responsibility to remind their staff that the fundraising and advancement profession is a team sport.

Who, other than the Chief Advancement Officer, Is Responsible for Leading Advancement Organizations?

Shell recognizes that the success or failure of Stanford's fundraising outcomes rests largely on his shoulders. But leadership manifests itself throughout the organization as broadly as it does deeply. "It is certainly not solely about me," he says. "The most successful development enterprises have a combination of people actively engaged and collectively working in the same direction toward its success." This, he says, requires strong, engaged, and active academic leadership:

> We have a very intelligent donor population. They lobby and invest in ideas, and they invest in individuals who can make those ideas become reality. They clearly invest in our university leadership. You are asking people to make phenomenal philanthropic contributions, most of whom I know would not do so without supreme confidence in the academic leadership of the institution. Leadership also comes from an engaged faculty. We are fortunate at Stanford to have an entrepreneurial culture that is embedded in the DNA of our faculty. They are critically important leaders for the advancement program.

In addition to academic leaders, Shell underscores the importance of volunteer leadership to the success of advancement and an institution as a whole. "Volunteers help our institution get better," he says. "They help our institutional and academic leadership refine ideas and think strategically. The cochairs of our current campaign care as much about our success as anybody on our campus."

Ultimately, however, Shell is keenly aware it is his responsibility to hire a talented group of staff and lead them toward fulfilling the mission and goals of the development program. And they are all crucial to his success. As he acknowledges, "It may be that the people who process gifts day in and day out do not consider themselves as leaders of an organization, but I think their contributions help ensure we continue to lead as an organization on campus."

What Competencies Make You an Effective Leader?

Shell says his strengths include listening, empathy, leading by example, and communicating effectively. But perhaps most importantly, his effectiveness, he says, comes from maintaining a strong sense of humor. "I had asked our HR team to list having a sense of humor as a requirement for every job posting. We also added that the successful applicant should have an appreciation for irony and the ability to live with ambiguity." Shell describes these competencies as vital components for success and survival in academic institutions, especially the development office.

In a nod to the many constituents contributing to his success, Shell describes his approach to leadership as client-focused. Shell's constituents include, among others, the three senior associate vice presidents and development legal counsel who directly report to him, the president, provost, deans and faculty, prospects and donors, the board of trustees, and the many other volunteers associated with Stanford. Accordingly, he says, "Understanding their motivations and interests and then responding appropriately is important."

Finally, Shell thinks his depth of understanding of advancement and development practices has contributed significantly to his success. He has made a deliberate effort to engage in focused training throughout his career in order to complement his existing experience. For example, he says,

> At Hendrix College, a lot of my time was spent in my car as I traveled the state visiting donors and prospective donors. I often popped in a cassette tape of planned giving lectures and listened to them as I drove from stop to stop. In hindsight, I think it was a very important training technique. Planned giving stuff can be deadly dry and boring. But understanding the difference between a lead trust, charitable remainder trust, and a gift annuity has been very helpful over time. I can sit down with our planned giving team and have a real sense of what they are talking about. Often, I can press them to think of strategies outside the box because I know the language. Understanding the nuances of this business has helped put me in good stead over time.

Shell says his leadership has been described as engaging, proactive, deliberative, and, as he laments, "sometimes too deliberative." One of his direct reports described him as confident without arrogance; as a leader with integrity, credibility, and passion for the mission of the organization; and as inspiring and motivating to colleagues in both small- and large-group settings. This subordinate went on to say,

> It is clear he is the leader in so many settings and situations, and that is a good thing. He takes accountability for the organization and steps up when things below him go poorly. At the same time, he has put other senior leaders in the organization in a position to lead, be visible, and share the responsibility. He is a storyteller and he believes in building rapport, both in one-on-one and group settings. His stories connect him with his audience in a compelling and genuine way. Sometimes his background in politics helps him as he can see every angle of a particular situation and take them all into account before making a decision or taking action.

Another direct report described Shell as a leader who is trustworthy, inspiring, persuasive, visionary, warm, compassionate, and highly intellectual—a relationship-builder with a sense of humor who acts with integrity and a clear and effective communication style. Regarding Shell's leadership style and philosophy, this subordinate said,

> His leadership style is hands-off. He sets a compelling vision for where he wants to go, and he lets you figure out how to get there, but he provides helpful guidance along the way to make the end result even better. He believes in developing talented people on his team, giving stretch assignments, and keeping people challenged and motivated. He pays attention to recognition and rewards and tries to thank people and acknowledge their contributions. He is also willing to take risks and question the status quo. He is not averse to change, but in fact often invites it. He also uses stories effectively to inspire and deliver a strong message. There is a certain charisma that is difficult to describe. There is something about him that builds trust and warmth quickly, and he inspires those around him.

Leadership Development and the Future of Advancement Leaders

As his subordinates accurately depict him, Shell has a magnetic personality that complements his deep understanding of operating complex advancement organizations. He praises his team's success publicly, while managing challenges privately. However, Shell acknowledges it has been difficult to let go of operations. He says he reflects often on his transition from chief development officer to vice president and struggles to resist the temptation of being insular. He explains,

> As you discovered, it was a challenge for us to even get this interview scheduled. In my current role, I don't feel like I do enough management by walking around. When I was COO of the law school, everyone was contained in one building. I wandered the halls with some frequency, and it is amazing what you pick up in the process. I don't do as much of that today. I don't feel that I am as visible, and it is troubling to me. Five times a year we do an all-hands-on-deck meeting, usually within a week or so of a trustees meeting, and the entire development organization from across the campus is invited. Part of what we try to accomplish is to keep people informed of the major decisions by the trustees. It also gives us a chance to communicate and keep people connected. Like many other places, we are a distributed development organization. When you have a few hundred people working in different places across campus, it is harder to maintain a sense of community.

To combat this challenge, Shell instituted a staff survey, which revealed what he had expected: the development staff wanted to hear more from him. Therefore, Shell has since instituted a question-and-answer session at various development meetings. He reinforces the importance of communication and teamwork, and he stresses that development is a very personal business. It is not only personal to donors, but also personal to development staff working with donors and with each other across campus. "I think there is a conundrum in our business," he says. "People expect real high touch, and they often expect it from the top person."

Existing Professional Development Programs for Chief Advancement Officers

Like many of his colleagues, Shell believes the leadership training and professional development environment in advancement has room for improvement. He attends the CASE chief development officer winter meeting on occasion, usually as a faculty member, but gains more from programs outside the profession or those that have sprung up organically across institutions. He says, "Stanford is in the Ivy Plus group, which is made up of the eight Ivy League schools plus Stanford and MIT, which I try to attend each year." Although the program is informal, he says it provides important training and information that he can't get elsewhere.

Beyond external programs, a few years ago Shell invested in and developed an internal training and professional development program for his staff at Stanford. "As long as I've been at Stanford, people have said, 'We've got to put a better training and development program in place,'" he explains. "We had multiple task forces address the issue, and at least three of those reports are probably sitting in my file cabinet as we speak." But Shell decided to take action and hire a full-time professional to manage a newly created Office of Learning and Performance, which provides a full spectrum of course offerings. In addition, Shell launched an effort to train managers of front-line development staff and better define the skill sets that most successful major gift officers possess. This effort not only trains managers to be more effective, but provides strategies for managers to help gift officers increase performance, effectiveness, and, ultimately, job satisfaction.

The Future of Leadership Development and Training

For Shell, there is no easy solution to the need for advancement leadership development and training. From his perch as chief development officer atop one of the most distinguished research institutions in the world, his most pressing need is to develop ways in which development can respond to future institutional needs, which are not always clearly defined. To that end, Shell thinks he needs more time to be thoughtful and strategic. "I am not sure how that might be embodied in a training program, but 'strategic anticipation' is an important aspect of leadership," he says, adding that development officers must maintain the longest horizon of anyone across a university campus. Today's students are tomorrow's prospects and, ultimately, the people who will ensure the long-time viability of our institutions. Strategies and actions implemented by today's leaders will impact their institutions well into the future. Shell wants to know more about trends and expectations lurking around the corner:

> This is an area that I am currently struggling with conceptually. For as long as I have been in this business, the response to calls for improvements to our development organizations has always been to hire more people. I hear people say, "If I had just one more major gift officer, just one more annual giving officer, just three more stewardship people, then I could do a better job. For me, the last two years of this economic downturn have taught me that this response is not effective. The right response is to consider what the future holds and to think more strategically about how we can be more effective. For instance, how can we leverage technology more strategically through social media platforms like Facebook, Twitter, or LinkedIn? How can we maintain high touch with donors during the evolution of these new communication platforms? I cannot envision a day, at least in my career, where high touch will not be the absolute prime mover of engaging people philanthropically in our institutions. However, we still need to consider the impact of social media and other outlets.

Shell thinks the industry needs more programming around organizational efficiencies and advocacy, especially in the current budget-cutting environment. Today's chief advancement officers also need tools to stay current in an age when information can be overwhelming. Sifting through the plethora of data and determining what is most important will be a critical skill for future generations. "A decade ago, the number of voice messages that came in per day was significantly greater," he says. "Voice messages have dropped precipitously but have been replaced three- or four-hundredfold with e-mail and text." Shell says that today's organizations struggle with information overload, causing real challenges among leaders and managers. Training programs that address these kinds of issues could be beneficial and certainly relevant for the future. He posits,

> I don't think that we are ever going to get caught up. Being harried and inundated with various forms of information and requests is the way of the world going forward. As a leader, are there things we can do to refine skills to better

manage and organize information? Likewise, are there ways to convey those
skills to our team members so we don't burn them out?

Challenges Facing Chief Advancement Officers

As the "Great Recession" gives way to a recovering economy, Shell questions
its consequences for the future. "We don't yet know what the long-term effect
will be from the economic reset that began two years ago," he worries. "I felt
like 2010 was one of the toughest years in my career, in part because my own
expectations of success based on prior results were pretty high." Additionally, he points to the considerable time constraints placed on today's chief
advancement officers. "You have a lot of constituents to serve in this role,
including the people who report to you, the people who report beneath them,
faculty, deans, the president, and the donor and volunteer populations. There
are a lot of people who have a piece of you." Working with various constituent groups and being responsive to them has always been a challenge, and will
likely remain so in the future. Moreover, as mentioned above, Shell ponders
the challenges of managing and responding to data and information. "We
have tremendous expectations to immediately turn around requests as they
come in." Shell thinks future leaders must calibrate their own expectations
and manage the expectations of others more effectively. Although fundraising
revenue has held relatively steady, he thinks future donors may make philanthropic decisions differently:

> During the downturn, some of our nearest and dearest donors who have made
> multi-million dollar commitments moved to the sidelines. You could pick up
> the *Wall Street Journal* or the *New York Times* or a number of publications over
> the past year and read about how the affluent were reassessing their priorities
> related to gifts, purchases, and lifestyle. It will be interesting over the next few
> years to see how discerning our donor population becomes. I had a conversation
> with one of our trustees a few months ago and he said, "You know, I think we
> may have moved from an 'and' economy to an 'or' economy." He meant that
> before 2008, people would consider buying this and buying that, making a gift
> here and making a gift there. It was an "and" way of thinking. Today, it is an
> "or" economy. People are considering buying this or buying that, making a gift
> here or making a gift there.

Finally, Shell cites what has become perhaps the most common topic of
discussion among current chief advancement officers: managing talent. He
thinks the recent explosion of not-for-profit organizations and resultant demand for more fundraising professionals has contributed to the talent shortage. It has certainly contributed to significant demand-driven wage inflation.
However, Shell is mostly concerned with identifying quality professionals to

fill current and future vacancies. "How do we continue to make this an attractive job opportunity for good people?" he asks. In addition, the profession has fallen short in making diversity a priority. As Shell points out,

> For the past several years, I've had the privilege of presenting at the CASE Summer Institute at Dartmouth. I was there twenty-five years ago as a student, and now I'm on the faculty. Each year I am taken aback by how few faces of color I see in that room. This is particularly so when you consider how well colleges and universities have done in the last twenty-five years of recruiting a more diverse student population. I don't know what the long-term impact of this will be to our profession, but it is a critical need that should be addressed.

Positive Aspects of Serving as a Chief Advancement Officer

Shell says he cannot imagine a more privileged job. As in most jobs, there are good days and bad, but working in an environment focused on the future is inspiring to Shell. He values his role as it relates to collaborating with faculty on projects and breakthrough research to cure cancer or autism; providing scholarship assistance to undergraduate and graduate students who are among the brightest in the nation and the world; and interacting with volunteers and donors who are interested in investing in the future of our institutions. "If our current students and faculty, and the donors who support them, are the future of this country and world, then I am very optimistic and hopeful about the future," he says. "It is a privilege to be part of the conduit that connects people who have the ability to philanthropically invest with the individuals and ideas of our institutions."

Preparation for Newcomers and Future Leaders in Advancement

Shell restates the critical importance of advancement professionals being knowledgeable about their institution. They must have enough knowledge to articulate the strengths of the institution, understand its organizational structure, and communicate funding priorities effectively. This requires both broad and deep knowledge of academic units and their programs.

Shell also worries that too many functions have become specialized. For example, advancement organizations recently have spent significant resources to hire more donor relations and stewardship professionals. These professionals are vitally important; however, Shell argues that fundraising field staff are often more knowledgeable and better equipped to sit across from donors and articulate how their gifts have been used. "There may be a lot of really strong personnel in the stewardship office who help provide material to field staff for donor visits," he says. "But at some point I worry that if fundraising field staff don't believe it is their job to also be stewardship officers, then we've lost some of our effectiveness." Shell has implemented a strategy at Stanford to push back against this over-specialization popping up in the profession. He encourages staff to move from schools and units to the central office, and vice versa. "I think some movement within the development enterprise is valuable," he argues. "Getting a broad perspective of what it takes to run a successful advancement operation is an important component of one's toolkit."

Shell's most sage advice for new professionals and future leaders is to never stop learning. He encourages staff to consider their weaknesses and identify ways to improve. Newcomers should never stop asking questions and never feel like they know everything they need to know. He expands,

> There is always something else to do in this business. Make yourself available and be the person who your boss goes to because he or she knows you will get it done. Nobody wants to go to the staff member who asks, "Is that in my job description?" or, "If I have to do these projects, what can I stop doing?" Make yourself available and do it in an upbeat, bright, and willing fashion. Make yourself indispensable. There will always be great opportunities for people like that.

Shell argues that advancement professionals at major research institutions should have some familiarity with science, engineering, and technology to be most effective. Reflecting on his career path, Shell underscores how helpful it would have been to have a greater appreciation and knowledge of the biological sciences. "We have two hospitals and a medical school at Stanford. I lived in law schools for a dozen years, and medicine was not part of my expertise."

Finally, he suggests that current and future leaders should be knowledgeable about the international landscape as it relates to higher education and the world economy. International students continue to flock to American postsecondary institutions. A confluence of factors, including increased wealth generation overseas and pressures to generate additional income at domestic colleges and universities, have contributed to the influx of students. As more and more international students attend American institutions, alumni will be spread out all over the world. Shell thinks domestic philanthropy will increase from foreign donors, especially as China, India, and regions throughout the Middle East become wealthier, and as laws change across the globe to encourage more philanthropic support—as is now evident in several European nations.

13

Curtis R. Simic: A Hoosier's Story

H IGHER EDUCATION AND NONPROFIT FUNDRAISERS often demonstrate gypsy-like professional behavior hard to ignore. The labor market is fluid and ever-changing, with job opportunities aplenty. The demand for competent fundraisers has been well documented, and it is not subsiding. Salaries, titles, and expectations have escalated to seemingly unsustainable levels. These are very real concerns for most chief advancement officers trying to build a sustainable and productive organization.

There are two underlying currents influencing movement in the advancement and development profession. One type of advancement professional, namely, the fundraiser, transitions into a new position every eighteen to twenty-four months because he or she has likely landed in the wrong profession. Poor fit leads to poor performance. And the plethora of career opportunities in the marketplace allows these individuals to find new jobs once their current job is no longer working out, resulting in a consistent cycle of turnover. But there is a second cohort of professionals who change positions because they are highly competent and productive. This group is in demand and recruited frequently to positions with significantly larger salaries and portfolios of responsibility. The seductive nature of frequent courting often becomes overwhelming and irresistible.

Curtis R. Simic exemplifies this second group. A highly talented, up-and-coming professional, Simic cut his teeth in the advancement profession in the mid-60s, a period when there was no prescribed advancement career path. Like so many others in the advancement industry, he says he "fell into" the profession, noting development in those days as a profession lacking organization and professionalism. As he describes it,

> I think it would be fair to say that back then, when institutions had people they didn't know quite what to do with, they would say, "Well, this person has a good personality so let's have them work with alumni or volunteers." One thing I saw early on is that development and alumni affairs were sort of bone yards for old coaches and people who were former deans or even former presidents. Institutions really didn't want to lose them, but they didn't have anything specific in mind to give them to do, so they would let them focus on connecting with people. It was almost serendipity that the field began to develop.

Simic entered the profession by happenstance. As a freshman at Indiana University, he participated in the Little 500 bike race run by the Indiana University Student Foundation, and the subject of the Academy Award winning movie *Breaking Away*. He recalls, "I didn't know anything about the IU student foundation, and I was never a bike rider, but I participated nonetheless." This chance experience engaged Simic with the life of the institution and exposed him to higher education philanthropy for the first time. Through many hours of volunteer committee work, he learned everything he could about the Indiana University Foundation and eventually became a member of the Indiana University Student Foundation Board of Directors. He was highly engaged and an increasingly active member, which culminated in his election as student foundation president his senior year. "Back then, the profession grew through mentorship," he says. "There was no formal path for working in development, but I had a strong mentor in my role as president of the IU student foundation."

At the time, Bill Armstrong was president of the IU foundation. He had served as president from 1953 to 1983, and the student foundation fell under the umbrella foundation's purview. Upon Simic's graduation, Armstrong encouraged him to consider a position as director of the IU student foundation. This individual served as the staff liaison to the student foundation, and Simic was a natural fit for the position. He knew little about major gift philanthropy, but he was eager to learn. The exposure and experience he gained from serving on the student foundation board and participating in the annual bike race gave him an immediate advantage over other candidates. The opportunity to engage in philanthropy for the institution as a student had had a profound impact on Simic. Engaging students in this way also helped Indiana University in their fundraising efforts:

> This is so important, and it's one of the places I think the profession falls short. We need to embrace the students while they are on campus and begin to teach

them that philanthropy is an important part of a public university. Private universities work hard on this from the very beginning, but most publics don't. We need to create basic opportunities, like event fundraising, and organize students in a way that gives them a structure to understand philanthropy. The IU foundation has been doing this for years. They structured an opportunity around a bike race that raises money for scholarships for working students. It was a very reasonable concept, and it started in 1950s. Now they have sixty years of experience to draw from. Today, over half of the board of directors of the IU foundation were members of the student foundation or participated in the Little 500. The whole idea was to build awareness around philanthropy, and the simplest way was to do it within the context of scholarships. It worked.

Although Simic initially had plans to be a basketball coach and English teacher (in that order), Armstrong convinced him to accept the position with the IU foundation. Naturally, Simic had early success, and it was only a year or two later that he was asked to assume more responsibilities and take over the annual giving program. He recalls, "In those days, we were mainly doing constituency based fundraising in the annual fund, so I had the law school, school of nursing, and school of dentistry. It was mainly direct mail." He eventually grew the program and recruited alumni to serve as "county chairman" for the law school's annual fund campaign, which evolved into a major giving program.

A loyal employee, Simic made his mark on the Indiana University Foundation. He appreciated his early experiences at the university and wanted nothing more than to help his alma mater be successful. It did not take long for him to fall in love with the profession:

I enjoyed what I was doing. It is very engaging to work with students. They are such great fun and so lively. I was close enough in age to connect with them and really enjoy being around them, but still had a clear understanding of my responsibilities. It was a great fit and a wonderful opportunity.

He goes on to say,

When I retired about two years ago, the students I worked with back in the 1960s got together and wanted to honor me. I told them I was interested in student leadership, so they raised 1.3 million dollars for a scholarship in my name to encourage student leaders.

It was a meaningful period in his life, which laid the foundation for what would become a highly successful career in development and advancement. But after more than six years working with the student foundation and annual fund, Simic decided it was time to move on and develop his skills. In the back of his mind, he knew he would be back.

Development positions can be risky, and one must take proper care in navigating potential job opportunities. Poor leadership, high turnover, and other organizational nuances can severely impact a development professional's success and livelihood. As Simic discovered, it can be difficult to assess an organization's true culture without experiencing it directly. Over the next several years, he made a series of moves that resulted in both personal and professional challenges.

In 1971 Simic was recruited from Indiana to the University of Tennessee to manage the medical campus's fundraising efforts. He was impressed by the institution's leadership, Chancellor Joe Johnson, who later became president of the University of Tennessee system. "To this day, he is one of the greatest people I've ever been around," Simic says. Johnson taught Simic that shortcuts are not an option. Building a quality institution requires a solid foundation and an infrastructure that makes sense. This concept led to the reorganization of the annual fund, which was moved to the alumni association, while major gift fundraising was moved to development. What emerged under Johnson's leadership was a more effective and efficient advancement structure. Simic describes it like this:

> The alumni association was charged to raise annual funds from alumni, which was a sensible thing to do. They developed a strategic plan and followed the four *I*s: Identify who cares or who should care; Inform them of what your aspirations are; Involve them in the life of the institution; and finally, they will Invest. And the *S* of the four *I*s refers to stewardship. The three *I*s are related to the alumni association, whether or not they are raising money. But eventually you begin to see a more formal advancement or external relations model emerge. The linkages became clear, and the institution did a great job of piecing it all together.

At Tennessee, Simic learned the value of fundamentals. He learned the importance of building an advancement program based on a strong foundation consisting of systems and processes that helped increase and sustain fundraising results. Without such a foundation, sustainability becomes threatened.

But Memphis, Tennessee, as a community presented a set of unexpected challenges for Simic. It was a period of high racial tension and civil unrest, and it caused angst for his young family. "I had this little blond-haired, blue-eyed first grader, and the school district wanted to bus her to North Memphis, a poorer area with high crime and other issues," he says. "We were caught in a conundrum. We couldn't afford private school, nor did we believe in private school. We wanted to use public education. But it was an untenable situation for us. So we made a decision to move."

Unfortunately, Simic's next move presented an entirely new set of challenges. But rather than personal, they were professional. Simic left Tennessee for the University of Southern Illinois, Carbondale, to work for a friend and close colleague. He laments, "SIU has a long history fraught with presidents who come and go. It's a highly political environment with a challenging culture." He assumed the position of director of development and worked as an executive to the foundation. But after only a few months, Simic's friend, the president of the university, was undermined by a board member and quickly decided that it was not in his best interest to stay. Simic's former chancellor at the University of Tennessee (Johnson's successor) knew of the situation and contacted Simic about joining him at Yale.

At Yale, Simic learned invaluable lessons about long-term prospect research and the impact it can have on an institution. "Yale's rich history and longstanding traditions provided centuries of data on donors, alumni, and their families," he says. "They knew where the money came from, how it was developed further, and even details about ongoing family dynamics. It was astounding to me because I had never seen such robust data." Simic developed new annual giving strategies at Yale, resulting in significant increases in annual gift fundraising. He considers his time at Yale a success, but was faced with an insurmountable professional challenge. After a short time, he discovered that if you are not a Yale graduate, you are not part of the Yale family. As a result, your credibility among alumni suffers. He acknowledges, "This was now my second bad career move, back to back, but I felt I had no choice but to look for a position at an institution with a better fit." Remaining optimistic, Simic was on the move again.

Undaunted, he connected with a colleague at the University of Alabama. Alabama was aggressively searching for someone to lead their development operation. Simic had ties to some of the administrators there, and his previous experience at Tennessee expanded his knowledge of the South. By this time, Simic was grounded in the fundamentals of higher education fundraising. His breadth of experience in the Midwest, the South, and at Yale made him an attractive fit. So after Simic had made multiple visits, Alabama offered him the job. Simic describes his time at Alabama like this:

> I supervised a staff that worked in constituency fundraising with some development officers reporting directly to deans rather than centrally. It's a common structure all over the country today. Most importantly, my experience at Alabama taught me how to be flexible and live with ambiguity. As you move up the ladder in development, you have to realize that the profession is not black and white. It's probably 10 percent black and 10 percent white, but 80 percent gray. It becomes more about working with people in ways that respect their positions in the organization, and then identifying their role in the whole

process. That is what I experienced at Alabama. It was a great learning opportunity. I learned a lot about minorities and the history of the South. As you
know, the South is where Governor Wallace stood at the school-house door,
on the University of Alabama campus, and defied President Kennedy in letting
black students enroll with white students. I learned a lot about race relations
and how people can get along, if they want to, recognizing that there are divisions that might never be healed.

Among other lessons he learned at Alabama, Simic found himself a white
male trying to penetrate black communities and organizations in support
of the institution. It was challenging back then, and he did not make a lot of
progress. But it did not deter his motivation. "I knew we had to engage those
communities, because our mission included them."

Each stop offered Simic new learning and professional growth experiences.
He credits his success to both the smart moves he made and also the bad ones.
Alabama provided him with the chance to manage a large development staff
in a highly decentralized organization. He learned the nuances of navigating
a major research institution where success hinges on multiple forces, influence, and people. After three years as assistant vice president for development,
Simic felt he was ready for a vice presidency and began exploring opportunities elsewhere. The University of Oregon recognized potential in Simic, and
once again after a series of interviews, he was offered the position of vice
president of university relations.

As vice president for university relations at Oregon, Simic had a broad
portfolio. He managed thirteen departments, including intercollegiate athletics. It was a unique organizational structure; however, as Simic describes it,
athletics did not come without its baggage:

> Anytime you can avoid having athletics report to you, you should. There are just
> too many loose ends, and you never know what's going on. You have to deal
> with six hundred or eight hundred athletes and fifty or more coaches. It's dif-
> ficult to manage and keep your finger on the pulse of what is happening. The di-
> rector of athletics reported to me, and it was a very distracting situation because
> you lose your focus on fundraising. I managed it the best I could. While I was
> there, we got the first big gift from Phil Knight for the university library, which
> is now named for him. It was largely the result of his relationship with the track
> coach and Knight's business partner, Bill Bowerman. It was a great lesson in
> relationship fundraising. Bowerman, who developed the concept for Nike shoes,
> is largely responsible for some of the significant gifts Phil Knight has made to
> the institution. It's related to the idea of engaging students in philanthropy while
> they are students. Knight was the runner, and Bowerman was the coach. They
> formed an incredible bond that grew into a business partnership, and now that
> relationship has had a profound impact on the University of Oregon. Knight has

donated hundreds of millions to the institution, both for athletics and academics. Many people don't realize how much money he has given to academics, but it is a very substantial amount.

Simic spent five years at Oregon before tiring of the state's inadequate support of higher education. "It was sad," he recalls. "State funding and support of higher education was, and still is, exceedingly low." But the breadth of his portfolio there strengthened his confidence as a leader and prepared him for the next phase of his career. Word spread that there was going to be a leadership change at the Indiana University Foundation. "I always had my sights on returning to my alma mater and assuming the foundation's top position, and I thought this might be my chance." Even though Bill Armstrong, the IU foundation's longtime president, announced his retirement, Indiana's president John Ryan told Simic the timing was not right for his return. "He called me, and I thought he was going to ask me to consider the position," Simic remembers. "But Ryan told me that whoever followed Bill Armstrong would have a tough time because the transition would likely last a couple of years." Simic had other options. At the time, he was being courted by the University of California, Berkeley, to serve as their chief advancement officer, and it proved to be a job with upward potential, so he accepted. "It was one of the greatest professional decisions of my career," he says. "I have made some bad decisions, but this was one of the great ones." He describes his time at Berkeley as "fantastic." UC Berkeley was, and still is, a highly decentralized advancement model with a lot of decentralized power. The power resides with the deans, and in fact, as Simic says, he initially turned down the position because of this:

> When I interviewed, I listened to what the deans said. We had a healthy conversation about the current model, but I sensed there would be trouble. After we finished, I called my wife and told her we were not moving to Berkeley because I felt the deans did not want any kind of centralization of fundraising. They wanted to continue doing their own thing. When I returned to Oregon, I withdrew from the search. The next thing I knew, the chancellor called and asked, "Why are you withdrawing?" I told him my sense was that the deans did not want a strong central operation. I told the chancellor that they would never raise big money if they continued down the same path, and that it would take a lot of credibility, strength, and resources to do the job right. After I gave him more specifics on what it would take to be successful, he countered with his support and said he would give me what I needed if I accepted the position. So after further consideration, I accepted the position and moved to Berkeley.

Before Simic's arrival, UC Berkeley raised about $25 million annually. It was mostly low-hanging fruit, with little organization and strategy behind it.

But five years into Simic's tenure, Berkeley crossed the $100 million mark, and today the institution brings in over $300 million annually. Chancellor Mike Heyman has said Simic's influence and impact on Berkeley's fundraising success was profound. However, equally important was the impact Berkeley had on Simic's career. While he was there, Simic says he refined his negotiating skills and learned how to work effectively within a complex operating environment with little control and authority. As vice chancellor for development and president of the foundation, Simic had to build linkages and productive working relationships with units across the entire campus, including the alumni association, the athletics department, and all of the academic schools, centers, and units. Reporting lines did not matter. It was the connections Simic made with faculty, deans, administrators, and staff that made the difference.

Perhaps most importantly, Simic points to his success in building a high-performing staff in support of UC Berkeley's comprehensive campaign. "I think this is the most important aspect of leadership," he says. "A leader's ability to attract and retain great people is crucial to his or her success." He hired people who became known as leaders in the industry, like Kent Dove. Dove's strengths included development operations, processes, and systems. "His organizational skills are unparalleled. I am not as interested in process because my strengths focus on engaging people," Simic says. "On a day-to-day basis, I don't read all of the contact reports and other details like that, but Kent was really good in those areas." Indeed, Dove has authored five books on various aspects of development. Another former Simic colleague is Rhea Turtletaub, who currently serves as vice chancellor of external relations at the University of California, Los Angeles. "We had some amazing team members," Simic recalls. "I think the true measure of a leader's success is recruiting great people. I believe Rhea is one of the most imaginative people in the country today." According to Simic, hiring people who compliment a leader's weaknesses rather than strengths is the key ingredient for leadership success.

Simic's tenure at UC Berkeley ended in 1988. It was a highly successful run and pivotal to Berkeley's future success. But an opportunity to follow his professional goal of returning to his alma mater as its chief fundraiser and foundation president lured him away. In 1988 he was given that opportunity, and he spent the final twenty years of his career at Indiana.

Simic has since received numerous awards for his contributions to the field, including the inaugural CASE Commonfund Institutionally Related Foundation Award for Professional Leadership, the Frank L. Ashmore Award for Service to CASE, and the Distinguished Hoosier Award presented by former Indiana Governor Frank O'Bannon. Furthermore, he recently received the state's highest honor, the Sagamore of the Wabash, from Governor Mitch

Daniels. And on his retirement, Simic was bestowed with Indiana University's highest honor, the University Medal, by President Michael McRobbie and the trustees. Most recently, in July 2010, CASE awarded him its Lifetime Achievement Award.

Beyond all the awards and honors, Simic points to the incredible impact mentors had on his professional development and rise to leadership. He has tried to pay it forward as much as possible:

> It is not just you, as a leader, working with some younger person who is looking for experiences and opportunities. It is about listening to them in terms of what their needs are, and then figuring out how to help them meet their professional goals. But it has to be a two-way street. Rod Kirsch, another colleague at Berkeley currently serving as the senior vice president for development and alumni relations at Penn State, is an example of someone who I had a strong mentoring relationship with. I think people like Rod and Rhea Turtletaub came to Berkeley because they knew they would grow. When Penn State was looking for somebody to fill their top position, the search firm came to me and asked what I thought about Rod. I fully supported Rod for the position and thought he was an excellent candidate. Eventually, Rod got the job. This is where it's a two-way street. You have to be able to attract high performers to your organization, but then you also have to look out for them and help them grow and move on when the time is right. They will come to your organization if they know they will develop and learn, and if you'll support them in their career. If a career move comes along that causes them to go someplace else, that's okay. You have to focus on them as professionals rather than just the institution. Some presidents would shoot me if they knew I was saying this, but it's true. Sometimes you have to go to grow. I want people to think that they can grow with us, and then when it is time for them to branch out, not only will I encourage them, but I will help them.

Reflecting on his own career path, Simic does not think everyone should change positions as frequently as he did. "I wouldn't advise it," he says. "As I said before, I made two false moves that were not particularly good for my career." But his focus was to build a set of credentials that Indiana could not ignore. As he recalls, "I was always thinking about where I would be when the Indiana job opened up." Fortunately for Simic, his timing was impeccable, and his ultimate career goals were achieved.

Perspectives on Leadership

For Simic, leadership is about articulating a vision and helping staff understand where the organization needs to be at a certain point in the future. The path might be long, but it is a leader's responsibility to chart the course. Once a clear vision has been established, Simic believes leaders must have the ability to disaggregate the big picture into more specific objectives and action items. It requires strategic thinking and planning. Once the strategic plan has been developed, Simic argues that it is the leader's responsibility to integrate the plan across the organization so that everyone knows their role in the process. But most importantly, the plan must relate to the vision. He states, "One thing I found at Indiana was that we did not have a strategic plan. So we went to the Kelley Business School and enlisted the best strategic planner they had to help us create one." It was an important process that helped Simic break down the elements of his vision. Eight strategic initiatives were developed that remained in place during Simic's twenty-year tenure. However, the plan was not developed in a vacuum. To encourage ownership, Simic recruited over twenty people throughout the organization to participate in developing the strategic plan. It was a collaborative process that, as he describes it, was equally as important as the end result. "A key piece of leadership is to get others to take ownership of the vision and process and determine what their role is," he says. And it does not stop there. Simic believes effective leaders give credit for successes to others throughout the organization. One way to do this is to allow subordinates the opportunity to participate in meaningful job assignments and gain exposure with multiple constituent groups both internal and external to the organization.

Leadership versus Management

Simic relates management more to systems and processes and leadership more to relationships and people. He also thinks they are inextricably linked; however, for Simic, leadership is about inspiring and motivating people, while management is about directing people. "They are both equally important," he says. "I don't diminish one with the other." He adds that leaders should be self-aware, identify their own strengths and weaknesses, and hire staff members who complement professional areas of weakness. But it all comes back to relationships versus process:

> Leadership can be played out in different ways. Management has a specific set of responsibilities. It might be generating contact reports or analyzing data. It's all important information that I use frequently, but I prefer to lead and let our managers focus on the mechanics.

Leadership Competencies Necessary for Success

Simic has served in senior leadership positions at three major research institutions and understands the various nuances that can make or break chief advancement officers. He believes they must first understand the mission of the organization and then articulate a vision that can be applied in specific ways throughout the advancement unit. Chief advancement officers must also be analytical and able to present important information to campus leaders in a way that helps them make sound decisions. "We must be able to provide tools and strategies to volunteers, staff, presidents, or chancellors that help them get to where they want to be by achieving desired goals and outcomes." For advancement professionals, it often entails significant preparation through research and data collection. By their very nature, faculty and academic leaders rely on, and are comfortable with, research in making decisions. Simic believes chief advancement officers must know when to invest resources in strategic planning, feasibility studies, and other forms of research to communicate messages strategically. He elaborates:

> Strategic communication really works. Engagement of multiple stakeholders, including volunteers, and getting them involved in the conversation is important. For example, when I was at Indiana, there were two or three faculty members who wanted to raise money for a free daycare center. I didn't know whether a fundraising campaign for a daycare center would work or not. My guess was probably not, but we took them through the process of a feasibility study. The results of the study said it would be challenging to fund a free daycare center through philanthropy. Having data to back this up was important because the people who wanted the center eventually realized they needed to identify alternative funding.

Simic thinks it is critically important how chief advancement officers interact with faculty. He encourages unit-based fundraisers to establish faculty development advisory committees so that they can communicate more openly about the fundraising process. "If you make faculty part of the process, then they become part of the solution. If you leave them out, they become your worst critics," he says. Chief advancement officers cannot operate single handedly. They must constantly be thinking about everyone who might be impacted—staff, faculty, donors, trustees, and board members—and bring together multiple constituent groups in the fundraising process.

Finally, having a close working relationship with the institution's chief executive is critical to Simic. One cannot be a burden to the president. He says chief advancement officers must present solutions to existing problems rather than look to the president for answers, adding,

> If you have a major issue and you tell the president you don't know what to do, it's not productive. In my position as a leader, that's not what I want to hear. I want to hear from the person who says, "We've got these problems, and I see three ways for us to handle it, what do you think?" You empower your staff to

think through problems and come in with what they think are ideas for solutions, then we'll talk our way through it together and figure out how to proceed as a team. Empowerment is a big piece of leadership. Staff must feel like they can actually disagree. They need to be able to say, "I don't think it will work for these reasons."

Leadership Competencies Most Difficult to Carry Out

According to Simic, it is difficult for chief advancement officers to determine exactly what information is best to present to campus leaders for making sound decisions. And how and when to present it is equally important. "There is a process that should be followed. Influencing the outcome of a decision sometimes has more to do with the process than the actual information presented." This theory also holds true when working with donors. Simic acknowledges:

> I've never influenced a donor to do something he or she did not want to do. We've had some very big gifts at Indiana. Each one those gifts was the result of a donor following his or her passion. Advancement professionals often talk too much about what the university wants to do. We don't listen enough about what donors want to do and what their dreams are. The really big gifts arrive when we listen to the interests of the donors. Our first big gift was $40 million from Mrs. Jacobs to endow the music school. Why did it happen? It happened because her son had a great experience at the music school. He was struggling but the dean took an interest in him, paid attention to him, and guided him appropriately. The experience had a major impact on him.

Who, other than the Chief Advancement Officer, Is Responsible for Leading Advancement Organizations?

Simic considers the advancement and fundraising process a partnership. He thinks the president must be empowered to participate in the process and serve as a leader and partner. "We want the president to say, 'Okay, how are we going to get this done together?'" Furthermore, the entire institution must take ownership of advancement's goals and outcomes. "The leadership team of the institution must be involved in the fundraising conversation. They must have a stake in the process," Simic contends. Ultimately, Simic believes, the president serves as the true chief advancement officer, but the president must have a partner who can help think through strategy and develop a plan. It is that type of partnership that leads to success, and the chief advancement officer is responsible for facilitating the partnership.

What Competencies Make You an Effective Leader?

Simic's answer to this question reveals a playful leader who does not take himself too seriously. "My staff would likely describe me as goofy," he quips. "But more importantly, I try to make them feel like they are real partners in everything I do as a leader." He says he tries to create a culture where no question is out of bounds. "During staff meetings, I let them ask whatever they want and try to give them a complete answer with a rationale behind the answer." This relates to transparency. Simic thinks one of his strengths is being open and transparent with staff, and also with faculty. Transparency with faculty and academic leaders helps chief advancement officers build credibility and trust across campus. And according to Simic, credibility, transparency, and ongoing communication lead to successful fundraising outcomes.

One of Simic's former direct reports had this to say about his leadership:

> Curt Simic is a charismatic leader who has the ability to make others feel special. Not long ago, I told Curt that whenever I'm with him, I always feel better afterward than when I arrived. I think that's true for most people who are around Curt. He looks you in the eye, asks questions about your family and things that are important to you, and makes you feel like you are the only person in the room, and the most important person in the world. He has an incredible memory for details. His interpersonal skills build loyalty and trust. There was rarely a day when Curt was in town and didn't beat the rest of the staff to the office. Seeing his car parked there before anyone else's, and typically on the weekends, clearly demonstrated his commitment, energy, and willingness to lead by example. Curt has the ability to bring people together, engage them in meaningful ways, and show his appreciation regularly and sincerely. His daily ritual of writing personal notes speaks volumes to his attention to detail.

Another former colleague said this:

> Curt truly likes people and finds contentment, even joy, in serving others and seeing others do well. He has tremendous interpersonal skills. People implicitly like him and trust him. He is a man of his word. He really knows the business. He is thoroughly honest, has complete integrity, and keeps his word without exception. He reads people and situations well. He is pleasant and humble. He loves people and has tremendous energy for them. He has character and holds true to his values.

It was a similar message repeated again and again. Loyalty, humbleness, and an innate ability to make people feel special were just a few consistencies among those who commented on Simic's leadership ability. But even more striking was the emergence of themes from subordinates that Simic himself said were important, such as making outsiders feel like insiders, collaboration and transparency, and having a genuine interest in developing staff. In short, Simic practices what he preaches.

Leadership Development and the Future of Advancement Leaders

Simic is a genuinely kind individual. Although he does not specifically list kindness as necessary for effective leadership, his subordinates point to it as one of his endearing qualities, or strengths, which likely has an impact. In thinking about areas of improvement, Simic says he needs more discipline when it comes to issues of process and ensuring the organization does not take on more than it can handle. He laments, "When you have limited staff, you have to be a little more disciplined in terms of what you will take on. However, I've tried to hire and keep good managers to ensure we stay on track."

Existing Professional Development Programs for Chief Advancement Officers

Simic's long tenure at Indiana gave him tremendous exposure to their Center on Philanthropy, a leading academic program offering degrees and professional development courses in nonprofit management and fundraising. As he observes, "The fact that there is a structured curriculum now is an enormous advantage today versus when I started. I think what happens in the fundraising school is really good and good for the profession." However, Simic acknowledges that Indiana's fundraising school is more focused on teaching people about philanthropy rather than developing advancement leaders. He also points to existing conferences and organizations like the Big Ten Institute as being helpful. But they too are typically focused on "how to" content more than anything else. "The profession is probably not doing enough regarding leadership development," Simic says. "There is a tremendous opportunity to develop comprehensive leadership development and training programs for CAOs. We tend to focus more on strategies for raising money than on leadership and management training."

The Future of Leadership Development and Training

Simic asserts that more research is needed to determine what kind of leadership development and training programs the profession needs. There simply have not been enough people addressing the issue. He thinks the industry should survey stakeholders and interest groups, especially college presidents, and ask them what types of programs are needed for the future. "For instance, one strategy might be to identify a group of college and university presidents and ask their perspective on what they think is important regarding their advancement leaders," he suggests.

Challenges Facing Chief Advancement Officers

The biggest challenge, according to Simic, is the impact of short presidential tenures on advancement. College presidents face insurmountable pressures, one being to raise a lot of money. As a result, short-term needs often trump long-term fundraising sustainability. The average fundraising campaign is nearly twice as long as the average tenure of presidents, which can be challenging for advancement staff. Chief advancement officers usually experience at least one cycle of turnover in the president's office during the life of a campaign. As Simic describes it,

> For the institution, continuity is important. At Indiana, I worked with four presidents and one interim president during a twenty-year period. However, I'm confident the continuity of our foundation board and in my position helped us sustain increased giving levels while I was there.

In addition, Simic points to the role of development and its relationships with key constituents as equally important. If these relationships are weak, challenges result. To maintain fundraising consistency during presidential turnover, it's important to build and maintain productive working relationships with volunteers and foundation trustees. "My view has been to build stakeholders in large numbers so that we had continuity in our fundraising effort. Presidents may have left, but our volunteer leadership remained in place, so we kept raising more money."

Looking to the future, Simic thinks funding will always be an issue, and the pressure to raise money through private sources will continue to increase. For example:

> In our early days at Berkley, staff was frustrated about the lack of big gifts coming through the door. But I said, "Look, we're doing the right things. We have to keep doing the right things and ultimately it will pay off in the end." And it did. We had a chancellor in place for ten years, followed by two more wonderful chancellors. There was continuity among the leadership, both at the institutional and volunteer levels. But today's advancement leaders need to be thinking about the next generation of volunteer leadership. They need to recruit younger family members of existing board members to engage with the institution and maintain continuity, which in turn will maintain and increase the future potential for major gifts.

Positive Aspects of Serving as a Chief Advancement Officer

For Simic, building relationships with a diverse cross-section of people brings him the most enjoyment as an advancement leader. And it is not just the relationships he builds with donors that he cherishes, but also those with faculty, staff, and other constituencies. Simic believes relationship-building is a leadership process, and one of his strengths is building meaningful relationships with the many people he comes in contact with. For example, he says, "I'm having lunch with two donors tomorrow. They may never give us another dime, and I don't really care. They are good people, and I care about them, and they understand that my feelings are genuine and sincere." Donors pick up on his sincerity, which has been a cornerstone of his success.

Preparation for Newcomers and Future Leaders in Advancement

Simic has clear instructions for newcomers and aspiring advancement leaders: Learn the fundamentals. "I don't think I would have gotten as far as I did in my career if I didn't know how to manage an annual fund and all the other important components of a fundraising operation. It just wouldn't have happened," he contends. He also believes it is important to establish credibility as a way to gain respect and effectiveness as a leader.

Perhaps equally important, he thinks future advancement leaders should learn how to better prepare institutions for the reality of what advancement is all about. According to Simic, institutional commitment to fundraising is just as important to a fundraiser's success as learning the fundamentals of the profession. "There is a significant need to get away from the tactics of fundraising and shift the discussion more toward longer-term strategies, which relates to leadership," he says.

> Presidents know how to work with faculty and deans on teaching and research, but many don't know how to work with faculty and deans from a fundraising perspective. They are very successful in the RFP (request for proposal) world applied by federal agencies, for example. But that world is not the same as the world of voluntary philanthropy—gift giving from personal wealth.

Therefore, chief advancement officers of the future need to not only develop their own leadership skills but figure out a way to develop the leadership skills of campus presidents and administrators from an advancement perspective—a challenging task indeed.

14

The Advancement Leadership
Competency Model

THE PURPOSE OF THIS BOOK is to make a case for the importance of successful, high-performing, and effective advancement leadership in higher education. As discussed at length, advancement organizations are among the most complex, dynamic, and ambiguous units on a college campus. Their reach is both broad and deep, and their success is highly dependent on the engagement and participation of a wide cross-section of both internal and external constituents. The knowledge, skills, abilities, attributes, and behaviors necessary to be an effective and high-performing chief advancement officer go well beyond deep domain knowledge of the advancement industry. As articulated in the previous pages, successful chief advancement officers are persuasive communicators, organizational developers, and strategic thinkers. They are skilled politicians and firm decision-makers. They must be able to speak on an array of topics and understand the nuances that make up diverse academic units, from medicine to humanities, law to education. Moreover, as the profession continues to grow and expand, chief advancement officers must be skilled managers of human and financial capital. And they must be able to do all of this with unflappable confidence and poise. These positions are not for everyone, but rather for those who have a passion for the mission of higher education and who want to make a difference in the world. It is a rewarding job indeed, but one that requires strong leadership.

To summarize the discussion of this book, the first chapter provided an overview of the history of the higher education advancement industry and the chief advancement officer position, followed by a brief literature review on general, higher education, and advancement leadership. It also outlined the context and approach for our data-collection and interview process and set the stage for the presentation of cases. In the remainder of the chapters we summarize narratives from interviews with ten highly regarded and effective chief advancement officers representing a professionally diverse cross-section of leaders at institutions around the country. These leaders provided intimate details of what they believe it takes to be a competent advancement leader in twenty-first-century academic institutions. Insight was gleaned on their career paths, philosophies and styles of leadership, professional strengths and weaknesses, and the future of the profession. These leaders were nominated by their peers and are considered among the best in the industry.

Up to this point, a strong case has been made for the need for competent advancement leadership in higher education, a case grounded and supported by anecdotal evidence, existing literature, and the research presented here. The following pages offer a competency model of advancement leadership informed by the preceding interviews and other supporting data. This model was created by identifying and tracking specific leadership competencies considered important for success as gleaned from the interviews.

An initial list of over sixty leadership competencies was identified. After review and analysis of the list, competencies were organized, consolidated, and narrowed further based on their similarity and parallel themes. The final model contains fourteen leadership competency categories representing this larger, more comprehensive list. This model is the first-ever research-based attempt at understanding what it takes to be a successful chief advancement officer in today's complex higher education organizations.

The Advancement Leadership Competency Model

The fourteen advancement leadership competencies contained in the model are listed below. For each competency, nearly all interview participants listed the theme, or at minimum a component or sub-competency of the theme, as important to the success and performance of an advancement leader. The competencies are presented below in no particular order. However, it is important to note that some competencies emerged with slightly more strength and frequency than others. This will be discussed later in more detail.

Intellectual Curiosity

For chief advancement officers, lifelong learning and an insatiable appetite for knowledge are important for leadership success. Effective leaders focus on staying current with the profession but also learn as much as they can about their institution. Furthermore, they possess an ongoing curiosity about life in general, expanding well beyond the reach of their profession. They read books frequently on a wide variety of topics, including management, leadership, and personal enrichment. They also learn by observing other successful leaders and try to emulate their positive leadership qualities and attributes. Conversely, they pay attention to and analyze poor leadership and make every attempt at avoiding what they perceive as negative leadership qualities.

Effective Communication Skills

Effective communication is an important leadership competency for chief advancement officers, including both oral and written forms. Chief advancement officers understand and think about new forms of communication, including social media and its potential for engaging future generations of donors. They listen well and communicate in clear, concise, and appropriate ways, which establishes credibility among diverse constituencies, including donors, volunteers, alumni, faculty, deans, and administrators. They actively learn as much as they can about their organization so they can articulate and clearly communicate the mission, vision, and goals of the institution effectively. In addition, they promote transparency through communication with both internal and external audiences in an effort to gain support and consensus. And finally, they possess savvy negotiating skills, making them effective at achieving desired organizational results and outcomes.

Self-Awareness

Competent chief advancement officers are keenly aware of their own strengths and weaknesses. They exude confidence but are willing to hire people who complement their own professional areas of weakness. They are comfortable in their own skin and maintain a sense of honesty with themselves about who they are as individuals and professionals. They reflect often about their own skills and abilities and seek to identify areas in need of improvement. They are open to feedback and always work to refine and improve their skills through professional development. Furthermore, they laugh at themselves frequently, try not to be too serious, and maintain a healthy sense of perspective on their careers and life in general.

An Ability to Think Critically

High-performing chief advancement officers are reflective and set aside time to think critically and analytically. They consider innovation a top priority and value creativity and fresh ideas. Great leaders are analytical thinkers and take the time necessary to consider big, high-impact decisions and the various implications of those decisions. They tune out peripheral distractions when necessary, giving thought and paying attention to what's most important to their organization and institution. While most wish they had more time, they make thought and reflection, or "thinking time," a priority, regardless of their busy schedule and the crises of the day.

Tenacity

High-performing chief advancement officers possess a determined spirit to move things forward, undeterred by challenges, obstacles, and roadblocks. They have an inner toughness, resolve, and competitive drive to succeed, and they hold others accountable to the same standard. They take initiative and display courage in the face of skepticism and doubt. They remain hopeful and maintain a positive outlook. Moreover, they are resilient, have a thick skin, and are able to withstand criticism while focusing on the mission, goals, and objectives of their respective institutions.

Thoughtfulness about Organizational Culture

Higher education institutions share a broad, unifying mission but are individually unique. As a result, effective chief advancement officers are savvy in navigating institutional culture, while maintaining thoughtfulness about context, situation, and environment. They focus on building a positive and productive organizational culture within advancement, while considering the greater needs of the institution. Furthermore, they have the wherewithal to continually assess and evaluate an organization and make changes when and where necessary. They are always thinking of ways to enhance culture and operating environment in an effort to improve productivity and moral, while moving their organization and institution forward toward strategic goals and outcomes.

A Focus on Excellence

Successful chief advancement officers maintain a laser focus on high performance, productivity, and sustained excellence. They never compromise on quality, which often requires tough decision-making, especially as it relates to personnel. Furthermore, they focus more on being effective than on being right, which requires a healthy dose of self-control and confidence when one's judgment is challenged. Their main focus is to promote excellence in an effort to improve organizational value to the campus, while balancing short-term initiatives and long-term objectives. They discourage the status quo while encouraging big ideas and new ways of thinking.

An Ability to Motivate, Inspire, and Influence

High-performing chief advancement officers lead by positively stimulating their staff and organization toward shared outcomes and goals. They are visionary. They have strong motivational skills and inspire people to reach beyond what they think is possible. Stretch, lofty goals are typical. They are savvy influencers and often leverage volunteer leadership to help achieve desired results and outcomes. Finally, they are highly optimistic, maintaining a positive attitude in the face of seemingly insurmountable challenges.

An Ability to Tolerate Ambiguity

The advancement industry requires its leaders to have an uncanny ability to operate within an environment that is often ill-defined and unclear. The work of advancement is rarely black and white. The most unambiguous and consistent aspect of a chief advancement officer's job is its ambiguity and inconsistency. Therefore, competent chief advancement officers are flexible and able to "roll with it" in the face of frequent change. They have a tremendous amount of responsibility with little authority and control, which requires political astuteness and savvy interpersonal skills to get things done.

An Ability to Accept Responsibility and Lead by Example

High-performing chief advancement officers understand the notion that success happens when preparation and opportunity are in alignment. They take responsibility for the success of their organization and expect the same of their staff and subordinates. They understand they have a responsibility to project leadership by nature of their position, but they also know when they must lead behind the scenes by facilitating the work of others. They are not afraid to get their hands dirty, and they seek to establish credibility by being engaged, available, and actively involved (without micromanaging) in the day-to-day work of the organization.

A Belief that Talent Management Should Be a High Priority

Successful advancement leaders understand the importance and impact of focusing on organizational development and talent management. Establishing high-performing organizations begins with making sound personnel decisions.

Effective chief advancement officers recruit and hire well but are also committed to helping staff grow and develop. They seek to create a learning environment and commit significant resources toward career and professional development. Moreover, they consider the development of future advancement leaders as one of their primary responsibilities. They encourage young professionals with high leadership potential to assume diverse portfolios early in their career and give them opportunities to take on stretch assignments. As noted, they also hire professionals who complement their own strengths and weaknesses.

A Passion for the Mission of Their Organization

Great chief advancement officers are concerned much more with the mission and goals of their organization rather than with their own status as a leader. They have reached a point in their career where money and title are less important than the overarching impact of their work and how it contributes to making society a better place by solving some of the world's most pressing issues. In fact, they couldn't be nearly as effective if they didn't have a firm belief in the mission of higher education. They never lose sight of doing what's best for their organization, even when it means making tough and sometimes unpopular decisions. In short, their passion for higher education is manifested in their role as advancement leaders and their impact on the institution as a whole.

Strong Interpersonal Skills

Savvy social skills are an important attribute of skilled chief advancement officers. They use interpersonal skills to gain commitment from their followers and to build bridges across the campus. They focus less on themselves and more on the team. Effective chief advancement officers are caring, sincere, and empathetic. They project a high level of sophistication, but as stated earlier, they do not take themselves too seriously and are able to laugh at themselves often. They believe it is important to stay positive and maintain a spirited sense of humor. They require this of their subordinates as well, and in many cases list "a sense of humor" as a requirement on job descriptions.

An Ability to Think Strategically

Successful, high-performing, and effective chief advancement officers are strategic thinkers and broad organizational planners. They are thoughtful of and reflect on the impact of their decisions and consider multiple options before acting. They manage the expectations of multiple constituent groups effectively and stay focused on the vision of both the advancement organization and institution. They have strong organizational skills and know how to delegate well. They engage multiple constituents in the strategic planning process and understand the importance of building consensus with internal and external stakeholders.

Implications of the Model

The research, data-analysis, and model-development process was focused solely on identifying core leadership competencies in general, as identified by the participants, rather than on determining if some competencies are more important than others. The chief advancement officers interviewed were not asked to provide a rank-ordered list, and thus, the data analysis focused specifically on emerging themes of leadership as presented in the model above. To determine which specific competencies are considered most important, future research surveying a large sample of chief advancement officers and asking them to rate these competencies based on importance is necessary. We intend to carry out this second phase of the research in the future. However, as mentioned above, some leadership competencies did indeed emerge with slightly more strength and emphasis during the interviews and deserve further mention here.

All ten chief advancement officers interviewed stressed the importance of intellectual curiosity and lifelong learning in one form or another. Intuitively, this makes sense. Higher education institutions are, at their very core, intellectual environments. Chief advancement officers must have a broad understanding of the entire campus, including its many centers, academic programs, research endeavors, sports teams, and student-life activities. But beyond the campus, chief advancement officers must also be able to speak intelligently with volunteers, donors, and other important stakeholders about current events, business matters, finance, politics, religion, and so on. Chief advancement officers must push themselves to become knowledgeable on topics that extend well beyond their formal training, education, and experience. Therefore, without a genuine interest in and curiosity about the many wonders of the world and the people who populate it, a chief advancement officer would most certainly find success fleeting.

Not surprisingly, effective communication skills consistently ranked very high among all ten chief advancement officers. Leaders who serve in the chief advancement officer position cannot operate effectively in a vacuum and behind closed doors. Rather, success requires the cooperation and collaboration of many stakeholders and constituents. Chief advancement officers must be able to articulate a clear vision to both internal and external audiences, speak and write in a compelling way that motivates and inspires, and listen attentively to donors in an effort to engage them with the mission, goals, and funding priorities of the institution. Without good communication skills, chief advancement officers will surely fail.

Another key factor worth discussing further is self-awareness and an understanding of one's own strengths and weaknesses. The complexity of an advancement organization requires a strong team of managers and staff to carry out the work of the department successfully. The ten chief advancement officers profiled here seem to have a keen sense of their own skills and abilities, and they emphasize the importance of recruiting team members, especially managers, who are competent in areas where they are not. Self-awareness was also emphasized consistently within the context of professional and career development. Nearly all of the ten chief advancement officers profiled said it is important to consciously focus on learning new things and to consider ways to improve as a professional and leader.

A thoughtfulness about organizational culture was the fourth leadership competency that emerged with more weight than the others. The interview participants suggested fairly unanimously that higher education institutions each possess very different and unique organizational environments. While they may have a shared sense of purpose, colleges and universities operate with their own set of norms, values, and traditions; therefore, it is important to consider culture strategically when leading advancement organizations. Lack of cultural awareness can have catastrophic career results.

If the day-to-day work environment of chief advancement officers had to be described in one word, that word is *ambiguous*. All of the interview participants made reference to the importance of being able to work within an operating environment that is often unclear and ill-defined. It's not unusual for higher education institutions to be referred to as "complex matrix organizations." Advancement leaders must be able to move in and out of multiple units effectively; work with a diverse cross-section of faculty, deans, and administrators; and have the flexibility to change course when necessary. Strategic plans must be based on broad, malleable themes that allow for flexibility in specific goals, objectives, and priorities. Rigidity is not a welcomed characteristic in advancement.

A belief that talent management should be a high priority also emerged repeatedly. Strategically recruiting, hiring, developing, and retaining the very best employees were mentioned as having a big impact on the overall success of organizations. The idea that attracting competent people who are both a fit with the organization's culture and specific positions rang true for nearly all chief advancement officers profiled. While not everyone stated they had formal talent management programs in place, they recognized the value of focusing on their people and the impact this has on developing a high-performing team of professionals.

Finally, it should come as no surprise that strong interpersonal skills consistently emerge as one of the most important competencies necessary for the success of chief advancement officers. While chief advancement officers do not necessarily need to be overly extroverted, it's important that they be able to build strong, meaningful relationships with people both internal and external to the institution when necessary. For ultimate success, advancement organizations require contributions from multiple constituencies. Therefore, chief advancement officers must be able to leverage relationship-building skills to help them move the organization toward desired goals, objectives, and outcomes.

Broad Themes

Beyond the frequency of specific competencies, the advancement leadership competency model, when viewed from a macro-perspective, touches on a few broad themes and domains worth deeper discussion. Padilla (2005) introduces his book on leadership of higher education presidents by stating, "Humans are primarily social creatures." While strong interpersonal skills are singularly important, many of the other fourteen leadership competencies relate to social skills and interpersonal competence to some degree as well (e.g., effective communication skills, and an ability to motivate, inspire, and influence). It is a conundrum of sorts. Chief advancement officers are expected to leverage interpersonal relationships within an environment where specialists and researchers—who sometimes fall on the opposite side of the social spectrum—dominate. Regardless, it's the responsibility of the chief advancement officer to leverage his or her social skills to engage faculty and other academic professionals with donors in meaningful ways, and vice versa.

Conversely, there is a critical thinking component whereby leaders must use analytical skills to effectively move organizations forward. Leaders must have a thirst for lifelong learning and a desire to continually improve themselves through the expansion of their own knowledge. This develops a more sophisticated leader, and in turn improves that leader's credibility among constituents and stakeholders. Fundraising programs in particular have become much more strategic and data-driven. Therefore, it is not enough for chief advancement officers to rely on social and interpersonal skills alone. Rather they must be able to balance both the external and internal demands of the job effectively and have the wherewithal to move in and out of both domains in a seamless manner as the job requires.

Another broad theme is success and accomplishment. It is clear that high-performing chief advancement officers consistently focus on results. They understand the blueprint of what success looks like and work tirelessly toward achieving desired goals and outcomes. In some ways, they are innately high achievers, while recognizing that the overarching success of their organization rests solely on their shoulders.

Finally, there is a component of human capital management and organizational development that underlies the model. Organizational culture, context, and environment are important considerations, but equally so is hiring and developing staff. As emphasized in the book *The People First Approach* (Croteau 2009), successful advancement leaders make this a priority, committing resources and thoughtful strategic planning toward a coordinated talent management program consistent with the mission, goals, and culture of the organization. They understand the importance of surrounding themselves with high-performing employees, and they commit resources toward recruiting, developing, and retaining the very best people in the industry.

Summary

The model presented here represents a broad leadership spectrum for chief advancement officers. It is the first step toward understanding this complex position more deeply. There are no magic ingredients or prescriptions for success. Leadership strategies employed at one institution might be very different from the leadership strategies employed at another. However, as the competency model exemplifies, what is most important is having the wherewithal and ability to understand that *leadership strategies* in general must indeed be considered and employed. Leadership is not about subscribing to specific methods and tactics. It is much bigger than that. Leadership does not imply knowing exactly what to do and what to say in every situation. Rather, leadership is knowing that it is often more important to know *when* to do it and *how* say it. It's about knowing your audience and considering ways to influence, motivate, and inspire that audience. It's about being able to analyze an organization and figure out what type of talent is a good fit for a specific position within that organization. Effectively communicating is generally important, but how and when one communicates with different constituent groups to achieve desired results and outcomes is more important. Leadership is about being strategic, thoughtful, and analytical in the face of significant challenges and responsibilities. These competencies are relevant and applicable regardless of institutional culture, organizational structure, academic focus, student population, funding models, research activities, or any of the other variables that make universities distinctly different. Leadership is leadership. The advancement leadership competency model detailed here provides a foundation and framework for studying this important topic further and, ultimately, for developing competent advancement leaders for the future.

15

Lessons Learned and Thoughts for the Future

T HE LEADERS INTERVIEWED FOR THIS BOOK represent a small sample of chief advancement officers employed at higher education institutions across the country and the world. Although there are more females than males in our sample, this does not represent the true makeup of current chief advancement officers, as males generally hold more top positions than females. However, it is evidence that a growing number of influential female leaders are making an impact on the profession, which is certainly a positive development. What is missing in our sample is ethnic diversity. Many of the leaders profiled spoke on this issue, suggesting the profession needs to do more to encourage and promote advancement as a career path to younger cohorts of professionals, especially college students. Higher education institutions have taken significant steps to provide more access to students of underrepresented minority groups over the past few decades, yet the advancement industry has not followed this trend with its own professionals.

Six of the leaders profiled currently serve, or previously served, institutions that are consistently ranked in or near the top twenty for fundraising revenue year after year, and two leaders come from institutions that are not far behind. Some readers might question the application of the aforementioned leadership competency model to and its practicality for smaller institutions. We argue that leadership is leadership, regardless of how many digits populate an institution's fundraising totals. In fact, the model presented here may have even more relevance for leaders at smaller institutions, as they typically work just as hard, if not harder, for every dollar raised, making effective, high-performing, and competent leadership critical to their success.

Beyond the model, there were many lessons learned from the interviews worth discussing. First, upon our reviewing the career paths of the interview participants, an obvious consistency emerged. All ten chief advancement officers held multiple and often very diverse positions early in their careers but then maintained longevity once they reached the top post. In addition, most leaders (but not all) held diverse positions at multiple institutions. Many of the leaders assumed management roles and leadership positions at an early age. They were open to trying new things and taking on stretch job assignments with high exposure and in some cases high professional risk. They developed diverse skill sets along the way and learned the anatomy of what a successful advancement operation looks like. This suggests that there is value in having broad, high-level exposure across advancement during the formative years of one's career because it may ultimately have an impact on future leadership potential and success. It also suggests that once the top position is reached, success and accomplishment take time to fully develop and realize.

Second, there were many positive and fulfilling aspects of the chief advancement officer position discussed by the interview participants. All the leaders said they enjoy having the opportunity to interact with and learn from some of the most interesting and successful people in the world. This was a theme repeated over and over, and it seemed to provide an energizing lift to the chief advancement officers in their day-to-day work. Calvert said she specifically enjoys linking donor passions and interests with the needs of the institution; May acknowledged he is motivated by all the external components of the job. Jackson, Pearson, and Shell commented on their enjoyment of interacting with and impacting students; Pearson, Shell, and Simic listed their interactions with faculty as particularly meaningful and inspiring. Pelzel suggested that the diversity and complexity of the responsibilities of the job are stimulating and interesting in their totality. But Michael Eicher summed up the collective belief among all interview participants well when he said, "What I absolutely enjoy the most is regularly coming into contact with some of the best and brightest people in the world." He added, "These are wonderful and amazing experiences. I don't think there is another job where I could experience so much with so many interesting people."

Conversely, the chief advancement officer position certainly comes with its challenges. Many interview participants said that high salaries continue to make it difficult to recruit and retain the best fundraisers and advancement professionals in the industry. Eicher and May questioned how long salaries can continue to escalate within an operational environment of increasing scrutiny and belt tightening. Furthermore, development turnover was overwhelmingly mentioned as an ongoing problem in need of a long-term solution. Turnover has plagued advancement organizations for years. The "Great

Recession" caused a pause in turnover and an increase in retention, but only temporarily. In 2011, the job market for development professionals picked up substantially and may have become even stronger than before the recession, creating a "buyer's market" for those interested in advancing their careers. Decreased funding for higher education, ever-increasing fundraising goals, and management of fundraising expectations were also listed as challenges by nearly every interview participant. Pelzel rightly observed that higher education institutions have an insatiable need for more funding, noting that higher education's current business model is sometimes inefficient and potentially unsustainable for the future. Multiple leaders said that it has become increasingly difficult to be responsive to the large number of constituents and stakeholders who demand the chief advancement officer's time. May's observation that today's donors require a high level of personal touch resonates throughout the profession. And Shell acknowledged the same phenomenon with regard to internal constituents, noting that he wished he had more time to give them the personal attention he thinks they deserve. As technology evolves and shapes the way we communicate, interpersonal relationships have become even more difficult to build and maintain. In a profession dependent on a high level of social interaction, this presents a significant challenge. Other concerns included presidential turnover, managing within the complex organizational structure of highly decentralized environments, and the need to consider newly emerging and influential donor groups, such as international and female constituencies.

The Future of Advancement Leadership

There is a lot to consider when thinking about the future of advancement leadership and preparing the next generation of advancement leaders. Many of the leaders profiled in this book suggested that future leaders must communicate better, know how to influence constituents effectively, understand various uses of social media, be competent advocates of their institutions, and get to know younger generations of professionals and donors better. They said it is important for future leaders to have strong mentors and supervisors, make smart job selections, and consider every professional situation—both good and bad—as a learning experience and growth opportunity. New professionals should observe current leaders and know what success looks like. They should be open to feedback and have a willingness to make changes and improve. And they should focus less on moving up the ladder and more on learning the fundamentals of advancement and establishing credibility within the industry. The leaders profiled in this book provided invaluable insight related to advancement careers, especially as it relates to assuming the chief advancement officer position.

However, there is an important issue that has remained an ongoing problem throughout the advancement industry, and one that was made abundantly clear during the interviews. There are few, if any, relevant leadership development programs, based on sound research and design, available to prepare current and future generations of advancement leaders. Few organizations engage in succession planning and even fewer systematically prepare and train their top talent for potential leadership positions. There is a broad array of leadership programs and organizational consultants available in many other industries, but not in advancement. This has partly contributed to the current void of well-prepared, holistically trained chief advancement officers ready to assume leadership vacancies. And it will likely become an even greater issue as the baby-boom generation exits the workforce.

As the chief advancement officer position continues to grow in complexity, scope, and responsibility, collective thought and resources must be committed toward this issue. The chief advancement officer is a highly visible professional overseeing a division in which the slightest error has the potential to cause significant organizational damage and damage to the chief advancement officer's career. On-the-job training is not a good solution for the chief advancement officer position. High-performing, successful, and well-prepared advancement leaders are needed to serve as partners with institutional presidents to help them guide the future of their colleges and universities. There is perhaps no position more important to a president's cabinet than that of the chief advancement officer. Historically, this has not always been true, but it is arguably true today. Thus, professional development programming is needed that focuses on the fourteen competencies of leadership outlined in the model presented in this book. A program of this nature would improve the leadership effectiveness of current chief advancement officers and provide future leaders with insight on what it takes to be successful.

This book provides a sound, research-based model of advancement leadership for the future, filling an important practical and theoretical void. It makes the case for why competent advancement leadership is so important and for the potential impact advancement leadership can have on higher education institutions. There are obvious organizational benefits that result from great leadership, and these have been discussed at length. But there are also significant and lasting consequences associated with poor leadership. This book shines a bright light on many important topics, but perhaps no topic is more important than what needs to be done to prepare the next generation of advancement leaders. And with a bit of irony, strong leadership is necessary to frame this important topic in a way that makes it a priority for the profession in the future.

So what's next, and where do we go from here? As both practitioners and scholars in the field, we hope to take the results from our research a step further and develop a thoughtful, strategic, and educational leadership-training program for advancement professionals. Our hope is to one day offer a program based on our model's fourteen competencies of leadership that helps sharpen and focus a leader's strengths, while offering strategies and tactics to improve upon his or her weaknesses. The program might include self-assessments, case-study analyses, and group projects. We envision a program that provides opportunities to learn from leaders both within and outside the field—touching on both success factors and mistakes—while offering learning modules focused on the challenges (and the potential solutions to challenges) that chief advancement officers will surely face today and in the future. There is no better time than the present to create and implement a program of this nature.

We hope the ten chief advancement officers profiled here inspire current leaders to think about their own leadership effectiveness, while motivating others to consider their leadership potential. Leadership is not for everyone. Understanding what it takes to be successful in an advancement leadership position is important. And for those who think they have the passion, interest, and competencies necessary to be a successful chief advancement officer, this book provides important points to consider. More broadly, developing the next generation of outstanding advancement leaders is critical for higher education institutions if they wish to meet current and future educational demands of the twenty-first century. As operating costs for colleges and universities continue to rise, expectations for more philanthropic support are also increasing. Thus, the leaders of advancement divisions—large or small, public or private, urban or rural—will continue to have the significant responsibility of keeping our nation's institutions of higher education among the best in the world. There may be no other position on a college campus with such an important role. And understanding the leadership competencies presented here, while ensuring that people within the field are provided with learning opportunities to develop them, is and will continue to be essential.

Bibliography

Foreword by Peter Hayashida

Gross, William H. (2009). "On the 'Course' to a New Normal." www.pimco.com/EN/Insights/Pages/Gross Sept On the Course to a New Normal.aspx (retrieved 8 May 2011).

Tavernise, Sabrina. (2011). "Numbers of Children of Whites Falling Fast." *New York Times*, April 6. www.nytimes.com/2011/04/06/us/06census.html?_r=1&ref=us (retrieved 8 May 2011).

CBS News. (2011). "Income Gap between Rich, Poor the Widest Ever." September 28. www.cbsnews.com/stories/2010/09/28/national/main6907321.shtml (retrieved 8 May 2011).

Avon, Natalie. (2011). "Why More Americans Don't Travel Abroad." CNN Travel, February 4. http://articles.cnn.com/2011-02-04/travel/americans.travel.domestically_1_western-hemisphere-travel-initiative-passports-tourism-industries?_s=PM:TRAVEL (retrieved 8 May 2011).

United States Census Bureau. (2011). www.census.gov.

Chapter 1

Cohen, A. M. (1998). *The Shaping of American Higher Education: Emergence and Growth of the Contemporary System*. San Francisco: Jossey-Bass Publishers.

Cutlip, S. M. (1990). *Fund Raising in the United States: Its Role in America's Philanthropy*. New Brunswick, NJ: Transaction Publishers.

Education.com. (2011). http://www.education.com/definition/institutional-advancement/.

Elliot, D. (2006). *The Kindness of Strangers: Philanthropy and Higher Education*. Lanham, MD: Rowman & Littlefield.

Herbst, J. (1981). "Church, State and Higher Education: College Government in the American Colonies and States before 1820." *History of Higher Education Annual* 1:42–54.

National Center for Education Statistics. http://nces.ed.gov/ (retrieved 9 March 2011).

Oliver, F. H. (2007). "The Roots of Academic Fundraising." In *Philanthropy, Volunteerism and Fundraising in Higher Education*, edited by A. Walton and M. Gasman. New York: Pearson Custom Publishing.

Pray, F. C. (1981). *Handbook for Educational Fundraising*. San Francisco: Jossey-Bass Publishers.

Rudolph, F. (1962). *The American College and University: A History*. New York: Knopf.

Snyder, T. D. (1993). *120 Years of American Education: A Statistical Portrait*. Washington, DC: National Center for Education Statistics.

Whitehead, J. S., and Herbst, J. (1986). "How to Think about the Dartmouth College Case." *History of Education Quarterly* 26 (3): 333–49.

Worth, M. J. (1993). "The Historical Overview." In *Educational Fund Raising: Principles and Practice*, edited by M. J. Worth. Westport, CT: Praeger Publishers.

Worth, M. J. (2002). "The Historical Overview." In *New Strategies for Educational Fund Raising*, edited by M. J. Worth. Westport, CT: Praeger Publishers.

Chapter 2

Bass, B. M. (1985). *Leadership and Performance beyond Expectations*. New York: Free Press.

Bass, B. M., ed. (1990). *Bass and Stogdill's Handbook of Leadership: Theory, Research, and Managerial Applications*, 3rd ed. New York: Free Press.

Bass, B. M. (1998). *Transformational Leadership: Industry, Military, and Educational Impact*. Mahwah, NJ: Lawrence Erlbaum Associates.

Bennis, W., and Nanus, B. (1997). *Leaders: Strategies for Taking Charge*, 2nd ed. New York: HarperBusiness.

Bensimon, E. M., and Neumann, A. (1993). *Redesigning Collegiate Leadership: Teams and Teamwork in Higher Education*. Baltimore, MD: Johns Hopkins University Press.

Bensimon, E. M., Neumann, A., and Birnbaum, R. (1989). *Making Sense of Administrative Leadership: The "L" Work in Higher Education*. Washington, DC: School of Education and Human Development, George Washington University.

Birnbaum, R. (1992). *How Academic Leadership Works: Understanding Success and Failure in the College Presidency*. San Francisco: Jossey-Bass Publishers.

Burns, J. M. (1978). *Leadership*. New York: Harper & Row.

Cohen, M. D., and March, J. G. (1986). *Leadership and Ambiguity: The American College President*, rev. ed. New York: McGraw-Hill.

Collins, J. (2001). *Good to Great: Why Some Companies Make the Leap . . . and Others Don't.* New York: HarperCollins.

Day, E. E. (1946). "The Rôle of Administration in Higher Education." *Journal of Higher Education* 17 (7): 339–43.

Elliot, D. (2006). *The Kindness of Strangers: Philanthropy and Higher Education.* Lanham, MD: Rowman & Littlefield.

Fiedler, F. E. (1967). *A Theory of Leadership Effectiveness.* New York: McGraw-Hill.

Fisher, J. L., and Koch, J. V. (1996). *Presidential Leadership: Making a Difference.* Phoenix, AZ: American Council on Education/Oryx Press.

Fisher, J. L., and Koch, J. V. (2004). *The Entrepreneurial College President.* Westport, CT: American Council on Education/Praeger Publishers.

Fisher, J. L., Tack, M. W., and Wheeler, K. J. (1988). *The Effective College President.* New York: American Council on Education/Macmillan.

Graen, G. (1976). "Role-Making Processes within Complex Organizations." In *Handbook of Industrial and Organizational Psychology,* edited by M. D. Dunnette. Chicago: Rand McNally.

Green, M. F., ed. (1988). *Leaders for a New Era: Strategies for Higher Education.* New York: American Council on Education/Macmillan.

Heifetz, R. A. (1994). *Leadership without Easy Answers.* Cambridge, MA: Belknap Press.

Hersey, P., and Blanchard, K. H. (1969). "Life-Cycle Theory of Leadership." *Training and Development Journal* 23:26–34.

Kezar, A. J., and Lester, J. (2011). *Enhancing Campus Capacity for Leadership: An Examination of Grassroots Leaders in Higher Education.* Stanford, CA: Stanford University Press.

Moilanen, J. H. (2002). "Leader Competency and Army Readiness." *Military Review* (July–August): 56–63.

Nehls, K. (2008). "Presidential Transitions during Capital Campaigns." *International Journal of Educational Advancement* 8 (3/4): 198–218.

Northouse, P. G. (2004). *Leadership Theory and Practice.* Thousand Oaks, CA: Sage Publications.

Peck, R. D. (1983). "The Entrepreneurial College Presidency." *Educational Record* 64 (1): 18–25.

Pollard, J. (1958). *Fund-Raising for Higher Education.* New York: Harper & Brothers.

Raines, S. C., and Alberg, M. S. (2003). "The Role of Professional Development in Preparing Academic Leaders." *New Directions for Higher Education* 124 (Winter): 33–39.

Reck, W. E. (1976). *The Changing World of College Relations: History and Philosophy, 1917–1975.* Washington, DC: Council for Advancement and Support of Education.

Smith, Z. A., and Wolverton, M. (2010). "Higher Education Leadership Competencies: Quantitatively Refining a Qualitative Model." *Journal of Leadership and Organizational Studies* 17 (1): 61–70.

Stogdill, R. M. (1974). *Handbook of Leadership,* 1st ed. New York: Free Press.

Chapter 3

Athey, T. R., and Orth, M. S. (1999). "Emerging Competency Methods for the Future. *Human Resource Management* 38 (3): 215–26.

Birnbaum, R. (1992). *How Academic Leadership Works: Understanding Success and Failure in the College Presidency.* San Francisco: Jossey-Bass Publishers.

Goleman, D. (1998). "What Makes a Leader?" *Harvard Business Review* (November–December): 93–102.

Hoppe, S. L. (2003). "Identifying and Nurturing Potential Academic Leaders." *New Directions for Higher Education* 124 (Winter): 3–12.

Kouzes, J. M., and Posner, B. Z. (2003). *Academic Administrator's Guide to Exemplary Leadership.* San Francisco: Jossey-Bass Publishers.

Krahenbuhl, G. S. (2004). *Building the Academic Deanship: Strategies for Success.* Westport, CT: American Council on Education/Praeger Publishers.

Marrelli, A. F., Tondora, J., and Hoge, M. A. (2005). "Strategies for Developing Competency Models." *Administration and Policy in Mental Health* 32 (5/6): 533–61.

McClelland, D. C. (1973). "Testing for Competence rather than for 'Intelligence.'" *American Psychologist* (January): 1–14.

McDaniel, E. A. (2002). "Senior Leadership in Higher Education: An Outcomes Approach." *Journal of Leadership and Organizational Studies* 9 (2): 80–88.

Merriam-Webster's Collegiate Dictionary. (2004). 11th ed. Springfield, MA: Merriam-Webster.

Montez, J. M. (2002). Developing and Piloting the Higher Education Leadership Instrument (HELI): "Bootstrapping" Theory and Measurement. PhD diss., Washington State Univ.

Smith, Z. A., and Wolverton, M. (2010). "Higher Education Leadership Competencies: Quantitatively Refining a Qualitative Model." *Journal of Leadership and Organizational Studies* 17 (1): 61–70.

Stanley, T. J. (2000). *The Millionaire Mind.* Kansas City: Andrews McMeel.

Wolverton, M., and Gmelch, W. H. (2002). *College Deans: Leading from Within.* Westport, CT: American Council on Education/Oryx Press.

Yin, R. K. (2009). *Case Study Research: Design and Methods.* Thousand Oaks, CA: Sage Publications.

Chapter 14

Croteau, J. (2009). *The People First Approach.* Washington, D.C.: Council for the Advancement and Support of Education (CASE).

Padilla, A. (2005). *Portraits in Leadership: Six Extraordinary University Presidents.* Westport, CT: Praeger Publishers.

Index

About the Authors

Dr. Jon Derek Croteau is a senior consultant with Witt/Kieffer, the single largest leadership solutions firm specializing in health care, education and not-for-profit organizations committed to improving the quality of life. Prior to joining Witt/Kieffer, he served as assistant vice president for campaign planning and operations, assistant vice president for advancement services, and director of organizational development and human capital management at Carnegie Mellon University. He is the author of *The People First Approach: A Guide to Recruiting, Developing, and Retaining the Right People* and has published numerous articles on strategic talent management in higher education. He is a sought-after speaker on the topic and a cochair of the national Strategic Talent Management Conference for the Council for the Advancement and Support of Education (CASE), and he serves on the editorial board of the *International Journal of Educational Advancement*. He has also served as adjunct professor at Carnegie Melon University and the University of Rochester.

Dr. Zachary A. Smith is assistant vice chancellor of development at the University of California, Riverside. He also consults with higher education institutions on talent management and organizational research projects (www.edusmith.com). Previously, he was the senior director of strategic talent management and initiatives for university advancement at the University of California, Irvine, and worked at the University of Nevada, Las Vegas, in a variety of advancement capacities while completing his PhD in educational leadership with an emphasis in higher education administration. His dissertation was titled "Creating and Testing the Higher Education Leadership

Competencies (HELC) Model: A Study of Athletics Directors, Senior Student Affairs Officers, and Chief Academic Officers." In addition to this book, he has authored numerous publications on leadership and talent management and presents regularly at national conferences and seminars. His work has been highlighted in the *Chronicle of Higher Education* and the *Chronicle of Philanthropy.*

Chief Advancement Officer Biographies

Lisa D. Calvert

Since September 2010, Lisa Calvert has led Purdue University's fundraising efforts as vice president for university development. Calvert leads a staff of 135 full-time employees and oversees annual, major gift, and planned giving programs, as well as alumni, corporate, and foundation relations. She serves as a senior member of the president's leadership team. Prior to her appointment at Purdue University, Calvert had been Creighton University's vice president for university relations since 2003. Under her leadership, Creighton received the 2007 and 2008 Council for the Advancement and Support of Education (CASE) overall fundraising performance award for superior programming over a three-year period. Earlier in her career, she held fundraising positions at Wichita State University, Kansas State University, and William Jewell College. Lisa has a BA from Oklahoma State University and has done graduate work at Oklahoma State and Wichita State. She has also completed business leadership programs at Harvard University and the University of Chicago.

Michael C. Eicher

Michael C. Eicher became vice president for development and alumni relations at Johns Hopkins University on September 1, 2006. He has overall responsibility for attracting private financial support for the university and Johns Hopkins Medicine, and for strengthening Johns Hopkins' relationships with alumni and other supporters. On his arrival at Johns Hopkins, Eicher assumed leadership for the Johns Hopkins University Knowledge for the World Campaign, an eight-year, multi-billion-dollar fundraising effort that had been under way since 2000. On December 31, 2008, the campaign concluded after raising $3.741 billion. Prior to joining Johns Hopkins, Eicher had been vice chancellor of external affairs at the University of California, Los Angeles, since 1998. He began his career at UCLA in 1986, rising from associate director of development in the school of medicine to deputy director and director, and from there to vice provost for medical science development, and assistant and associate vice chancellor. Campaign UCLA, a ten-year effort completed in 2005, raised $3.05 billion, a record for a U.S. university according to the *Chronicle of Higher Education*. Eicher graduated from the University of California, San Diego, in 1979.

Susan K. Feagin

Susan K. Feagin served as executive vice president for university development and alumni relations at Columbia University, overseeing the Columbia Campaign, a university-wide $4 billion fundraising initiative, which was later increased to $5 billion, that ran through 2011. As part of her portfolio, she also directed the university's alumni relations programs. Feagin stepped down from her post in January 2011 and assumed the role of special advisor to President Lee C. Bollinger. She spent her development career at three universities: Columbia, Harvard, and the University of Michigan. She held leadership roles at institutions during three major, university-wide development campaigns. In 1990, she was named the first associate dean for development in Harvard's Faculty of Arts and Sciences, comprised of Harvard College and the Graduate School of Arts and Sciences. She was named director of university development in 1996. From 1998 to 2002 she served as vice president for development at the University of Michigan. Feagin received a BA cum laude from Columbia University's School of General Studies in 1974.

Patricia P. Jackson

Patricia "Trish" Jackson is vice president for advancement at Smith College and has served in this role since September 2005. She began her career at Scripps College in 1983, serving as assistant director of annual giving. She then spent four years at Claremont McKenna College coordinating a wide variety of campaign activities and publications, as well as overseeing the corporate fundraising program during CMC's successful $50 million campaign. In 1988, Jackson assumed the position of director of major and leadership gifts at Mount Holyoke College during the institution's $139 million campaign. From 1991 to 1998, she served as director of development at Wheaton College in Norton, MA, and in 1998 she became vice president for education at CASE. At CASE, she managed all conferences and awards programs originating out of Washington, DC, and served as the organization's primary contact with the media on issues surrounding philanthropy. Later, Jackson spent four years at Dartmouth College as associate vice president for individual and organizational giving before assuming her current leadership position at Smith. Jackson earned her BA in psychology from Scripps College in 1982 and completed an MBA with an emphasis on the economics of nonprofits in 1991 at Claremont Graduate University's Drucker School of Management.

Connie Kravas

Connie Kravas has served as the University of Washington's vice president for university advancement and president of the University of Washington Foundation since 2001. As chief advancement officer for the university, Kravas is a strong proponent of an integrated model of advancement that brings together fundraising, alumni relations, and marketing at both central and peripheral levels. Previously, she served as vice chancellor for university advancement at the University of California, Riverside. She also held a variety of positions at Washington State University, including that of vice president for university advancement (1997–99) and president of the Washington State University Foundation (1981–99). Kravas has been recognized with numerous awards both within and outside the advancement profession. She holds a BA in English literature from Pacific Lutheran University, an MA in sociology from Indiana State University, and a PhD in educational leadership from Washington State University.

Jerry A. May

Jerry A. May is vice president for development at the University of Michigan. In this role, he is responsible for all fundraising activities at the university, including policy formulation, strategic planning, and program implementation. He also manages the university's fundraising programs and works with a staff of 450, including development officers in schools and colleges, regional major gift and planned giving officers, corporate and foundation officers, annual giving staff, constituent giving staff, and development support professionals. Before joining Michigan, May was vice president for development at Ohio State University and president of the Ohio State University Foundation from 1992 to 2003. From 1993 to 2000, May planned and implemented the second university-wide campaign in Ohio State history, setting a goal of $1 billion and concluding with more than $1.23 billion in gifts. Previously, May was director of principal gifts at the University of Michigan and helped manage Michigan's first billion-dollar campaign, the Campaign for Michigan, which began in 1990. He also served as director of the major gifts program at Michigan, as senior associate director of an earlier campaign, and as director of the business school's $15 million campaign. May holds a BA in English from Hope College and an MA in higher education administration from the University of Vermont. He also did PhD-level graduate work at the University of Michigan Center for the Study of Higher and Postsecondary Education.

Sarah R. Pearson

Sarah R. Pearson has been in the advancement profession since 1980. She is currently chief development officer for the Broad Institute of MIT and Harvard, where she oversees fundraising for one of the world's leading biomedical research institutes. Prior to her arrival at the institute, Sarah served as vice president for alumni relations and development at Northwestern University. Pearson began her development career in 1980 at Harvard University. Later, she assumed the position of director of the Cornell Fund during Cornell's $1.5 billion campaign. Moving on to the University of Chicago, she served as associate vice president of development and alumni relations and as campaign director during the launch of the university's successful $2.3 billion campaign. Pearson received her BA from Bates College, where she currently serves as a member of the board of trustees. Pearson received her MFA in theater from Brandeis University. Pearson is a member of the board of trustees of CASE and serves as chair of the Philanthropy Commission.

Carolyn A. Pelzel

Carolyn "Carrie" Pelzel was appointed senior vice president for advancement of Dartmouth College in June 2010. She oversees a staff of two hundred in alumni relations, development, and public affairs. Previously, she served nine years at Dartmouth as vice president for development and four years as director of development. As vice president, she led the college's $1.3 billion Campaign for the Dartmouth Experience, which exceeded its goal on December 31, 2009. Pelzel began her career in fundraising at Northfield Mount Hermon School in 1975. There, she worked in alumni relations, served as director of development, led a capital campaign, and eventually became director of external affairs, overseeing development, alumni relations, and communications. She then became director of development and information services at the National Association of Independent Schools (NAIS), traveling across the country to work with development officers, heads, and trustees of member schools. Next she served as executive vice president of the Williamson Group, a computer systems company with vertical market expertise in providing information systems in fundraising to schools, colleges, museums, and hospitals. During these years, she was also a partner in the Franklin Group, a fundraising consulting firm. In 1986 Pelzel joined the development staff of Harvard University. She spent eleven years at Harvard and became associate director of university development, participating in the planning and kickoff of the university's $2.3 billion campaign that concluded in 2000. Pelzel received her BA from Trinity College.

Martin Shell

Martin Shell is vice president for development at Stanford University, reporting directly to the president, John Hennessy. He is responsible for all of the university's development activities and for working closely with the president, the provost, and the school's deans to set the development agenda and oversee fundraising operations across the university. He also serves as executive vice chair and lead staff member to the Stanford Challenge, the university's $4.3 billion fundraising effort launched in October 2006. The campaign surpassed its goal well ahead of schedule. Previously, Shell served for two years as associate vice president for development at Stanford. He joined Stanford's development team in 1998 as senior associate dean for external relations and chief operating officer at Stanford Law School. Prior to his move to Palo Alto, he was associate dean for development and alumni relations at the University of Pennsylvania Law School. Shell has been an advancement officer for more than twenty-five years, serving institutions of higher education in Arkansas, Pennsylvania, and California. In addition, he was an executive with a public utility company, a press secretary to a U.S. representative, and a newspaper reporter. Shell graduated from Hendrix College in 1980 and started his fundraising career there in 1983.

Curtis R. Simic

Curtis R. Simic has more than forty years of experience in development at both public and private institutions of higher education. He started his career at the Indiana University Foundation and returned seventeen years later as its president. He retired after twenty years of service and leadership in August 2008 to become president emeritus of the Indiana University Foundation, and he continues to assist the development program of Indiana University. In the years he spent building his career outside of Indiana, Simic worked in increasingly more responsible positions in development, alumni, and external relations at public and private institutions in all parts of the country, including Yale, the University of Tennessee, the University of Alabama, the University of Oregon, and the University of California, Berkeley, where he served as vice chancellor for development and president of the University of California-Berkeley Foundation. There he directed the largest fundraising campaign ever conducted at a public university at that time. He is a national leader in development and has served on multiple professional association boards and committees for CASE, the Association for Governing Boards, and others. Simic graduated from Indiana University with a BS in 1964.